T0295734

Mastering Global Business Development and Sales Management

The Global Warrior Series

Series Editor:
Thomas A. Cook

Mastering the Business of Global Trade
Negotiating Competitive Advantage Contractual Best Practices,
Incoterms, and Leveraging Supply Chain Options
Thomas A. Cook

Driving Risk and Spend Out of the Global Supply Chain
Thomas A. Cook

Managing Growth and Expansion into Global Markets
Logistics, Transportation, and Distribution
Thomas A. Cook

Growing and Managing Foreign Purchasing
Thomas A. Cook

Excellence in Managing Worldwide Customer Relationships
Thomas A. Cook

Enterprise Risk Management in the Global Supply Chain
Thomas A. Cook

Developing Masterful Management Skills
for International Business
Thomas A. Cook

Mastering Global Business Development and Sales Management
Thomas A. Cook

For more information about this series please visit: https://www.crcpress.com/The-Global-Warrior-Series/book-series/CRCTHEGLOWAR

Mastering Global Business Development and Sales Management

Thomas A. Cook

CRC Press
Taylor & Francis Group
Boca Raton London New York

CRC Press is an imprint of the
Taylor & Francis Group, an **informa** business

First edition published 2021
by CRC Press
6000 Broken Sound Parkway NW, Suite 300, Boca Raton, FL 33487-2742

and by CRC Press
2 Park Square, Milton Park, Abingdon, Oxon, OX14 4RN

Library of Congress Cataloging-in-Publication Data
Names: Cook, Thomas A., 1953- author.
Title: Mastering global business development and sales management / Thomas A. Cook.
Description: First edition. | Boca Raton, FL : CRC Press, 2020. | Series:
The global warrior series | Includes bibliographical references and index.
Identifiers: LCCN 2020015538 (print) | LCCN 2020015539 (ebook) | ISBN
9781482226232 (hardback) | ISBN 9780429272370 (ebook)
Subjects: LCSH: Sales management. | Marketing. | Strategic planning.
Classification: LCC HF5438.4 .C668 2020 (print) | LCC HF5438.4 (ebook) |
DDC 658.8/1—dc23
LC record available at https://lccn.loc.gov/2020015538
LC ebook record available at https://lccn.loc.gov/2020015539

ISBN: 978-1-4822-2623-2 (hbk)
ISBN: 978-0-429-27237-0 (ebk)

Typeset in Minion
by codeMantra

To Lindsay and Ayana … who are beautiful, articulate, creative, determined, detailed, and artistic … make me proud everyday … and now you are fantastic MOMs! Love you, Dad.

Contents

Foreword

Tom is one of the best salesmen I know, and is maybe the best-ever business development strategist I ever worked with.

He understands the psychology of people with an intense level of emotional intelligence. He is able to think through the challenges of both domestic and international business modeling and develop strategies to leverage strengths and minimize weaknesses.

This book capitalizes on Tom's strengths, expertise, and wherewithal and lays out a concise understanding of business development along with the necessary skill sets to achieve overwhelming favorable results.

I am impressed and continue to learn from Tom and his many business books and the consulting work he accomplishes for so many businesses and company executives. But this book has "raised the bar" of his writings and brings a whole new level of expertise delivered in a very readable, friendly format.

Business development internationally is a comprehensive and detailed process which Tom goes to great length to capture in this highly recommended read.

This book is a must-read for any person with responsibilities in sales, marketing, customer service, business development, or senior management in companies seeking growth and expansion on a global scale.

Kelly Raia
Managing Director
Dragonfly Global, LLC
New York

Preface

Sustainability is a mediocre goal. Growth, expansion, and profit enhancement are much better goals, designs, strategies, and business development objectives.

When they happen ... sustainability will follow. A company that only sustains is in trouble and may not have a long-term future.

A company must always be growing, expanding, and enhancing its margins and profits. This is a much better strategy in dealing with:

- Risk
- Spend
- Competitive pressures
- Sustainability
- Mastering technology
- Maintenance of existing personnel
- Attraction to quality personnel
- Ability to be a leading-edge organization

All the above requires a specific sales and business development strategy, which is outlined in this book in great detail.

This book encompasses an array of strategies, tactics, business models, and action plans that are guaranteed to grow and sustain any business model domestically or globally.

Successful sales management requires comprehensive skill sets, resources, and training which this book outlines and reviews in a very constructive and easy-to-read format. This book can be considered a "blueprint or foundation" for any company or business executive to follow or utilize as a guide to achieve growth, expansion, and long-term sustainability.

Achieving growth means having a specific sales management strategy that combines marketing and sales prowess with the art of closing a deal by talented sales personnel.

What I achieved in this book was a compilation from A through Z ... of what it takes to create a sales strategy and what is necessary to execute specifically designed tactics for achieving sales success. This book walks the reader through a series of steps that logically outlines just what it takes a company and business executive to think through a plan and deliverables to make growth, increased margins, and long-term sustainability a reality.

Always keep in mind that businesses are run by people. Improve the skill sets, the attitude, and functionality of people ... and the business will grow and expand.

Knowing what to do, how to do, and when to do ... is a good idea on what this book is all about in sales, business development, and overall global trade management.

> Almost everything worthwhile carries with it some sort of risk, whether it's starting a new business, whether it's leaving home, whether it's getting married, or whether it's flying in space.

Chris Hadfield, Astronaut

Author

Thomas A. Cook is the Managing Director of Blue Tiger International (bluetigerintl. com), a premier international business and management consulting/training company on leadership, general management, strategic planning, supply chain, freight operations, port and terminal services, risk management, divisional alignment, trade compliance, purchasing/sourcing, global trade, eCommerce, logistics, and business development/sales.

Tom was former CEO of American River International in NY and Apex Global Logistics Supply Chain Operation in LA.

He has over 30 years of experience in assisting companies all over the world to manage their business models, supply chain risk and spend, sales and business development, purchasing, business decision-making, vendor/contract management, and import/export operations.

Tom's practice includes business mentoring in sales, leadership, project, presentation skills, risk management, supply chain, purchasing/sourcing management, trade compliance, international and management capabilities enhancement.

He has been working for many industry verticals in mitigating the impact of duty and tariffs on global trade. Since 2017, this initiative has included the 232 and 301 Tariffs.

He is a member of the NY District Export Council, sits on the board of numerous corporations, and is considered a leader in the business verticals he works in, such as ISM, CSCMP, DEC, to name a few of the organizations he works with.

He has now authored over 19 books on Business Management, Global Trade, and Business Development. This is the eight book in *The Global Warrior Series: Advancing On the Necessary Skill Sets to Compete Effectively in Global Trade*. Tom is also a veteran advisor, developer, and instructor of the AMA (American Management Association) in NYC, the largest corporate training association in the world. His previous book, *Enterprise Risk Management in the Global Supply Chain*, is receiving great praise and accolades from the professional community.

Tom is also the Director of the National Institute of World Trade (niwt. org), a 30-year-old educational and training organization, based here on Long Island.

Tom is a frequent lecturer and keynote speaker several times a year at various management, leadership, transportation, supply chain, insurance, and business development venues here and abroad.

Tom is also a professor/lecturer/teacher and course developer at Stony Brook University in Long Island, Baruch College, and the Fashion Institute of Technology in NYC.

He graduated from Maritime College where he holds both a BS and MS/MBA in international transportation management. He additionally received his commission in the U.S. Navy where he served from 1971 to 1984, honorably discharged.

Tom also founded and chairs *Soldier On* (soldieronathome.org), a non-profit organization engaged in helping wounded combat veterans and wounded combat dogs and supporting specially trained dogs to assist soldiers with PTSD.

Tom can be reached at tomcook@bluetigerintl.com or 516-359-6232.

1

The Importance of Business Development

The importance of business development in both domestic and global business is that it assures sustainability. And simultaneously creates a track to growth and expansion. This chapter creates the foundation for companies to prioritize sales and business development management and practice.

It is amazing to me how many companies do not have a structured and concerted effort in business development. It is rather a by-product of existing relationships, good customer service, or of reputation or of the persona of the organization.

All those areas are good and important, but they fail in creating a pathway to long-term sustainability and expansion. Most of these types of companies will have stunted growth and, at some point, begin to lose market share.

And even if the growth is good ... the real questions are ... how good could it be? Are we maximizing our opportunities?

THE CRITICAL IMPORTANCE OF BUSINESS DEVELOPMENT

A company needs to continually grow and expand. I have heard it said by seasoned businessmen for over 35 years ... if you are not growing ... you're dead!

While I believe a company goes through cycles, where some cycles have "downturns" ... I firmly embrace the idea that over a longer time frame, a company must be growing.

Growth is a number of areas that are expected, as follows.

GEOGRAPHICALLY

A company is best when it diversifies its markets over the entire United States and the World. Diversity in geographical locations is both a risk and opportunity management benefit to any organization.

You can take advantage of multiple locations, which potentially allows "scalability" that, in turn, lowers cost and increases margins.

Geographic diversity also allows a more balance to the variables which happen in politics and the economy which may have volatility in some areas while other areas do not.

Geographic diversity also allows for leveraging the variables that occur in other markets, which might have more favorable nuances for business development opportunities and sales.

GROSS REVENUE

Gross sales demonstrate how a company is maintaining and/or expanding market share. Its significance lies in over periods of time where that gross number continually evidences expansion, growth, and business development targets and goals being met.

Though gross revenue is not a true or only indication of the financial health of an organization ... it does demonstrate a company's ability to be competitive in a specific space. Additionally, it indicates the potential strength of customer services, sales, and business development initiatives.

Gross revenue is just that ... gross revenue. It does indicate what margins are being developed, which are a much better indicator of the financial health of any organization.

Having a good balance of both strong gross and high margins is really the best scenario for a company's financial picture.

NET REVENUE (MARGIN)

As just discussed, net revenue or sometimes referred to as margin is typically a more important dynamic in the financial well-being of any organization.

Example

A company needs to make an 8% margin on its sales in order to break even and to cover its operational expenses.

In 2018, it accomplishes that goal. In 2019, it grows its gross sales by 10%, but net revenue falls to only 5% of gross sales.

This leaves the company with a 3% shortfall. It either has to borrow money from its reserves or from a third party to meet expense requirement allocations.

This will reflect poorly on the P&L (profit and loss) and possibly the balance sheet, as well.

Decisions will have to be made on how best to maintain gross sales growth but … move margins minimally to cover expenses … and optimally to generate net profits into the company's coffers.

It is said that gross sales are like the engine in the car that propels it forward, but the margin is the fuel that allows the engine to function … (Thomas Cook, June 2013).

PERSONNEL

A company grows from both within and externally.

Internally, they train, develop, and provide empowerment to their management teams to propel them forward along with the organization's growth strategy.

More often than not, a company must train from external resources as they internally do not have the bandwidth, time, or expertise to manage training. More seasoned companies have dedicated personnel overseeing training as an independent silo in the company.

It becomes their pathway to career development, more authority, power, money, and security in the organization.

Additionally, the organization brings in "talent" from other organizations, which should greatly add to the diversity and strength of an organization. "New blood" with new ideas, resources, and know-how can be of great value to an organization that becomes somewhat stagnated with its existing personnel.

Personnel acquired from external resources can also be problematic, and if the hiring and vetting process is on solid foundation ... the risks should be minimized.

Over the years, I have observed a number of companies that only promote from within. While I do believe existing personnel should be given certain preferences ... the policy of only hiring from within is like "incest" ... and it can only lead to issues, down the road.

Hiring and bringing in talent from external resources can only:

- Make the company stronger.
- Diversify when managed well equates to stronger gene pools among the staff and management teams.
- Bring in new ideas, resources, and strategies.
- Utilize varied experiences gained elsewhere to your company's benefit.

PRODUCT AND SERVICE DIVERSITY

A company grows and expands as it diversifies its product and service offerings. It is ok to have stable and core business products and services ... but these can get old real fast. Companies that lie back on their success and rest on their laurels can soon be in trouble, when they react too late.

Innovation is at the heart of a company's ability not only to sustain but to grow. That growth must bring in new product and service offerings into its portfolio. It demonstrates to clients, prospects and the marketplace that your company is competitive, innovative, and contemporary.

I too often hear in the marketplace "they are too old", "their ideas are prehistoric", "their staff are cavemen", "the last new idea I saw out of them was before 9/11".

Too many companies have fallen by the wayside getting too comfortable with the status quo.

The key to survival is to diversify both your product and service offerings. This requires:

- Creativeness
- Innovation
- Development of new and companion products and services

Creativeness is generally led in the following company silos:

- Senior management
- Marketing
- Sales
- Customer service
- Research and development (R&D)

New products and services will typically be at the forefront of innovation, but companion products and services also can be a successful pathway in diversifying a company's business model.

Companion products and services are those that have a direct relationship to the primary product but offer a potential alternative purchase as its design is to supplement or add to the value of the primary product or service.

Some examples of companion products:

Primary Product	Companion Product
Cell Phone	Cell Phone Case
Car	Remote Starter
Lawn Mower	Grass Cutting Basket
Lipstick	Matching Eye Shadow

Primary Service	Companion Service
Real Estate Broker	Mortgage Financing
Banker	Currency Exchange
Furniture Retailer	Carpet Sales
Pharmacy	Flu Vaccinations

These examples outlined above demonstrate how an innovative approach utilizing companion sales of products and services can easily be orchestrated to provide expansion and growth that fall in line with your existing product and service portfolio.

This methodology also creates leverage and opportunity with existing clients, trade lanes, business verticals, and existing sales outlets.

Additionally, this widens the sales personnel reach to existing clients and markets without having to expand by cold calling and/or developing new sales leads. Its success is its penetration into existing clients.

The next outline shows expansion with new product and service offerings through existing sales and partner channels.

Primary Product	New Product
Audi 8	Audi 8 Hybrid
Coke	Carbonated Water
Electric Tools	Battery Remote Tools
Manufacturing Garage Doors	Manufacturing Outdoor Sheds

All these examples outlined above show how through innovation and creativity one can bring new products, and companion products and services to help a company grow and expand.

PRODUCT AND SERVICE ENHANCEMENT AND DIFFERENTIATION

Product diversity outlined in the preceding section is one way to develop. Another option is to expand by offering similar products but with:

- Enhancements
- Differentiation
- Value Addition

A number of examples:

Existing Product	Enhancement/Differentiation/Value Addition
Supermarket	Home Delivery
Eat-In restaurant	Catering Offsite
Bank	Tax Services
Doctors Office	Fulfills Basic Prescriptions Onsite
Car Dealer	Includes Maintenance
Boutique Clothing Shop	Free Tailoring
Manufacturer of Widgets	Customized Widgets

I have outlined enough examples of everyday products and services that could easily be enhanced through some innovative and creative ideas. This will drive growth and expansion and keep a company competitive.

THE CASE FOR BUSINESS DEVELOPMENT IN EVERY COMPANY

The argument for every company to engage in practices that instill growth are numerous:

- It allows companies to become stable, tenured, and sustainable.
- It assures continuity.
- It protects when downturns occur.
- It enhances competitiveness.
- It strengthens the company to withstand risk.
- It creates a structure for employees to grow upward and increases the opportunities for advancement.

It Allows Companies to Become Stable, Tenured, and Sustainable

All companies should have such noble goals ... stability, tenure, and sustainability. It would always be a perfect scenario for any company to operate where those goals are achieved.

But when a company accomplished business development successfully ... then the doorway is kept open wide ... for these noble goals to actually be realized.

Business development creates the conduit for capabilities, funding, and resources be brought to bear that makes a company be stable, tenured, and be a sustainable organization.

It Assures Continuity

Continuity is best achieved when business development is accomplished keeping a company growing and moving forward. It becomes a demonstrated avenue for progression, meeting all the challenges and risks that a company faces from competitive pressures, and surrounding events that impact operational success.

It Protects When Downturns Occur

Successful business development protects a company when business downturns are happening.

Economic downturns, industry depressions, and all kinds of scenarios that can impact a company's risk to have business fall off … are best protected when over the longterm that business has been growing and expanding.

It creates resilience within the organization that strengthens to resolve and deal with hardship, downturn, and various challenges it will face at various points in time.

It Enhances Competitiveness

Competition makes the company stronger when they adopt a business model to embrace "competitive pressures" rather than shy away from them.

As a company grows and expands through proactive business development, it can only sustain that by adopting competitive strategies.

An aggressive company growing becomes a target for all other competitors. It must then raise the bar of its competitive structure to stay ahead of its competitors.

Competition makes those who engage become even more competitive. It can be a vicious cycle, but it does create a continuity and sustainability.

It Strengthens the Company to Withstand Risk

The challenges of business are huge, to name a few areas of many:

- Personnel
- Regulation
- Political
- Economic
- Geophysical
- Competition
- Technology
- Trade disruptions
- Cyber security
- Risk and insurance issues

These risks and challenges can bring a company to their knees. To combat these challenges a company that is growing, developing business is in the best position to one that is not.

This enables the company through the strength of its successful business development model to manage risk and successfully meet all the challenges it faces.

Business development will typically mean robust infrastructure and well-positioned marketing and sales initiatives along with financial resources. All of that translates to an ability to meet risk head-on and make the challenges all manageable.

If a company is in a weakened financial position … any of the challenges outlined above could easily be negatively consequential. On the other hand … a sting financial position makes a company be more tolerant and resilient in the face of risk and business challenges.

It Creates a Structure for Employees to Grow Upward and Increases the Opportunities for Advancement

How do personnel grow and expand their company horizons? How do they make more money, move their career forward, and provide additional levels of job security?

A company that has a successful business development model creates the best opportunity for its employees to:

- Be more secure
- Make more money
- A better-defined career path upwards and beyond
- Better perks and incentives

At the end of the day, secure, happy, and prosperous employees typically become more loyal and better employees.

A win-win scenario is created where the best interests of the company and employees are aligned and in sync with one another.

A company where the staff is aligned with management which is aligned with company goals is the best formula for success. Sustainable business development is an important ingredient in making all of that happen.

Continuous business development makes it happen over long periods of time, through various ups and downs in business, the economy, etc., which at the end of the day is the best situation for everyone's (the company and the employee) interests to be protected and to prosper.

Prosperity is another "noble" goal that positions well with the characteristics of stability, tenure, and sustainability. All well supported by the fundamental nature of a company with successful business development practices and initiatives.

SENIOR MANAGEMENT OVERSIGHT OF BUSINESS DEVELOPMENT

Business development in any organization has to start from top … down. Senior management has to create a culture that moves the organization and the employees in the direction of acknowledging how important business development is and design an overall strategy to make it happen.

Our experience in assisting corporations all over the world in this subject matter has allowed us to develop a ten-step process for senior management to follow:

1. Create the culture
2. Establish a point person
3. Identify the stakeholders and appoint a committee
4. Draw up a budget
5. Allocate resources
6. Set clear goals, deliverables, and expectations
7. Set up lines of accountability and responsibility
8. Set deadlines
9. Maintain transparent and open lines of communications
10. Provide senior management visibility and support

CREATE THE CULTURE

Senior management must take a leadership position in creating a culture in the organization from top down that both charges and encourages business development.

Employees, managers, and staff look to senior managers to provide direction, influence, and control on how the company moves forward.

There is an expectation of staff that they will receive this direction from the top management and usually will follow sound, responsible guidance. When this is clearly communicated and an outline of the reasons why and the importance to the organization is demonstrated, there is an increased opportunity for the managers, employees, and staff to follow along and be active participants.

The culture also sets the tone for their engagement. With the right culture, the personnel will be much more responsibly engaged in any business development initiatives.

This makes for the best opportunity then for business development to happen successfully.

ESTABLISH A POINT PERSON

One person has to be appointed by senior management to take charge and ownership of any new business development plans.

Typically, this individual will have a sales, marketing, or business development expertise and have the basic skill sets to inherit this business development responsibility.

This individual will take ownership of the plan and lead the strategy created by senior management to make new business development happen for the organization.

The "point person" will be supported by various managers and personnel within the organization. This is imperative to obtain support as the task particularly in larger organizations would be too daunting for one person to accomplish independently.

Identify the Stakeholders and Appoint a Committee

The point person in reaching out to colleagues … will identify who are the true stakeholders in the organization and form a committee of these personnel.

The stakeholders will:

- Have a vested interest in the outcome of any business development strategy, plan, or initiative
- Be impacted by any decisions or consequences/results of any new business development program

Once the committee is formed, they will share the following responsibilities:

- Be available for scheduled meetings.
- Provide constructive input and advices to the committee.
- Make the time to understand the related activity and underlying issues of what the committee is established to accomplish.
- Bring the interests of the vertical/fiefdom that the committee member represents to the committee for review and assessment.
- Create a conduit of information flow in both directions ... to and from the vertical/silo/fiefdom represented by that committee member.
- Provide input, direction, and counsel to the committee on the related subjects.
- Be supportive in the committee's goals and outreach.
- Work with the other committee members to achieve all deliverables and expectations within the time frame required by the committee lead and senior management.

Draw Up a Budget

Senior management will need to allocate funds based upon a drawn-up budget. In any business development initiative, there may be costs in any of the following areas:

- R&D (research and development)
- Marketing efforts ... assessment, branding, outreach, and sampling
- T&E (travel and entertainment)
- Additional sales and/or customer service personnel
- Required technology advancements
- Communication costs
- Consulting support

The budget, in nature, may be both short term ... that is 6–9 months ... and long term ... that is 1–3 years.

Keep in mind, many times business development can be transactional, which places it in the short-term basket, or long term, placing it in the strategic basket.

Transactional is more short term ... specifically targeted marketing and sales initiatives seeking immediate results.

Strategic business development is looking for longer-term results following a much more comprehensive and well-thought-out approach. This might include entering a new market, introducing a new product, or a big change in how sales are being conducted.

Strategic planning will most likely longer at a longer-term view, and in-budgeting may create a bigger expense with a longer-term ROI (return on investment) anticipation period.

This must all be contemplated in the budgeting process.

The ultimate goal of new business development is to make money, so this must be figured into the budgeting process.

This would include the potential of creating a P&L grid to show at what point new business initiatives will start to bring in revenue and how long it will take to cover the expenses which went into the costing on the front end of the overall strategy.

This established financial and operational accountability between operations, senior management, and the Board of Directors.

The budgeting process brings the financial interests of the organization into the business development strategies which in public companies would be a SOX (Sarbanes–Oxley) requirement and in the private company … a best practice.

At the end of the day, financial considerations will ultimately drive most business decisions and in particular, those related to business development.

ALLOCATE RESOURCES

Senior management will have to allocate various resources within the organization to support and business development initiatives.

This starts with communications to management teams and operating staff advising them on the importance of business development, gaining their support and participation.

Resources that need to be mustered might be:

- Personnel time
- Management oversight
- Technology capabilities
- Funding

- Shared services
- Operational capabilities
- Obtaining vendor/supplier, customer, and channel partner support

Internal and external resources create potentially both direct and indirect expenses to the organization and may be specifically allocated or absorbed in already established operating budgets.

Resource allocation must be carefully managed because you are drawing from various silos in an organization that may already be "stretched" with personnel wearing numerous hats and having extensive responsibilities. And keep in mind, resource allocation can be costly!

Set Clear Goals, Deliverables, and Expectations

Senior management should be patient and make the time to set clear and concise goals, deliverables, and expectations.

This allows the managers, the point person, and their team, along with the support group to clearly understand what is expected of them and what they ultimately need to achieve.

Setting these clear and concise goals will set up the specific tactics the committee and the leadership will utilize in making sure they can accomplish all the deliverables.

Set Up Lines of Accountability and Responsibility

The ultimate success of any internal business development initiative will be determined by how the effort and the personnel involved are being held to a strict level of responsibility and accountability.

Person	Action	Status	Next Step
John	Allocate funds to the new vendor	Will do by May 16th	Accounting to follow up
Sally	Put out the request for proposal to assigned participants	Completed on April 8th	F/u on May 15th, after 30-day mark
Ted	Deliver management review	Have draft ready by next week	Committee to view the draft after next week
Mary Jo	Visit the Raleigh office next week to see new product demonstration	Confined by Friday	Obtain T&E approval from CFO

This is achieved by following all the previous outlined steps and adding into the mix ... an Excel spreadsheet that outlines the committees' goals and actions ... with a status and who is responsible. This allows the committee to stay aligned with each other and to be utilized as a reporting mechanism up the line to senior management for oversight.

For example:

XYZ Company ... New Vendor Committee
Leader: Ed Walsh
Date: April 3

This sample accountability Excel-based document keeps everyone on the same page, creates a path to accountability to the person and action item, and when distributed up the line, creates a management oversight tool.

Set Deadlines

All strategies in any area of business including business development require deadlines when goals and deliverables need to be met.

Deadlines will also include "milestone" reference points, which might be dates established between start of the project and when it is finished.

Deadlines coordinated with milestone reference points keep everyone on track to complete the project on a timely basis.

One needs to build into the milestones ... to outreach communications that will keep everyone involved with updates and status as outlined in the Action Excel sheets.

Deadlines, milestones, and timely communications are the best triage for responsible management of business development activities in any company.

Maintain Transparent and Open Lines of Communications

A complaint often voiced by managers and staff is the lack of communication and transparency in any organization from the top ... to down.

And it is true that this creates an atmosphere of angst, mid-trust, and even fear.

The best-run organizations through their leadership drive for an environment that is open, straight forward, communicative, and transparent.

This builds confidence in the management teams, the staff, and all employees. This then creates the best patch to success to Business Development Projects supported by senior management.

PROVIDE SENIOR MANAGEMENT VISIBILITY AND SUPPORT

The leadership in business development projects is best utilized to move the initiative forward by being visible and openly providing support ... for managers, teams, and employees.

This outward reach, visible to all parties engaged or impacted, becomes a leadership skill set and a prominent factor in the project on business development being successful.

Personnel are more likely to participate, be engaged, and give it their all when they see senior management involved and providing support.

CASE STUDY IN BUSINESS DEVELOPMENT: COOKSON TECHNOLOGIES

Cookson Technologies, located in NYC, is 26 years old and manufactures and distributes satellite communication systems for internal uses ... intercompany for utilization in closed technology spaces. Meaning how a company can communicate to itself without any external access from third parties. This becomes an alternative to AT&T, Verizon, etc.

Over 99% of their sales are in the United States, but their domestic market is plateauing, and a number of new competitors have joined in the fray.

Their sales team believes there is growth and market potential in some overseas markets as has approached senior management to move forward on this business development initiative.

After several internal discussions by the management and senior management teams, it is decided to move forward with this project and initiative.

The CEO calls in his management team to outline a specific management strategy for overseas business development expansion. They name the project ... **Foreign Destiny**.

During the meeting, a SWOT (Strengths/Weaknesses/Opportunities/Threats) analysis is accomplished. The sales VP ... Jack leads the conversation.

He outlines ...

SWOT

The strength of Cookson Technologies is that they have a strong financial position and have an internal funding capability.

The weakness is a lack of expertise in global markets.

The opportunity is that the foreign market could represent as much as 80% of the total market. Additionally, many of their domestic clients could utilize their services within their own foreign operations. Also, as domestic sales are flat, selling overseas will create the best path to maintain growth in the 15%–20% area, where they have been in the previous 10 years, but not in the last where sales dipped to 7% growth.

The threats are several:

- Entrance into an unknown and unproven foreign market(s).
- There are some already strong established companies in this market servicing Europe, Asia, the Middle East, and Africa.
- Potential financial exposures on assets and receivables.
- Lack of Global Supply Chain experience.

In the meeting, Jack requests everyone's input in how to discuss the SWOT Analysis ... and ask the questions ... what else do we need to think about, and what steps do we need to tack to manage what we have developed from the SWOT Analysis.

At the end of that meeting, an Action Plan is concluded which starts to deal with all the issues and opportunities outlined in the SWOT Analysis.

Team Assembly

The CEO structures a team made up of his managers who would be of value in this project:

- VP marketing
- VP sales takes the lead
- Legal counsel
- Controller
- Director of supply chain
- Manager of customer service
- Compliance director

The team is led by the VP of sales, who is new to the company, and the CEO wants to see how he moves the project forward. Plus, he has had some prior experience in his previous company in export sales.

The Project Lead convenes the meaning with an Excel spreadsheet ... Action Plan as outlined:

The Action Plan:
Foreign Destiny Project
March 3, 2019

Person	Action	Status	Due Date
John B	Attend the Communications Trade Show in Frankfurt next month to evaluate market potential	John, Mary, and Denise have booked to be at the event and are setting up meetings with various potential prospects	30 days
Alice K	Will set up a draft budget for the committee to review in two weeks	Meeting with CFO and Controller on Thursday to set up what is needed for the budget	March 15
Joan A	Identify 2–3 consultants who have experience in this vertical with helping companies on overseas business development projects	Joan will reach out to the entire management team, plus our counsel, broker, and existing consultants to see if anyone can make some recommendations on who we should be talking to	March 30
Tommy B	Know one of our clients who may need our support in this area and will speak with them	Tom to make the call ASAP and let us know how they respond, ... if we go into this market	ASAP
Sam E	Evaluate all our exposures and complete a "Generally Accepted Accounting Principals" ("GAP") analysis	Sam to meet with our CFO and Risk Manager to start the questioning and analysis	Report back by April 10
Denise P	Will determine what expertise we have in our existing staff who may have global or international skill sets	Denise to meet with Human Resource Director to take first step and create an outreach initiative to see who may be an existing internal resource	President to send out memo next week to all staff soliciting a response on their experiences and skill sets in regard to global

This Action Plan begins the responsibility and accountability structure between the team and management on the project.

The team meets again in 30 days, and all the actions are updated and new ones are added. The updated Action Plan matures as follows:

The Action Plan:
Foreign Destiny Project
April 1, 2019

Person	Action	Status	Due Date
John B	Attend the Communications Trade Show in Frankfurt next month to evaluate market potential	The three team members attended the event and overwhelmingly determined there are significant opportunities and have developed at least 19 specific leads and/or prospects. Additionally, they acquired a lot of intelligence which has been filtered and disseminated to all the other team members and the CEO	This will all be updated again in 30 days
Alice K	Will set up a draft budget for the committee to review in 2 weeks	Budget was competed as a draft and sent to the team and the CEO on 3/16	Everyone needs to review and give their comments by the end of next week
Joan A	Identify 2–3 consultants who have experience in this vertical with helping companies on overseas business development projects	We met with three consulting companies, and after the interviews, we unanimously chose Blue Tiger International, as they have very direct experience in our vertical and can cover all the challenges we are facing. They will provide final costing and meet with the entire team on 4/15	April 15
Tommy B	Knows one of our clients who may need our support in this area and will speak with them	Tom did speak with Vertogos Communications, and they are definitely interested in our expansion into Europe, more specifically the Mediterranean Coast. Additionally, they referred us to their lawyer who has helped a number of companies going global. I referred them into our General Counsel	Will require follow-up as we get ready to go into Europe towards the end of the year

(Continued)

Person	Action	Status	Due Date
Sam E	Evaluate all our exposures and complete a "GAP" Analysis	Sam to meet with our CFO and Risk Manager to start the questioning and analysis	This process is taking longer than expected …and new completion date – April 30
Denise P	Will determine what expertise we have in our existing staff who may have global or international skill sets	Human Resources identified five persons on our staff with global experience. All of them are set up for interviews next week	President did send out a memo to those persons who responded are part of the five we are interviewing next week
Lauren	Determine what marketing channels are available to create a client outreach platform	Work with Blue Tiger to see what options they recommend	April 5
Hanjin Q	Start to plan out how we are going to move product from the United States to various destinations	Blue Tiger has made some recommendations … and plan to meet with them on Friday	April 15
Lisa A	Began to prepare how we will handle marking, packing, labeling, and quality control standards	This will be determined once specific markets are agreed to	To be determined
Anthony A	Evaluate which market to handle our first test sale and shipment	Anthony to call meeting with Blue Tiger sales and marketing next Wednesday to present recommendation on starting with Italy as we have a very interesting prospect in Genoa	ASAP

The Action Plan is growing as the project moves forward. It also becomes more granular as the subject matter becomes more intense and detailed. This is all great news as it typically means the project is aging traction.

The committee meets again at the beginning of May, … and now the project is gaining steam.

The Action Plan:
Foreign Destiny Project
May 5, 2019

Person	Action	Status	Due Date
John B	Attend the Communications Trade Show in Frankfurt next month to evaluate market potential	All the prospects were contacted, and proposals have begun to go out. Two deals have been closed. One in Italy and the other in Greece	The sales team will provide another update by mid-June but is on track to close at least 5–6 more deals
Alice K	Will set up a draft budget for the committee to review in two weeks	Budget was modified slightly and approved by the committee and the CEO	Everyone needs to be aware of the budget as it will be reviewed every month at our meetings to make sure we are on budget
Joan A	Identify 2–3 consultants who have experience in this vertical with helping companies on overseas business development projects	Blue Tiger has been very helpful in the following areas: • Marketing and sales • Proposal writing • Supply chain needs	On-going
Tommy B	Knows one of our clients who may need our support in this area and will speak with them	We coded Vertogos and the first shipment will happen on August 1, once we complete their customized order	Net f/u on July 1
Sam E	Evaluate all our exposures and complete a "GAP" Analysis	Sam is still working on the GAP Analysis but identified two concerns he is addressing with our CFO and general counsel: Export Receivable and Foreign sales Contract	We expect to have these two issues managed by June 1 and the balance of the GAP Analysis completed by July 15

(Continued)

Person	Action	Status	Due Date
Denise P	Will determine what expertise we have in our existing staff who may have global or international skill sets	We moved three of the five to positions on the new international sales team and 1 into the new global supply chain position. The other preferred to stay where she was in domestic payables.	HR has put out some marketing efforts to see if we can find additional three to four persons with international experience in customer service and trade law. ASAP
Lauren	Determine what marketing channels are available to create a client outreach platform	Blue Tiger recommended another three trade shows for us to go to, but we will exhibit and promote: September ... Milan Communications Exhibit October ... Sydney Broadcasters Conference November ... Toronto Communication and Satellite Exhibition	Details finalized by July 1
Hanjin Q	Start to plan out how we are going to move product from the United States to various destinations	Blue Tiger has introduced us to Apex Global Logistics who can meet all our shipping needs. We will have a contract in place when our first shipment happens in August	July 1
Lisa A	Began to prepare how we will handle marking, packing, labeling, and quality control standards	This will be determined once specific markets are agreed to	TBD
Anthony A	Evaluate which market to handle our first test sale and shipment	We created a priority list of countries we will initially market to: Italy Greece United Kingdom Netherlands Australia Malaysia Canada Chile South Africa	Currently conducting outreach through marketing and sales and reviewing results every 30 days when we meet. Question has been revised about South Africa which needs to be evaluated from our CFO

The Action Plan is continuing to mature, grow, and become much more comprehensive. It is a solid tool to be utilized by the committee, impacted parties, stakeholders, and senior management … to know where everyone is at, issues, resolutions, and next steps.

It is a spectacular Management Instrument to give the project the best opportunity to succeed and/or to determine what changes need to be made or when to "pull the plug".

MANAGING THE CHALLENGES OF BUSINESS DEVELOPMENT

Every business development initiative will have challenges pop up that have to be dealt with.

These may fall into the following areas:

Personnel

Finding qualified personnel with the necessary skill sets to manage business development on a global scale is very arduous and difficult … and in some verticals nearly impossible.

Companies need to create creative and aggressive campaigns to attract seasoned and qualified sales personnel.

This challenge is not easy and requires the full support of senior management, operations, and Human Resources to find and keep good sales management talent.

Sales talent may be the most difficult "find" for any company, particularly with international or global experience.

Some companies take inexperienced and younger MBA-types and train them into sales managers.

That process requires a lot of patience, risk, and cost.

The author's experience does not favor that option as the risk is high and the learning curve is long.

The author favors the quest to find seasoned-experienced sales talent, with books of contacts and business opportunities … tied into already established and effective sales techniques and skill sets.

While seasoned are more difficult to find … like diamonds, which are extremely difficult to find and mine … they are much more valuable once possessed.

Financial

The sales process has a cost attached. The old expression … "you cannot save your way to prosperity" is true. Likewise, you have to spend money to make money.

The sales process has an expense in:

- Prospecting
- Marketing
- Branding
- Outreach
- Social media
- Hiring
- T&E
- Networking

All the above are necessary sales process costs that have a financial impact on any organization. Sometimes the "ROI" will not be very clear or not have a defined window of eventual success.

Each area has risk associated with an unknown opportunity.

Always keep in mind that international business, which has significant potential, also, can be significantly more expensive to sell to and operate in. This means budgets need to be well thought out for those additional costs.

Many Consider Sales a "Roll of the Dice" … to Some Extent that is True …, But:

When sales expense is going to be incurred … the risks can be mitigated, as follows:

- Take only well-thought-out risks. Be cautiously aggressive.
- Gain insight, information, and fact-gathering in each area of sales initiative, so calculated decisions are made.
- Hold sales personnel accountable both with incentives and de-incentives along the way of the sales process.
- Establish costing and timing parameters to some extent whenever possible.
- Track the sales process, along the way and be prepared to "tweak" as necessary.

Manufacturing

The typical sale is selling something manufactured, distributed, and/or service offered.

Your success in sales becomes the basis of that manufacturing process being able to deliver … what the customer ordered … on time and in working order.

The very best salesperson and sales initiative will fail if the manufacturing, operations, and customer service side fail.

The sales team and sales management must have a direct line of communication into a receptive manufacturing management team to advise and consult on customer complaints, needs, and future areas of product development.

The best organizations have total collaboration between sales and manufacturing as companion silos and not divisions with an independent sole.

Distribution

Following the manufacturing process is tying in the accessibility, availability, and delivery to the customer. That is "distribution", and it is necessary for the sales initiative to be successful.

The big issue between sales and distribution is "tight and accurate" communications defining client needs and the delivery system emanating via the company's distribution system.

Supply Chain

Each company defines the supply chain differently. Academia defines supply chain as follows:

> A supply chain is a defined system of organizations, people, activities, information, and resources involved in moving a product or service from supplier to customer. Supply chain activities involve the transformation of natural resources, raw materials, and components into a finished product or service that is delivered to the end customer.

Supply chain incorporates manufacturing and distribution along with a host of additional features and add-ons.

Successful sales management becomes an extension of any company's supply chain as it creates the sale and the connection to the end user.

Many senior and seasoned executives make sure all aspects of the supply chain work well ... but would agree that "sales" drives the supply chain forward.

> As business moves into the third decade of the new millennium ... it is widely acknowledged by most senior management in international companies just how important managing the global supply chain is to reduce risk and cost and create the best path to growth and sustainability.

Regulation

Business in the United States domestic market and markets abroad has a huge impact on how a company operates its supply chain and sales management process.

One always must pay attention to "regulation" as a necessary evil to business success.

Those companies that integrate "regulatory management" into the sales process as a "value-add" will do better than those that attempt to minimize regulation or try to circumvent it.

The consequences that face regulatory issues can be enormous and even threaten the existence of certain business models.

Managing "regulation" is an integral aspect of any company's supply chain that will have a huge impact on sales.

Manage it better than your competition and ... utilize it to your advantage, and a marketing differentiator ... increases your business development opportunities greatly.

Numerous organizations will utilize the "management of regulation" as a "value-add" and service differentiator.

This aspect can better define sales into a more integral component of how clients feel about their vendor relationship in a more favored way.

Some areas of regulation impacting client relationships:

- EPA (Environmental Protection Administration)
- OSHA (Occupational Safety and Health Administration)
- USDA/FDA (United States Department of Agriculture/Food and Drug Administration)
- ATF (Alcohol Tobacco and Firearms)
- DOT (Department of Transportation)
- HR (Human Resources)
- HAZ-MAT (Hazardous Materials)
- And dozens of others, unique to specific business models and supply chains

Keep in mind that on an international scale ... regulatory concerns cross borders and can have multiple complexities.

Competition

There are companies that set the mark in their verticals, such as but not limited to Starbucks, Microsoft, Google, and Blue Tiger International.

These companies drive the verticals they operate in. Other companies follow.

Leading and following are two contrast strategies ... but also successful business models.

Many companies combine the two strategies to work to their advantage.

Competition will usually set the mark, control pricing, and set the stage for services offered and at what price. Companies that follow ... these strategies often relate closely aligned to all of that.

Companies in the lead set the price, the services, and value-adds and are always innovating to stay ahead of the competition.

These leaders can more easily develop their business models with potentially more risk but with seasoned teams minimizing those risks along the way.

Having said all of that ... we must always pay attention to what our competition is doing, even when we are a "leader" because that can change in a heartbeat. Ask companies such as Oldsmobile, Polaroid, Netscape, Compaq, Tower Records, Kodak, Circuit City, Radio Shack ... to name a few ... all of who learned some very hard lessons.

FUTURE PLANNING: CURRENT CLIENTS AND PROSPECTS

Current Clients

Planning is creating a strategy for the future. The future can be next month, quarter, year, or maybe out for 5 years.

Every industry and business model has its own planning time frames.

It becomes a predictive process only mastered by a few. It is ½ Voodoo and ½ Hard Core Metrics.

It combines qualitative and quantitative business processes that hopefully with a high degree of accuracy and can offer some guidance on what the future will hold.

Knowing what the future will hold ... provides you the information to strategize properly that will impact the opportunity for better outcomes.

There is no 100% proven method or forecasting. There are only tried and proven guidelines, all with variables that impact the percentage of correctness.

Planning is applying a mix of judgment from experience tied into futuristic data from historical and predictive information flows.

Then it is ... YOUR BEST-INFORMED GUESS!

Those who have a successful track record in business planning create a strategy that focuses on what delivers the best odds of favorable outcomes.

They acknowledge that 100% accuracy is not viable but look to achieve percentages in the 60%–70% range … when higher that is even better.

They utilize **quality**, **comprehensive**, **and timely** information from an array of sources, one principally being historical purchasing and sales detail over the past time period, likely to be a year or two.

That data is combined with information obtained from the clients on anticipated needs (one must always keep in mind, most clients will be conservative on their needs, making sure there will be no inventory shortfalls).

The qualitative process is engaging "experience" for which time and trial is always the best teacher.

Experience validates the hard data to estimate the need for future planning.

Prospects

Prospect planning is creating the strategy to:

The pipeline delivers a flow of opportunity!

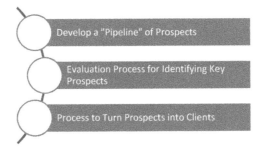

- Develop a "Pipeline" of Prospects
- Evaluation Process for Identifying Key Prospects
- Process to Turn Prospects into Clients

Clients drive strategic planning!

Develop a Pipeline of Prospects

Successful sales managers create a continual flow of opportunities into an organization. These opportunities should be warm leads, not developed by "cold calling" as outlined in various sections of this book.

Planning a strategy for that continual flow is based on a number of critical evaluating steps:

1. Identifying the goals that senior management has established

2. Identifying your areas of strength through a SWOT Analysis

	Helpful	Harmful
Internal	Strengths S	Weaknesses W
External	Opportunities O	Threats T

3. Identify key market segments, geographies, key prospects, demographics, and who on the team to best approach. Maybe a "tandem" initiative?
4. Determine the competitive markets and how they impact your goals and ultimately the strategies you are developing
5. Set up lines of responsibility and accountability in all directions of the sales pipeline. This will mean managing in four directions:

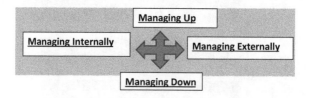

Managing Up is working with your senior management team to obtain their goals and expectations and receive the financial and resource support necessary to achieve the desired results.

Managing internally with colleagues is a collaborative process … manufacturing, operations, customer service, finance, legal, import/export, IT, etc.

Managing externally includes … service providers, vendors, suppliers, channel partners, distributors, agents, and customers.

Managing down is typically working with subordinates in marketing, sales, and customer service.

In managing all these directions, you are becoming a focal point that controls or influences a collaborative process that increases the best opportunity *to achieve the desired results in prospecting, managing the pipeline, and closing deals.*

Evaluation Process for Identifying Key Prospects

Key Prospects are those that meet the following criteria:

- Larger, important players that not only mean revenue but offer higher margins ... and more importantly become "marquis" that will open the doors for many other opportunities in that industry vertical.

  Starbucks in the coffee business, Coke in the beverage industry, BMW in the automotive vertical, etc. ... would all be great examples.

- You have quality and tight existing relationships with the prospect that will open the door for opportunity.
- The prospect is one that is right in the middle of your "wheelhouse".
- Your prospect vertical is very defined, and it is clearly transparent with key companies to go after, that fit perfectly in the model.
- Companies that have shown interest in your products or services through inquiry, contact, or in your prospecting methods.

Process to Turn Prospects into Clients

Closing the deal becomes the critical stage of the sales process. This is a process where prospects are turned into clients.

For some people in sales, this is a very difficult task and, in some cases, poses an insurmountable challenge or issue.

In my experience, if you have to ask for the order then you are less likely to close.

The "order" ... and the "close" ... should be a natural by-product of the sales process. It should arrive and be berthed without asking.

If you have created the overwhelming or compelling argument that your firm is the right choice ... then it will happen with ease, grace, and poignancy.

The client should be asking closing questions:

- How do we start?
- What are your payment terms?
- Who will be servicing our account?
- What is the next step?

All the above are questions indicating ... to ... have successful close.

An intuitive sales manager will gain a sense of where you are at with the client, at the sales process moves along and forward.

Not too many times is the sales manager surprised that they obtained the account. More often then not ... they are surprised ... they did not!

While we must always be positive and hopeful, we must also be pragmatic and cautious.

Closing the deal also requires implementation and on-boarding into your organization. You want to make this process as smooth as possible.

You can lose a deal when implementation fails. At the end of the day, a deal is not closed until it is successfully implemented between the vendor and the client.

Suggestions for a Successful Implementation Process:

- Be prepared proactively for issues to be raised.
- Make sure all the vested interests are engaged on both sides ... the vendor and the client.
- Create an "Action Plan" ... which clearly list all the steps in the implementation process, identifying who is responsible for what, when, and how?
- Stay on top of everyone intently.
- Make for tight and timely communications, follow-ups, and status meetings.

- Stay on top of the client's responsibilities in the implementation process.

Prospects drive the business model … follow these guidelines and you create the best business model for business development success.

The only strategy that is guaranteed to fail is not taking risks.

Mark Zuckerberg, Founder, Facebook

2

Domestic versus Global

Over 95% of consumers and 85% of commercial opportunities exist outside the United States. This chapter reviews and details the opportunities and steps necessary to sell in foreign markets. Resources, skill sets, and cultural balance are very relevant factors.

THE CASE TO GO GLOBAL

A large share of the consumer and commercial market in foreign locations ... that alone is a justification for export sales and/or foreign business development (FBD).

Going global is also a risk management strategy in diversifying your market to a much larger demographic with potentially different economics, politics, and customer basis, which may prove to be of great value when the domestic market has a downturn.

FOREIGN BUSINESS DEVELOPMENT

FBD is different from export sales. Export sales have goods originating in the United States or being shipped from the United States to foreign destinations.

FBD is a U.S.-based entity that creates sales in a foreign country by:

- Finding alternative suppliers in that country and controlling the local selling and delivery process

- Establishing their own manufacturing and distribution capability within that country
- Managing and owning a local entity sourcing from other countries than the United States and selling into that country

EXPORTING AND FOREIGN SALES

Most companies will tend to export from the United States and then as the business expands will look to controlling the distribution into that country and even manufacture locally, as a natural business progression.

Export sales are a good beginning to an overall export business and development model.

The basis for exporting and expanding to overseas markets is outlined as follows:

Large Customer Base in Foreign Markets (95%)

The clear majority of consumer and commercial markets lie outside the United States boundaries.

So as we plan to expand our business, foreign markets can present a much greater market potential.

We restrict our potential sales expansion when only selling domestically. Countries in Europe and Westernized Asia have similar cultural needs as in the United States with rich middle-class growing segments.

Countries in Latin America, such as Chile, Brazil, and Argentina, present significant opportunities in both consumer and commercial sales. As does certain markets in Africa and the Near and Middle East … Egypt, Algeria, South Africa, Saudi Arabia, UAE, Dubai, Qatar, Pakistan, and India.

In Asia, China is a huge opportunity with the fastest and largest growing consumer base in the world. Along with growing countries such as but not limited to South Korea, Vietnam, Taiwan, and Malaysia.

And right next to the United States and as part of North American Free Trade Agreement (NAFTA) [United States Mexico Canada Agreement (USMCA)] … Canada and Mexico are large trading partners.

Diversifying Your Risk Portfolio from Political and Economic Issues

Selling in the United States is lucrative but limiting. And we have to consider the competition, which is vast, creative, and aggressive here.

When we sell and expand into foreign markets, we become less subject to what happens here in the United States. When our economy is strong as it has been in 2018/2019 … sales are strong, but we know that the economy is cyclical.

There are times when our economy is weakened, and some foreign markets are doing much better. Selling in foreign markets, therefore, can reduce our risk of political and economic issues as they develop around the world.

There are times that the U.S. Dollar ($) is strong. We can take advantage of when it is weak, which will allow U.S. exports to be less expensive for countries to buy in those times.

Expanding Upon Market Opportunities

Some products sell well in the United States but do much better in foreign markets. It could be a cultural issue, or a formulization or regulatory factor … that will make the U.S. product or service sell better on foreign shores.

We can take advantage of that opportunity by allowing a certain percentage of our sales to be directed to foreign markets.

Foreign markets also can allow for:

- Ease of access to various marketing platforms
- Have lower distribution costs
- Have less expansive service and warranty programs
- Deal with less regulation and government control factors

Some Products and Services are Better Sold in Foreign Markets

It is just a simple fact, we have numerous products and services we produce here in the United States that sell better outside of the United States.

Some U.S. products have a "panache" in the foreign market and also in the United States.

The "sex appeal" of certain brand names is more attractive to the foreign consumer.

Brand names from the United States, such as but not limited to, do very well in export markets: Estee Lauder, Cadillac, John Deere, Microsoft, and Sara Lee.

Potential for Enhanced Margins

With all the competitive pressures in the United States, margins can be on the thin side. This opens the door for potentially greater margins in export markets.

EXPORT SALES CASE STUDY

We recently worked with a U.S.-based manufacturer of Commercial and Household Generators, based in NY.

Their margin on U.S. sales mainly because of competition was originally 10 years ago at 30%–35%. But over the last 5–7 years that amount has decreased to 15%–17%.

Through an engagement we had, we analyzed overseas market opportunities. We found a market in two African countries where there was a crisis related to their power grid and energy infrastructure.

We identified a distributor serving with a strong foothold in both the commercial and retail markets.

After 6–9 months of trial sales, that company now has over a $1,000,000 + in export sales averaging a 25%–30% margin, a lot more than their U.S. sales.

The following year we identified another six markets in Africa, the Middle East, and Southeast Asia, where sales potential, i.e., in excess of 4 million USD and the margins will be higher than 30%.

Export Margin Assessment

Margins are the key ingredient for sustainable growth and business development. In not all situations will export margins be greater than domestic sales.

Each product vertical and country of destination must be evaluated on the merits of the trading opportunity.

We have found over time that margins in export sales have a greater potential for being more robust from domestic sales mainly when markets are chosen carefully, as follows:

- A market study was accomplished that clearly identified:
  - Less competition
  - Product or service needs
  - Easy access to the market
  - Regulatory compatibility
  - Pricing affinity
- Pricing was studied and analyzed carefully to choose appropriate pricing for market entry as compared to longer-term pricing strategies.
- Value-add was clearly defined that allowed for better margins.
- Terms of payment were offered on more competitive options which became a real benefit and allowed higher margins to occur.

THE DEPARTMENT OF COMMERCE RESOURCE

The Department of Commerce is an excellent source for building an export sales program (DOC.gov).

Our tax dollars contribute to a government initiative that works on the premise that the best interest of the country is served by U.S. companies being engaged in export sales.

This is based upon:

- Exports bring in foreign currency and balance our trade deficit.
- Our expansion into global commerce serves the countries national interests.

- Trade crosses cultural differences and promotes relationships that foster camaraderie between the people of the trading nations.
- Global trade reduces the opportunity for war.

Specifically, the DOC has the following areas of support and assistance:

HOW TO EXPORT

- eCommerce
- Export education
- Finding foreign markets
- Legal considerations
- Logistics
- Financial considerations
- Product preparation
- Trade agreement guides

CUSTOMIZED SERVICES

- Services for U.S. exporters
- Plan and assess
- Promote and expand
- Locations

MARKET INTELLIGENCE

- Find market intelligence
- Export guides
- Industry information
- Trade leads
- Trade data and analysis

EVENTS

- Events and trade missions
- Webinars

TRADE PROBLEMS

- Get help with trade problems
- Report a foreign trade barrier
- Foreign trade remedies
- Foreign safeguard activity involving U.S. exports
- U.S. products subject to Anti-dumping/Counter Vailing Duties (AD/CVD) measures

FAQS

BOARDS

About Us

- International Trade Administration
- Federal Trade Partners
- Programs for Trade Promotion Partners
- Trade Initiatives
- Contact Us
- Social Media
- Privacy Program

U.S. Offices			
Anchorage, AK	Chicago, IL	Fort Worth, TX	Jackson, MS
Atlanta, GA	Cincinnati, OH	Fresno, CA	Jacksonville, FL
Austin, TX	Clearwater, FL	Grand Rapids, MI	Kansas City, MO
Bakersfield, CA	Cleveland, OH	Grapevine, TX	Knoxville, TN
Baltimore, MD	Columbia, SC	Greensboro, NC	Las Vegas, NV
Birmingham, AL	Columbus, OH	Greenville, SC	Lexington, KY
Boise, ID	Denver, CO	Harlem, NY	Libertyville, IL
Boston, MA	Des Moines, IA	Harrisburg, PA	Little Rock, AR
Buffalo, NY	Detroit, MI	Honolulu, HI	Long Island, NY
Charleston, SC	El Paso, TX	Houston, TX	Los Angeles, CA
Charleston, WV	Fargo, ND	Indianapolis, IN	Los Angeles (West), CA
Charlotte, NC	Fort Lauderdale, FL	Indio, CA	Louisville, KY

(Continued)

U.S. Offices			
McAllen, TX	Oakland, CA	Rochester, NY	Tacoma, WA
Memphis, TN	Oklahoma City, OK	Rockford, IL	Tallahassee, FL
Miami, FL	Omaha, NE	Sacramento, CA	Toledo, OH
Middletown, CT	Ontario, CA	Salt Lake City, UT	Trenton, NJ
Midland, TX	Orlando, FL	San Antonio, TX	Tucson, AZ
Milwaukee, WI	Peoria, IL	San Diego, CA	Tulsa, OK
Minneapolis, MN	Philadelphia, PA	San Francisco, CA	Ventura, CA
Missoula, MT	Phoenix, AZ	San Jose, CA	Virginia (Northern), VA
Monterey, CA	Pittsburgh, PA	San Juan, PR	Washington, DC
Montpelier, VT	Pontiac, MI	San Rafael, CA	Wheeling, WV
Nashville, TN	Portland, ME	Savannah, GA	White Plains, NY
New Hampshire, NH	Portland, OR	Seattle, WA	Wichita, KS
New Orleans, LA	Providence, RI	Shreveport, LA	Ypsilanti, MI
New York, NY	Raleigh, NC	Sioux Falls, SD	
Newport Beach, CA	Reno, NV	Spokane, WA	
Northern New Jersey, NJ	Richmond, VA	St. Louis, MO	

This is an array of services outlined above that will help both the new and seasoned exporter wanting to expand into global markets.

An area we have found to be of real value to companies seeking global expansion is the U.S. Commercial Service.

U.S. COMMERCIAL SERVICE

The U.S. Commercial Service (CS), part of the U.S. Department of Commerce's International Trade Administration, offers companies a full range of expertise in international trade. Companies can find assistance locally in more than 100 U.S. Commercial Service offices nationwide and in more than 70 international offices.

They have offices in key business centers in the United States and overseas.

International U.S. Commercial Service Offices		
Albania*	Gabon*	New Zealand
Algeria	Gambia*	Nicaragua*
Argentina	Georgia*	Nigeria
Angola	Germany	Norway
Australia	Ghana	Oman*
Austria	Greece	Pakistan
Azerbaijan*	Guatemala	Panama
Bahamas*	Guinea*	Paraguay*
Bahrain*	Haiti*	Peru
Bangladesh*	Honduras	Philippines
Barbados*	Hong Kong	Poland
Belgium	Hungary	Portugal
Belize*	Iceland*	Qatar
Benin*	India	Romania
Bolivia*	Indonesia	Russia
Bosnia and Herzegovina*	Ireland	Rwanda*
Botswana*	Israel	Saudi Arabia
Brazil	Italy	Senegal*
Brunei*	Jamaica*	Serbia
Bulgaria	Japan	Singapore
Burkina Faso*	Jordan	Slovakia
Cambodia*	Kazakhstan	Slovenia*
Cameroon*	Kenya	South Africa
Canada	Kosovo*	South Korea
Chile	Kuwait	Spain
China	Latvia*	Sri Lanka*
Colombia	Lebanon	Swaziland*
Congo – Kinshasa*	Lesotho*	Sweden
Costa Rica	Liberia*	Switzerland*
Cote d'Ivoire*	Lithuania*	Tanzania
Croatia	Macedonia*	Taiwan
Cyprus*	Madagascar*	Thailand
Czech Republic	Malawi*	Trinidad and Tobago*
Denmark	Malaysia	Tunisia*
Dominican Republic	Mali*	Turkey
Ecuador*	Malta*	Turkmenistan*
Egypt	Mauritius*	Uganda*
El Salvador	Myanmar	Ukraine
Estonia*	Mexico	United Arab Emirates
Ethiopia	Mongolia*	United Kingdom
European Union	Montenegro*	Uruguay
Fiji*	Morocco	Uzbekistan*
Finland	Mozambique	Vietnam
France	Namibia*	West Bank
	Netherlands	Zambia*
* Limited services		

EXAMPLE IN THE UNITED STATES

Central Ohio

- Central Ohio Home
- About Us
- Our Services
- Trade Events
- Exporter's Resource Database
- Press Room
- Contact Us

Welcome to the Columbus U.S. Export Assistance Center

The Columbus office of the U.S. Department of Commerce's U.S. Commercial Service is located in downtown Columbus and serves exporters in a 16-county territory:

• Franklin	• Perry
• Delaware	• Muskingum
• Union	• Morgan
• Madison	• Guernsey
• Pickaway	• Noble
• Licking	• Belmont
• Fairfield	• Monroe
• Hocking	• Washington

Our in-depth industry and tradecraft counseling coupled with an array of export-related services allow us to specialize in providing customized international business solutions. By leveraging our network of experienced tradecraft staff in 150+ cities and over 70 countries worldwide, we can connect Ohio exporters to buyers and international partners.

EXAMPLE IN FOREIGN LOCATIONS

Mexico

- Mexico Home
- Doing Business in Mexico
- Services for U.S. Companies
- Trade Events
- Business Service Providers
- Leading Industry Sectors
- Border Program
- Contact Us

Our Worldwide Network

- About Us
- Press Room
- Other American Markets
- Other Worldwide Markets
- Contact Us

If you are unsure of where to start, contact your local U.S. Export Assistance Center, you can find the nearest one to you here: http://export.gov/usoffices/index.asp

As an example, if you have specific questions about customs and documentation issuing Mexico, **ASK MANNY**. Manuel Velazquez, Commercial Specialist in our Monterrey office counsels U.S. companies on a daily basis in the customs and shipping areas. He can be reached at manuel.velazquez@trade.gov or +52-81-8047-3248.

What are the things you need to know when exporting to Mexico? Click here to review frequently asked questions.

Interested in learning more about opportunities for a specific sector in Mexico? Click here to review our growing list of podcasts on the Mexican market.

Our Offices

We have offices in the major commercial centers of Mexico City, Monterrey, and Guadalajara.

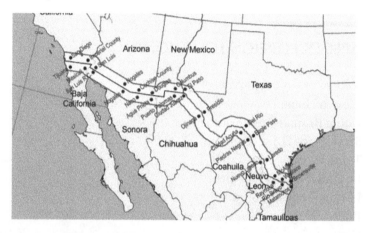

Contact your Industry Specialist

The Commercial Service Mexico offers a number of specialists covering virtually every industry to assist you in entering the Mexican market. Contact the specialist for your industry today.

DOC: OF GREAT VALUE

The U.S. Commercial Service, International Trade Administration, and the overall Department of Commerce can be of great value to helping U.S. companies build an export business with numerous informational flows such as:

CHINA – eCOMMERCE

Describes how widely eCommerce is used, the primary sectors that sell through eCommerce, and how much product/service in each sector is sold through eCommerce versus brick-and-mortar retail.

Includes what a company needs to know to take advantage of eCommerce in the local market and, reputable, prominent B2B websites.

Last Published: July 14, 2017

OVERVIEW AND CURRENT MARKET TRENDS

China is the world's largest eCommerce market and is projected to reach $1.6 trillion in 2 years. Over 40% of total global eCommerce spending comes from China. In 2015, China's online retail transactions reached $622.5 billion. In 2016, the number of digital buyers in China reached over 460 million and continues to increase, with the total number projected to surpass 650 million by 2018. By 2020, China's eCommerce market is predicted to be larger than those of the United States, the United Kingdom, Japan, Germany, and France combined, according to Dezan Shira & Associates. Research firm iResearch, China, forecasts that China's eCommerce market will grow 27% annually over the next 4 years.

DOMESTIC eCOMMERCE (B2C), CROSS-BORDER eCOMMERCE, AND B2B eCOMMERCE

The eCommerce space in China is dominated by domestic platforms, namely Alibaba's Taobao, Tmall, and JD.com, which hold 57% and 25% of the market share, respectively, according to Dezan Shira & Associates. Other platforms such as Suning, Vipshop, Gome, Yihaodian, Dangdang, Amazon.cn, and JMei make up for the majority of the remaining market share. Cross-border eCommerce is experiencing significant growth. China's Ministry of Commerce (MOFCOM) projected that cross-border eCommerce transactions would increase to RMB (Yuan Renminbi) 6.5 trillion by 2016.

U.S. companies targeting to sell products in China's eCommerce platforms can choose either to establish a firm presence in China or use cross-border eCommerce to sell products directly from abroad. A presence in China can be a subsidiary company, a joint venture, a wholly owned entity, or a local distributor/agent. However, within the massive growth of eCommerce, American firms can take advantage of China's cross-border eCommerce-bonded warehouses. These special bonded zones create a streamlined pathway, which makes it easier for China Customs to manage and potentially easier for buyers and sellers to conduct cross-border eCommerce transactions. There are more than a dozen cross-border eCommerce-bonded zones in China and growing. Through this channel, Chinese consumers can purchase no more than 2,000 RMB per sales transaction and no more than 20,000 RMB per year. American companies seeking to sell through one of these special zones will need to partner with local authorized partners who have integrated systems to record transactions with China Customs. The eCommerce landscape is rapidly changing hence it is of the utmost importance for companies to stay current with the newest rules and regulations.

MOBILE eCOMMERCE, POPULAR MOBILE PLATFORMS, AND SOCIAL MEDIA

Online wallets are the top payment method of choice, with 33% of Chinese shoppers utilizing the technology to complete transactions. Roughly half of all China's eCommerce sales are made on mobile devices, nearly 16% more than the global average, according to the U.S.–China Business Council.

There are dozens of mobile eCommerce platforms, but in 2016, Taobao had the most monthly active users at 253.2 million, according to Walkthechat.com. Other platforms like Meituan, JingDong, WeiPin, Tmall, eLeMe, Baidu NuoMi, and DianPing all play an active role in the market, but none are nearly as popular as Taobao in terms of active monthly users.

Understanding how to utilize the advantages of social media can raise your company or product's profile and accelerate your company's ability to sell online. The three biggest social media players are WeChat, micro blog Weibo, and social network QQ Zone. WeChat allows retailers to feature online stores and has a convenient third-party payment function. It also features push messages to introduce new product lines or deliver promotions. U.S. companies interested in exploring social media avenues and working with these sorts of social media players should seek working with a local marketing partner to develop a strategy and support execution.

MAJOR BUYING HOLIDAYS

"Singles Day", November 11, is the busiest online shopping day of the year when huge discounts are offered. For some brands, up to 80% of revenue is generated on that day. In 2015, Alibaba recorded sales of about $9 billion on Singles Day, with shipments of 278 million orders, 43% of which were placed on mobile devices. In 2016, approximately $14.3 billion was spent on Alibaba as the company beat its own record by selling 36 billion RMB in one hour. Other holidays such as Valentine's Day and Chinese New Year are also aggressive online shopping periods.

eCOMMERCE INTELLECTUAL PROPERTY RIGHTS

Intellectual property rights (IPR) infringement across eCommerce platforms is common in China. Registering your intellectual property is essential. The registration process for a trademark can take up to 18 months and can only be protected once the application process has been completed. U.S. companies should conduct due diligence to see if similar trademarks have already been registered. Current trademarks can be found in the China Trademark Office's official database. U.S. companies experiencing serious eCommerce IPR concerns should consult with the U.S. Department of Commerce's Patent & Trademark Office who has offices in Beijing, Shanghai, and Guangzhou.

Prepared by our U.S. Embassies abroad. With its network of 108 offices across the United States and in more than 75 countries, the U.S. Commercial Service of the U.S. Department of Commerce utilizes its global presence and international marketing expertise to help U.S. companies sell their products and services worldwide. Locate the U.S. Commercial Service trade specialist in the United States nearest you by visiting http://export.gov/usoffices

FINDING FOREIGN BUYERS: CUSTOMIZED SERVICES

One of the challenges U.S. exporters face in expanding their export sales is how to find international buyers. This is especially true for smaller U.S. companies, as they often don't have the in-house resources to locate reputable overseas partners. The U.S. Commercial Service has a global network of trade experts across the United States and "boots-on-the-ground" trade professionals in foreign countries. Through their customized services, trade experts can pre-qualify and identify the best prospects in your country of interest and arrange face-to-face meetings. To learn more, view Customized Services, the second of five videos in the Finding Foreign Buyers at DOC.gov.

U.S. Government Export Help

Visit: Export.gov, which provides numerous resources to help a company sell their products in foreign markets.

U.S. Commercial Service Tailored Services

The U.S. Commercial Service helps U.S. businesses find overseas buyers and export partners around the world. Their trade professionals – located in countries that represent 95% of the market for U.S. products and services – are experts on the business environments in their respective regions. We can assist with your international selling strategy through their many services: export counseling, navigating customs and documentation issues, international market research, advocacy, business matchmaking, due diligence on prospective foreign partners, export trade show and trade mission support, and more. Each year, thousands of businesses leverage the U.S. Commercial Service's portfolio of customized services; you can too. Find and establish relationships with foreign buyers today by taking advantage of the following services:

International Partner Search

- Identify potential partners and get detailed company reports.
- Determine the marketability of your product or service.

Gold Key Service

- Meet one-on-one with pre-screened sales representatives or business partners deemed compatible for your firm by our trade professionals.
- Leverage customized market briefings, research, and advice.

Single Company Promotion

- From product launches to technical seminars, trade experts can help you organize a promotional event to reach target audiences and key decision-makers in worldwide markets.

International Company Profile

- Learn more about potential foreign partners of interest from trade professionals who conduct due diligence and background checks.
- Order an international company report containing available sales, profit figures, potential liabilities, and other financial information.

U.S. Exporter Directory

- Feature your U.S. products and services on U.S. Commercial Service websites worldwide through our online directory.
- Local buyers, distributors, and agents see your company's profile and send inquiries to our embassy office. Trade experts confirm the local company's viability, purchasing interest, and contact details, and send you the sales lead for follow up.

Get Help

Export.gov, the U.S. federal government's export portal, links to many resources, including the following:

- Locate a trade expert and learn about the services of the U.S. Commercial Service's global office network.
- Country Commercial Guides provide the latest market intelligence on more than 140 countries from U.S. embassies worldwide.

- *A Basic Guide to Exporting* provides additional information on export resources.

Prepared by the International Trade Administration. With its network of 108 offices across the United States and in more than 75 countries, the International Trade Administration of the U.S. Department of Commerce utilizes its global presence and international marketing expertise to help U.S. companies sell their products and services worldwide. Locate the trade specialist in the United States nearest you by visiting http://export.gov/usoffices.

FOREIGN STANDARDS & CERTIFICATION

Member countries of the World Trade Organization (WTO) are required under the Agreement on Technical Barriers to Trade (TBT Agreement) to report to the WTO all proposed technical regulations that could affect trade with other Member countries.

Notify U.S. is a free, web-based e-mail subscription service that offers an opportunity to review and comment on proposed foreign technical regulations that can affect your access to international markets.

Agriculture-Specific Requirements and Certifications

Agricultural exports require a number of unique documents and certifications from both the United States and destination country (Foreign Agricultural Service Regs, USDA).

European CE Marking Guidance

Conforming in Europe (CE) Marking and certification are required on most manufactured goods marketed in the European Union. Learn if your product requires a CE Marking and how to go about getting one.

China Compulsory Certification (CCC Mark)

CCC Marking and certification are required on many manufactured goods marketed in China.

ISO Standards

The International Organization for Standardization (Organisation internationale de normalisation), widely known as ISO, is an international standard-setting body composed of representatives from various national standards organizations.

Packaging and Recycling Laws

Many countries have passed packaging and recycling laws that affect U.S. exporters. Please refer to the Country Commercial Guides' labeling and marking section for more information. U.S. exporters need to ensure that their packaging materials are compliant with their importer's domestic regulations.

Onerous or Discriminatory Certifications, Standards, and Regulations

Where particularly onerous or discriminatory barriers are imposed by a foreign government, a U.S. company may be able to obtain help from the U.S. Government to press for their removal. In these cases, the firm should:

- File an online complaint with the Trade Compliance Center
- Contact the U.S. Trade Representative (USTR) in Washington, DC at 202-395-3000

Prepared by the International Trade Administration. With its network of 108 offices across the United States and in more than 75 countries, the International Trade Administration of the U.S. Department of Commerce utilizes its global presence and international marketing expertise to help U.S. companies sell their products and services worldwide. Locate the trade specialist in the United States nearest you by visiting http://export.gov/usoffices.

RULES OF ORIGIN

To take advantage of the reduced-duty benefits under a Free Trade Agreement (FTA), an exported product must originate from an FTA party or must contain a specified percentage of U.S. inputs and components. Each FTA has its own Rules of Origin (ROOs) that describe how exported goods shipped to a country, or a region may qualify for duty-free or reduced-duty benefits. Because the ROOs are FTA- and product-specific, they need to be followed carefully.

To receive preferential treatment under an FTA, the exported good:

- Must be made in the FTA territory
- Must meet the appropriate Rule of Origin pertaining to specific products and the specific FTA
- Must be documented as originating via appropriate certifications or information provided to the importer or its representative broker. Each FTA contains a specific chapter on ROOs procedures and lists all product-specific ROOs according to "Harmonized System" (HS) numbers. Qualifying a product for duty-free or reduced-duty benefits requires:
  - Obtaining the product's HS classification number
  - Determining the duty (tariff) rate
  - Qualifying the product for an FTA
  - Identifying the specific ROO for the final product
  - Determining whether the foreign content meets the ROO
  - Certifying the origin of the product
  - Retaining information about how the product was qualified in case of a customs audit

ROOs are used to determine whether or not a product qualifies to receive preferential tariff treatment under the FTA. The rules determining country of origin can be very simple if a product is manufactured and assembled primarily in one country. However, when a finished product includes components that originate in many countries, determining origin can be more complex.

Rules of Origin and Why They Matter

There are two types of ROOs: non-preferential and preferential. Non-preferential ROOs are used to determine the origin of goods exported to countries that are WTO members and therefore grant one another duties (tariffs) on a most-favored-nation (MFN) basis. FTA ROOs are preferential. They are specific to each FTA and generally vary from agreement to agreement and product to product. They are used to verify that products are eligible for duty-free or reduced duties under U.S. trade preference programs, even though they may contain non-originating (non-FTA) inputs.

Sorting through the ins and outs of ROOs can be complicated. There are percentage-based rules and regional value content-based rules. There are also various methods of calculating content under the different types of rules, including the net-cost, transaction value, buildup, and build-down methods. In addition, while ROOs are generally product- and FTA-specific, some general categories also apply. Several other rules and considerations apply as well, including sector-specific considerations covering industries such as automobiles, chemicals, agricultural products, and textile products. There are also generic Certificates of Origin for products that do not qualify for an FTA. Refer to *A Basic Guide to Exporting* for further information on the ROOs.

SUMMARY FOR THE DEPARTMENT OF COMMERCE

When utilizing the DOC and their resources, as we have outlined above some of their most important topics, one should understand that all information has to be scrutinized as to its last publication date and the political slant that might be portrayed.

This well established a prolific Washington-based resource like all government agencies needs always to be combined with other resources and sources to make sure you are obtaining full, complete, and the most comprehensive information flow.

Motivation is the catalyzing ingredient for every successful innovation.

Clayton Christensen, Economist and Harvard Professor

3

The Sales Business Model

The creation of the sales business model is a comprehensive initiative to position an organization into the best possible situation to grow its business into the future.

This chapter reviews the various types of business models for sales and business development and provides detail on each one assisting the reader with a guide on options and the decision-making process.

ORGANIC GROWTH VERSUS INORGANIC BUSINESS DEVELOPMENT

There are several ways an organization can develop business models to grow its footprint and increase sales and revenue:

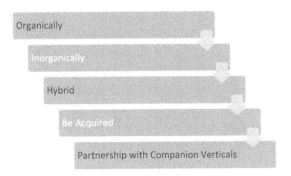

ORGANICALLY

Organic growth is from "within". In other words, a company grows its new business from:

- Existing relationships and clients
- From its own marketing and sales initiatives
- Utilization of its own sales force

This method has its pros and cons. The challenge that is the biggest hurdle … is that it usually works more slowly than other options.

The other challenge is it becomes totally dependent on internal capabilities, manpower, and resources. If they are not up to the challenge … then a slow failure may ensue.

The only other area of concern with organic growth is the threat associated with competitors who may be utilizing the other methods of growth that may hamper organic methods and strategies.

The positive side of organic growth is as follows:

- It allows you to be in direct control of your destiny.
- If organic sales in the past have a good track record, you have an established base that can lead to even greater success.
- You are utilizing the talents and capabilities of a known sales force.
- Better control of the "tweaking and flexibility" required to close deals.
- Usually a much less expensive method than inorganic strategies

In our experience, as long as senior management can exercise patience … organic growth has its value, but it will typically lead to slower leaps in growth and has a dependency upon existing staff, which will need to be up for the challenge.

It has been said that the turtle will win the marathon and the rabbit will win the 100-yard dash. Most business models want sustainability over time … Organic will win in that race!

INORGANICALLY

This process is usually led by M&A (Merger and Acquisition) activity led by the Host Company.

M&A can be an expedient way to grow a business. You access sales personnel, resources, capabilities, prospects, and clients, along with a host of additional benefits.

The acquisition model typically has an upfront expense associated with the purchase, with a trust factor built in that the "return on investment" (ROI) will come after a certain agreed period of time.

Acquisitions also have other concerns:

- Expected benefits never get realized
- Transitional issues interfere with the effectiveness of the M&A
- Clients leave the new business model
- Key managers and staff exit the company

All above are serious and potentially damaging impacts of M&A activity. They all can be mitigated in the acquisition process by exercising due diligence, reasonable care, and common-sense practices as the "take-over" is being planned and occurring.

The big benefit of inorganic growth is the immediacy of growth and market penetration.

The challenges, when successfully navigated can be significantly minimized, making M&A a very viable option.

HYBRID

In many companies, they will pursue a strategy that combines a mix of initiatives that include both organic and inorganic growth components.

They will have defined personnel chasing prospect and client opportunities directly, then another team chasing M&A opportunities.

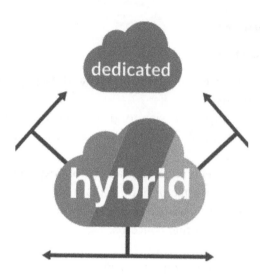

The author likes the "hybrid model" because it opens the door for leveraging both options simultaneously.

This will maximize growth potential as it takes advantages of both direct and M&A options, which can both prove to be successful strategies and not interfere with each other in the pursuit.

This "hybrid" approach can also be a "risk management" approach because it potentially reduces the exposure if only one option is pursued, and it does not work.

It is when both approached do not work ... where you have to go back to the drawing board and reassess your overall approach, leadership, and pursuing strategies.

Keep in mind, multiple strategies at one time can also be an overall strategic position. More difficult to manage but minimizes the risk if ... the chosen strategy fails?

BE ACQUIRED OR ACQUIRE

There are many companies after complete review and assessment that they will have a very difficult time in competing, growing, and developing business opportunities in their corporate structure and state ... as is.

As an option, if they become part of a larger organization, by merging or being acquired, they would see huge benefits, as follows:

- Financial resources to provide funding for growth activities and initiatives
- Operational resources for more robust capabilities
- Access to certain IPR (Intellectual Property Rights) … that might prove beneficial to business development opportunities
- Better management structure which provided enhanced leadership to make business development strategies happen
- Access to technology that makes business development easier to move forward
- More robust value-adds.

In this option, both the new parent company and the acquired merge and gain from the new entity. It is a mutually beneficial strategy that creates advantages for both parties.

The acquisition may not be accomplished as a "savior or vanquish" but one that creates a stronger company for both interests.

PARTNERSHIPS IN COMPANION VERTICALS

This option is a favored for one of the authors … because the upfront costs are minimized and results can be seen very quickly.

In 2018/2019 … the merger of CVS and Aetna would be a great example of a companion market for both companies coming together to leverage opportunity, resources, and strengths.

For which "mutual clients and products" would be of combined synergy.

My firm Blue Tiger International in 2018 involved in global trade consulting and business development formed a companion partnership with a logistics company … Sparx Global Logistics to the mutual benefit of both our organizations.

This enabled both companies:

- To share resources
- To share leads and opportunities
- To leverage strengths
- To minimize and supplement weaknesses
- To integrate technology advantages
- To combine management prowess
- To minimize costs where purchasing and costing can be reduced or shared

This initiative as we approach 2019 has been very successful in achieving all those benefits.

In the past 20+ years, we have utilized this from business development strategy as a very effective process to grow our business with minimum expense and risk.

Another example of companion relationship is in building an international sales model:

BLUE TIGER INTERNATIONAL

Blue Tiger International is a specialized and boutique consulting company with headquarters in NY that provides expertise in global supply chain, trade compliance, logistics, and international business management areas.

Many of their clients in accepting their advice and counsel will always question which service providers they should be utilizing to maximize the efficiencies in their supply chains.

So, Blue Tiger aligned itself up with several service providers that they can refer clients into developing a synergy where these service providers will now refer business into Blue Tiger International.

This will work best in cases where it makes sense for both parties to gain without compromising client interest principals.

You had one company providing consulting on global supply chain and the others in a more "hands-on" capacity in the physical movement of the goods ... often referred to as logistics.

The actual import and export companies benefited from these "companion" relationships as the related parties ended up typically in better serving their needs and interests.

eCOMMERCE: INTERNATIONAL SELLING IN THE NEW MILLENNIUM

eCommerce is becoming an increasing bigger component of all business models, and sales management needs to adjust to this form of selling which is very different from the standard sales practices of the past.

It requires different skill sets, comprehensive technology, and innovative delivery systems.

Sales management in eCommerce needs to pay attention to several key areas:

- Technology
- The future of purchasing
- The eCommerce supply chain

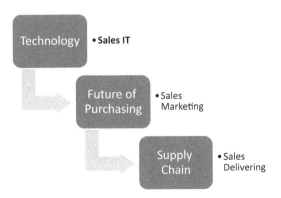

Technology

eCommerce's foundation is technology based. Those companies that have done well, i.e., Alibaba, Amazon, Netflix, etc., have mastered both the art and science of technology to gain huge market shares.

In eCommerce, those companies that have mastered the technology interface follow these sales management principles:

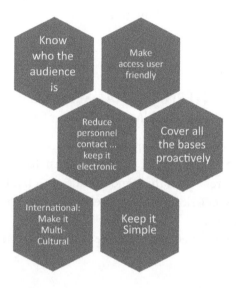

Know Who the Audience Is

eCommerce primarily sells to millennials and business to consumer, both domestically and globally.

But this dynamic is changing as more business is being sold "business to business" and older and more seasoned individuals and executives are utilizing eCommerce for purchasing.

Once your audience is identified, the next step is to target market that group and customize the approach.

Make Access User Friendly

People are impatient and not very tolerant. If the website is not user friendly or has numerous challenges when accessed ... potential customers will move on.

So many companies have perfected the "customer experience" in website access and utilization ... that those companies become standards for everyone else.

This means that your website should be designed by very contemporary professionals, with state-of-the-art skill sets and creative juices running at full strength.

Reduce Personnel Contact ... Keep It Electronic

A business or person coming into the website for information or to purchase should be able to navigate the entire process with as little as possible ... human contact.

That is where the efficiency of eCommerce originates from ... reduced personnel count in sales and customer service.

What some companies are doing to be competitive and more user friendly is opening up a browser when they see someone who has entered the website and is browsing around.

They place an icon on the screen ... asking if they can be of assistance. This can be done electronically and then only a person needs to be involved if a question is asked.

It helps control costs and offers a "human-touch" if required.

Cover All the Bases Proactively

You need to think through what the customer experience is like when visiting your website. You must walk alongside them so that you can anticipate all the needs they have to make their visit a good experience.

You must anticipate, understand their questions, their challenges, and also provide competitive advantages ... all proactively.

The eCommerce sites and business models that think through the clients' needs in advance will grow and prosper ... and the ones that don't ... they won't.

International: Make It Multi-Cultural

The differences around the world are vast:

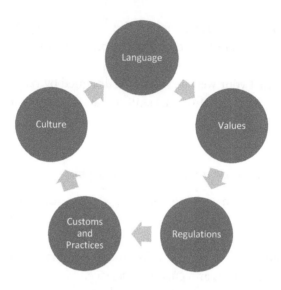

All these areas above … language, values, regulations, culture, customs and practices … all must be taken into consideration when building an eCommerce business that crosses international borders.

Sales management and global business developers must learn the specifics in each one of these areas when approaching any aspect of global trade and in eCommerce, as well.

These five areas must be built into the eCommerce business model in the website design, the communications, the messages sent, how goods and services are offered and delivered, and in every aspect of the eCommerce experience in that particular foreign market you are selling to.

It could be possible that if you sell in 30 markets overseas, you will have 30 variations in the eCommerce platform customized to any of the five areas outlined above.

Keep It Simple

Websites that are too expansive will make the buyers complicated and convoluted at some point.

There needs to be a "balance" obtained with being comprehensive but not to the anxiety of the buyer, who you will lose.

There is both an art and science in keeping the eCommerce model simple in areas such as:

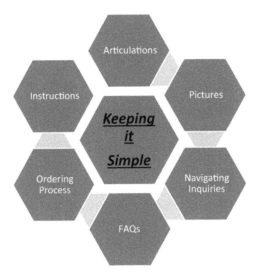

Managing the sales and business development aspects of eCommerce require:

- Access to expertise
- Paying attention to detail
- Being comprehensive and simple at the same time

The six areas outlined above are some of the primary areas of keeping eCommerce simple, which is the best practice on the road to global success, utilizing this mode of sales.

THE FUTURE OF PURCHASING

Purchasing managers are always charged with reducing risk and cost in their global supply chains. Sales teams need to pay attention to how the parties they sell to are changing and developing their purchasing strategies.

Their strategies will impact your strategies on how you approach the marketing, sales, and customer service process.

The eCommerce business model in certain product and service verticals does clearly offer price reductions and has seen significant growth in the past ten years.

eCommerce purchasing has many challenges:

Purchasing decisions and procurement business models impact the sales strategies.

- Less negotiation opportunity
- Less opportunity for relationship building
- Less mitigation opportunity when matters go awry

The eCommerce business model's foundation reduces human contact. Prices are more fixed. There is less room for negotiation if any at all.

If you are communicating with a website ... then the opportunity to build relationships between sales and purchasing is minimized.

Since the personal relationship is lessened in eCommerce when there is a problem, mitigations and problem resolution are also minimized, and the opportunity for favorable recovery is substantially reduced.

The expectations in these three challenges are reduced but not eliminated. The author believes as eCommerce continues to become more sophisticated and consumer favored, these challenges and their negative impact will not go away but will begin to dissipate.

THE eCOMMERCE SUPPLY CHAIN

The eCommerce Supply Chain has numerous elements as outlined in the following pictorial representation:

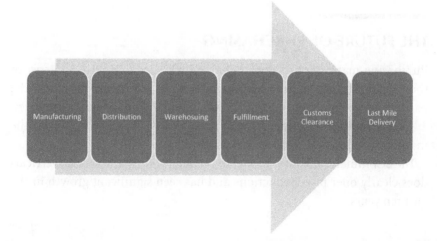

Manufacturing: In eCommerce on a global scale, the manufacturer has to develop products and specifications that meet all the unique requirements of the countries they are selling to.

Distribution: Products being distributed in eCommerce have a completely different supply chain than those companies involved in normal commercial trade. Smaller orders are likely and dealing with multiple carriers, and service providers become a more likely scenario.

Relationships with many of the integrated carriers like DHL, Federal Express, and UPS become increasingly important.

There are also specialty boutique eCommerce carriers designed and capable to handle eCommerce as an outsource function and third-party solution.

Warehousing: Warehouses need to be inventory, and materials handle products very differently in eCommerce as compared to normal commercial trade.

Fulfillment: eCommerce causes a very different approach to packing, marking, labeling, and shipping.

In going international, this process must be customized for each country you are shipping to.

Local regulations will also be another area of concern in dealing with in-country regulations and legal requirements.

Many companies outsource their fulfillment needs to third-party providers who specialize in this eCommerce and Global Marketplace.

Customs Clearance: The clearance of customs authorities in every country is a daunting responsibility. This is what makes international sales and eCommerce complicated, requiring extreme due diligence.

In normal business practice, the importer typically will handle the customs clearance process. In eCommerce, it becomes the responsibility of the seller/exporter.

Customs clearance will also include duties, taxes, and applicable fees. This is usually determined by the country of origin and product description, identified by the Harmonized Tariff Schedule (HTS).

This then becomes a sales management area of concern in coordinating how this will be accomplished in collaboration with internal or third-party logistics expertise.

There are costs involved in this process that needs to be brought into the "landed cost" of the product which will assist in deciding the selling price.

Landed Cost Elements in Export eCommerce:	
Selling Price FOB Origin	$38.00
Freight	$3.50
Export Handling	$2.00
Insurance	$.50
Customs Clearance	$2.50
Duties	$7.50
Local Delivery	$1.50
Total Landed Cost	**$55.50**

The landed cost modeling is important for international sales management to closely monitor. It controls competitiveness, sustainability, and margin protection.

Many countries around the world, such as Great Britain, the United States, China, Germany, to name a few … have special programs in easing the process of eCommerce passing through their borders.

HOW SALES PERSONNEL ARE "VIEWED" BY OTHER PERSONNEL IN YOUR COMPANY?

It is very important for any person to "see the forest through the trees" and to "have a realistic idea of how others view their being". It is for that reason this section from the book *Sales Management* is now discussed.

As a general statement, sales personnel in most organizations are:

- Not well liked
- Not well respected
- Viewed as not necessary "cogs in the wheel"
- Not taken seriously
- People who don't pay attention to detail
- People who move around a lot, but get very little done
- People who cut corners
- Not to be trusted
- Selfish
- Arrogant and condescending

Now, many of these character traits are true, some embellished a bit, and others absolutely perfect descriptions.

But we also know that there are a handful of sales personnel who have none of these traits and are outstanding corporate citizens at every level and in every way.

But more experienced management personnel and business executives would clearly outline many of these traits to hold water.

So are these good or bad attributes. The answer is not black and white … it is gray. It is gray because some are traits that "to an extent" could be valuable in sales doing what they need to do to … sell!

The key phrase "to an extent" is the critical aspect to understand. Being selfish as an example, for a salesperson could prove valuable as a motivating trait, but only to an extent. If the selfishness crosses the line of being obnoxious, insensitive, or impartial … then that makes them horrible traits.

Selfishness to an extent could be a positive characteristic or trait.

Another trait, which to an extent has value … "not paying attention to detail". This is controversial.

HUNTERS AND GATHERERS

In some circles, sales personnel are identified as "Hunters or Gatherers". Hunters are typically more aggressive and take on more complicated tasks.

Gatherers are more like customer service personnel, who "care-take" relationships, nurture, and hold on to.

It is the authors' opinion that "Hunters" present the better option for direct sales talent in most business development models. This is supported on the basis that developing opportunities and closing deals could be two of the hardest tasks that companies have to manage successfully in building their business models.

Hunters present the best opportunity for sales success in new clients and protecting higher margins.

Hunters are also a difficult hire. They are elusive and among salespersons are hard to find. They also can be somewhat of a prima donna, similar to a high-end trial attorney.

Hunters have the following traits:

- Motivated
- Big spenders
- Huge ego
- Creative
- Persistent
- Gregarious but not obnoxious
- Determined
- Can be detailed
- Patient, but not to a fault
- Relationship builder
- Great networker
- Possible, high in emotional intelligence... maybe

Additional Internal Perceptions

- Sales personnel "appear" to have special privileges and much about as prima donna's.
- Sales personnel travel a lot and are often out of the office, who many believe are then not working and become jealous of that external freedom.
- Sales personnel make a lot of money for doing very little.

These additional factors causing internal strife towards sales personnel are not well-founded and are a perception that creates all sorts of unnecessary angst.

Sales and senior management have to communicate and manage well to avoid this yep of stereotyping.

Though it is true that salespeople do not like operations and administrative responsibilities, typically, most of them, most of the time.

True salespeople who are "Hunters" are not going to pay attention to operational details, nor should they be elected to.

True "Hunters" are a scarce commodity, and their expertise is in meeting people and creating business development opportunities. Their skill sets are being gregarious, extroverted, and in the right place at the right time and knowing just what, when, and how to say things ... that create opportunity.

They should not have to fill out paperwork, complete applications, fill out reports, etc.

- It is a waste of their valuable time … you want them out selling not administering. Administer with support and administrative personnel.
- They will be "reluctant campers", resistant to paperwork, and therefore, they will always be late, you will have to follow-up and when done, it will be short-changed material.
- Hunting is a specialized skill set and talent. I think it is akin to higher-end trial attorneys … of which both need to be treated special, out of administration and allowed to focus on what they do best … hunt and kill! (Figuratively speaking ☺).

So why do I point out that sales personnel need to understand this perception of them?

It is important for an array of reasons:

1. Perception is reality when it comes to how people make judgment and decisions. If they perceive negative traits and character flaws … that will determine how they will react, interface and impact their relationship with you in a diminished or bad way.
2. Many of these traits … arrogance, condescension, not well respected, etc., are certainly not virtues from any perspective, and these are examples of traits that must be modified, corrected, and changed as soon as possible.
3. Change will take behavior modification, which is one of the hardest aspects of people's behaviors to deal with.
4. Change is necessary to "smooth out" internal personnel relations.
5. Change starts with a clear understanding of a realistic and forthright view of how others perceive you and understanding that bad behavior and traits have negative consequences and good behavior and traits have positive and enhanced opportunities.
6. Smoothing out relations will make you a more effective salesperson and allow for a more collaborative process in handling and managing client's needs.
7. Bad behavior may only be tolerated in the short term. Good behavior has a better opportunity for longer-term sustainability and increased sales and greater margins.

Corrective behavior of sales personnel is a very serious matter. It is a skill set all by itself and requires a lot of diligence and creative processes:

- Quality leadership by management creates the best opportunity to correct behavior. Said in another way ... "lead others to change" moves personnel into silos of corrective behavior
- Leadership demonstrates better character traits through their own actions and behaviors
- Leadership identifies a pathway with incentives for good behavior and consequences for bad behavior
- Ingrained negative behavior may take some very creative approaches to cause successful change:
  - Intense diligence
  - Serious perseverance
  - Immediate feedback on actions, changes, and consequences
  - Far-reaching approaches to cause change

CASE STUDY ... THE RIGHT WAY

JLN Engineering, located in the Midwest, sold high-end construction services for building stadiums, event and amusement parks, and outdoor theaters. All their sales personnel (six) reported to a VP of Sales (Bob). All were engineers by education and training.

They were supported by a team of customer service managers who helped to prepare bids, handle customer needs, and provide client support, when they were out on the road.

Five of the six sales team got along famously with the customer service team, with the exception of one (Jack), who struggled with several of the customer service account managers.

Bob made several attempts to work with Jack in smoothing out Bob's interaction with the customer service members but with little success. Bob worked hard to identify customer service membership who were more tolerant and might be able to work with Jack.

But these initiatives failed over time. Jack was the youngest member of the sales team and the least experienced but had managed to produce a very large account early in his tenure with JLN Engineering. The account produced a lot of revenue for JLN, had a high profile in the organization. But the client was demanding, difficult, and required a lot of attention.

This put stress on Jack and some of the account managers went matters became hectic or problems surfaced.

When stress levels rose … Jack became demanding, impatient, unreasonable, rude, and, to some extent … unforgiving.

Jack's handling of the client and his responsibilities caused an array of issues in the Customer Service Group.

This led to one of the customer service team, who was a valued member of the team, to leave the company, citing Jack's "attitude and demeanor" as the reasons.

The HR Manager and Bob's boss required an immediate action to resolve the problem, even if it meant Jack's termination.

Bob knew that he had to try and save Jack and that meant driving Jack to a serious dose of behavior modification.

Bob clearly understood he would have to exercise serious diligence and be creative in finding a solution.

He first met with Jack, put him on notice of the seriousness of the matter and advised he was going to come up with some suggestions and ideas on how this situation, which was not tolerable, was going to change.

He requested that Jack begin thinking about what he could do to begin to modify behavior to tone down his aggressive demeanor towards the customer service team.

He told Jack that he was a valued employee, a great salesperson and that he was committed to finding a pathway on how best to move forward.

Bob also spent considerable time explaining what the situation was serious, concerning, and intolerable. But left matters on positive reinforcement of believing a resolve would be forthcoming.

Bob decided he had to figure out what triggered Jack's bad behavior and move towards finding an implementing solution.

He did not want to lose Jack as he believed Jack could easily develop into one of their top salespersons.

Bob structured a strategy:

- Find out more about jack on a personal level to determine if there was anything in his history or background that would incite such behavior
- Meet with the other sales team members to obtain their input
- Meet with the customer service team members to receive their input

- Meet with HR to determine what he could and could not do
- Put all the data together and come up with a strategy to resolve the problem. It would include corrective behavior

The strategy was that Bob structured was as follows:

- Meet with Jack again and make sure he understands and accepts the level of concern
- Obtain Jack's commitment to do what he has to resolve the issues
- Commit himself and the resources of the firm to work towards a favorable resolution
- Set a time frame of 90 days to start to see results
- He placed Jack within the customer service team for 2 weeks with the hope that Jack would be more sensitive to their needs if he understood what they were dealing with each day. It would also help him develop better relationships with the people he was struggling with
- He met with Jack a number of times and through some intimate and deep dialogue determined that stress triggered a lot of his bad behavior

Bob found a local consulting company that acts as support to executives, who require support in what they do. He found an experienced consultant within that organization that had workshops in stress management and provided customized counseling for those managers in need. He had Jack meet the consultant and they agreed to meet two times a week over the next 60 days.

The consultant determined after several sessions that Jack became stressed believing that when he got busy not everything was going to get done and he would lose his most valued client ... leading to his failure and eventual termination.

The consultant worked on several fronts with Jack:

- Time management
- Effective delegation techniques
- Relaxation exercises to reduce stress
- Developing a better mindset to deal with pressure

The consultant tied in his work with Bob, as Jack's manager and mentor, teaching Bob how do be a better manager and leader in this type of personnel issue.

- Bob created a number of off-set social events … a dinner and an evening hockey game for both the sales and customer service teams to socialize with one another … causing bonding and better relationships both as a team and in favor of Jack's situation.
  - Bob also realized that this specific client was more demanding and problematic than any other clients and created a special support team for Jack to delegate to when the situation warranted.

Move ahead to the 90-day mark.

Bob's management initiatives worked, as follows:

1. Jack became more sensitive to and more aligned with customer service. Having spent two weeks, "walking in their shoes" paid off dramatically as he was now much more understanding of what they had to deal with daily and at the end of the day … how important they were to his team and more importantly … to be more respectful of them as individuals, friends, and colleagues.
2. Gaining support during peak client demand was a "godsend" and eliminated a lot of panic and stress.
3. His work with the consultant and supported by Bob's leadership allowed Jack to better manage his time, delegate more effectively, and to communicate more responsibly without causing stress levels to rise.
4. He had to still learn to better control his own fears and build confidence … but that will be a work-in-process to be accomplished over time.
5. The social activities created better harmony between the sales and customer service teams which helped all team members but also with Jack.

In conclusion, Bob utilized numerous resources, got creative, and manufactured a successful solution to getting Jack to change his behavior. It did require professional assistance, which is ok … as that is why they exist and can be very valuable in these more difficult circumstances.

Jack still needed continued professional support, and Bob will have to stay on top of matters more diligently, but the corrective path forward has been accomplished hopefully providing sustainable changes to avoid having to deal with this problem again.

Behavior change is a complicated and difficult process requiring skill set, experience, resource utilization, and lots of good management and luck.

CASE STUDY ... THE WRONG WAY

Arc Enterprises located in a business suburb of Philadelphia manufactures specialized medical equipment for dental surgeons all over the world.

There is a Director of Sales (Jenna) who has five sales personnel covering both domestic and foreign markets. The sales team are experienced, all coming from various aspects of the medical industry.

Their sale is direct to trade practitioners and is an expensive purchase that requires a much-focused sales process. The sales team is highly paid, they travel over 60% of the time and have mastered telecommunications to keep in touch with the office and transmit orders and client instructions.

Interaction with the home office is mostly accomplished electronically. The team rarely sees one another with the exception of an annual sales team meeting in January of every year.

Brian has been with the sales team for 3 years and is a good salesman somewhere in the "middle of the pack" in overall sales volume. He came out of the fetal field as he went to school to be a dentist, but in his last year, which he never finished, dropped out for personal reasons, and took this job.

He is somewhat arrogant and condescending in his approach internally, and though most communications are electronic ... it seems to "piss-off" someone in the company every day with an attitude that "his shit don't stink" and "yes, I am better and more important than you" approach.

Recently, his attitude has become increasingly unbearable by the operations team who process the orders, arrange shipping, and dialogue with the customers, once a sale is made.

The operations team has now dropped the ball a few times on Brian's accounts ... probably not intentionally, but certainly not as a result of caring about him and his accounts.

One client has been lost and another one is complaining and threatening to leave. Jenna needs to resolve this matter and understand she has to change Brian's behavior.

Every problem is a gift—without problems we would not grow.

Anthony Robbins, Motivational Speaker and Writer

4

Sales Skill Sets

Sales managers and their sales team have to acquire and master a number of skill sets to be successful in business development. This chapter identifies and highlights these skills and addresses their relative importance as a foundation area for global trade and business development.

THE IMPORTANT SALES MANAGEMENT SKILL SETS

Keep in mind that sales managers must have both management and sales skills to succeed.

In some cases, both skill sets are equally critical in other cases, one will need to dominate.

The sales manager must learn to work from both the management and the sales angles to the company's benefit and show the flexibility when to bring the skill to the table for access and utilization.

The Key Management Skill Sets are:

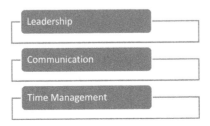

```
┌─ Problem Resolution      ├──────────
│
├─ Coaching & Mentoring    ├──────────
│
├─ Negotiation             ├──────────
│
├─ Sub-Skill Sets          ├──────────
```

LEADERSHIP

Leadership is the ability to influence and control others to follow a particular path. In business, this will mean following the mission, culture, and objectives of the company to the mutual benefit of the company, the shareholders, the employees, the clients, vendors, and to themselves.

Academicians will define as follows:

Leadership defined is a personal and business concept where both a research area and a practical skill encompassing the ability of an individual or *organization* to "lead" or guide other individuals, *teams*, or entire *organizations*.

The U.S. academic environments define leadership as "a process of *social influence* in which a person can enlist the aid and *support* of others in the accomplishment of a common *task*".

In business, it is coordinating a concerted effort to achieve desired goals.

Some business leadership resources characterize leadership with the following words:

Guidance, control, supervision, direction, management, power, influence, administration, captain, conduct, authority, initiative, command, skill, foresight, capacity, preeminence, conveyance, preside, supremacy, domination, superiority, hegemony, dictate, govern, sway, and *primacy.*

Leadership Embodies Many of the Following Traits

- Responsible
- Decisiveness
- Awareness
- Focused
- Communicative
- Accountability
- Empathy
- Loyal
- Confidence
- Problem solver
- Optimism
- Honesty
- Inspiration
- Transparent
- Cautious risk-taker
- No nonsense

Many people quickly assume that being a good leader means you're a good manager and vice versa. The two concepts are actually quite distinct and understanding that distinction can help you understand what it means to be good at either or good at both. As this chapter continues, we will highlight the differences and similarities.

COMMUNICATION STRATEGIES

Communicating with and about an organization is a critical skill set, developed by many, mastered by a few. Here are 14 substantive thoughts on communication skill set development:

Face to Face

Learn to know when "face-to-face" meetings are important and should be undertaken, millennials too often struggle and do not utilize this method.

Face to face allows the eyes to see what you cannot hear or read. Allows potentially true emotions to be identified and analyzed.

Understand What You Are Trying to Accomplish

Goals, objectives, and deliverables need to be set each time you communicate. Are you informing, incentivizing, instructing, delegating, influencing or what?

Knowing what you are seeking to accomplish, which may be multiple outcomes will impact your communication strategy, structure, and delivery mechanism.

Listening Skills

Most people do not listen well. It is the ability to listen to and incorporate others' views in your communication. Listening shows you value opinions outside of your own and are open to new concepts. As a result, your audience views you as an equal partner, and you can come to a solution that benefits the greater good. An active listener will allow pauses for interjections, repeat other people's words, and *ask questions* to affirm his or her engagement in a conversation.

Creating a Perception of Concern

The person on the other side of the communication will respond better if they sense you are seriously engaged, concerned, and involved in the purpose/substance of the communication involved.

Hopefully, you are really engaged, but if not so, a perception truly has to be developed so the communique will be more open to the subject matter at hand.

Expression and Writing Skills

You need to present a substantive discussion. Utilizing specific data and examples in written communication(s) that will make a solid case and in communicating proposed action items.

Quantitative positions over qualitative will work better.

Written communication for business should be brief but informative and helps an audience focus on only the most important points.

Good written communication also includes adequate follow-up, which closes the communication loop and shows proactive activity towards goals.

Accountability and responsibility concerns always should be outlined in good communications.

Speaking and Verbal Skills

It is the ability to communicate information (ideas, thoughts, opinions, and updates) in a clear manner verbally.

Like good written communication, good verbal communication in the workplace is also concise and specific (researchers have found that *today's attention span amounts to only 8.25 seconds*).

Verbal communication allows employees to engage with one another in-person and come to a mutually agreeable consensus.

Verbal can allow "interactivity" which allows a dialog and mutual engagement to take place. That will allow resolution, direction, or action to more easily follow.

Build Trust and a Solid Bond

Building trust and a strong personal bond will help any level or kind of communication become more likely to succeed.

Trust allows believability to come through. The sender is in a stronger position when the respondent believes they are honest and trustworthy two very defined character traits of "trust".

Interpersonal Communication Skills

"Soft skill", successful interpersonal communication allows employees to find common ground, display empathy, and build bonds with one another. Interpersonal communication means connecting on more than business level but a personal level as well.

Personalizing communications, though sometimes forbidden in some organizations, allows the door open for being politically incorrect over millennia has proven to be a more effective and believable way of influencing and informing.

Storytelling

Building stories, case studies, and analogies into communications often allows the sender to be more believable, and it affords the opportunity for the respondent to better identify with the substance of the communication.

Some of the best leaders in the world over the last 200 years have been great storytellers.

Group Management and Team Building

Taking a leadership role in communicating may mean addressing a team or group of individuals who need to be aligned for a common goal or expected outcome.

Effectively communicating with others who may have different agendas, goals, opinions, and capabilities is a good best practice.

In a business setting, this means putting aside personal differences and working towards a common goal. For teamwork to be successful, all parties must recognize that combined efforts are worth more than individual contributions.

You must be able to:

- Align the team to a common goal they all are working towards
- Eliminate any challenges caused by personalities or personal differences
- Cleary allocate responsibilities and structure an accountability system
- Have regular meetings and open a portal for timely information flow between all the team members
- Create transparency to all undertakings of the team and the related parties
- Make sure the "team members as a group" receive fair credit for all activities of the team, irrespective of who was more involved.

You can always show favor for those that are more involved and handle all the heavy lifting.

Presentation and PowerPoint Skillsets

It is presenting information and ideas to an audience in a way that is engaging, motivating, and effective. This method of business communication allows one individual, or a group of individuals, to share evidence to support an idea or argument.

A good presenter is also a good storyteller, using data, stories, and examples to influence an audience to act towards a desired outcome, as was previously discussed. These now need to be conveyed via the presentation format.

PowerPoint is the most contemporary resource available to deliver powerful and comprehensive presentations. It is user-friendly and extremely creative, flexible, and allows personalization.

All sales managers must be able to master the delivery of presentations and the utilization of PowerPoint.

Persuasion and Selling Capabilities

Selling and persuading are closely related skill sets. Sales will usually require a decision by the other party. Persuasion may just cause an alignment, as well.

Persuading stakeholders to pursue an idea, decision, action, product, or service, is a necessary business practice.

Selling skills extends beyond just those whose jobs fall under the sales department. Employees with selling skills can use these skills to influence other employees to buy into a project, team members to choose a side, or executives to offer new products or services.

True leaders will typically find it easier to persuade and sell as they have established:

- Credibility
- Trust
- Power
- Influence.

These characteristics make it much easier to persuade, influence, and sell ideas and action items.

Negotiation Skills

Negotiation is always a process that business development and all managers need to find success in. Good negotiators have a better opportunity at achieving their desired results and dealing with the typical challenges that will come up on any given day, in any project, or business initiative.

Reaching a mutually beneficial solution by understanding and leveraging the other side's motivations. A mutually beneficial or "win-win" solution is one that both sides find favorable and maintain positive relationships for future interactions. In order to achieve this outcome, you'll need to discover what factors would be most influential and agreeable for the other side.

Psychology of people's behavior is a great skill set to master in becoming a good negotiator, as we always negotiate with "people". Understanding their behavior is critical to finding ways to navigate that complexity.

Sales Management Is a "Collaborative Process"

When sales are truly successful within any organization, a defined component of that success is the ability of the sales manager to reach into the organization and create a "Collaborative Process".

Sales is not an "island" by itself. It is coordinating the delivery of products and services from the inside of an organization to the external benefit of the clients.

This process then has both a direct and an indirect interface with all the internal workings of the organization, such as but not limited to manufacturing, legal, finance, customer service, distribution, warehousing, marketing, and senior management.

The successful sales manager is like the "quarterback" at a football game. It is a leadership role that moves the team down the field eventually delivering a "touchdown"!

The "touchdown" is coordinated with all the team players:

- Being in synch
- Understanding each other's roles
- High degree of cooperation
- Moving ego to a less than important issue
- A coordinated and orchestrated initiative

Internal and External Relationship and Networking Skills

Having both internal and external relationships with people and other forms of resources is an important attribute to have in building a solid communication capability.

Displaying business value and encouraging others to enter into your business network is another best practice. In order to network successfully, you'll need to be interesting, important, or influential sufficiently that others desire to partner with you in some way.

A large business network can also be a safety net and means you have more people to rely on when you require help, information, or services.

Time Management

Time is both a precious natural resource and a huge commodity in business.

For successful business development managers, it is also a necessary component of being able to move forward on a consistent and reliable basis in the handling of all your scheduling, appointments, management responsibilities, and moving the company into growth and prosperity with long-term sustainability.

Managing time is allowed when two additional factors are mastered prioritization and organization.

A manager who knows how to prioritize and is highly organized than and only then can be successful in managing his or her time.

Since the recession of 2008/2009 every manager is working harder, longer hours, and with less support in personnel count. If you do not manage time well, your opportunity for achieving your desired goals is very limited.

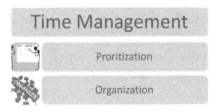

We need to learn a better way to prioritize and organize which has a direct impact on how we manage "time".

Managing priorities and organization is a highly personal issue, but there are some common and generic considerations.

Some of the following suggestions should be built into business development managers' daily routine.

1. Know what the goals are and the expectations of your senior management, board of directors, shareholders, partners, etc.
2. Prioritize your responsibilities and activities into two lists:
     One that outlines overall responsibilities, such as but not limited to:
     • Work with the sales team
     • Visit key clients

- Visit new business activity weekly
- Meet with the sales team monthly
- Send in weekly reports to the CEO

The second list with specific tasks, such as but not limited to:

- Call John at BWE Corp to review renewal numbers
- F/u with Karen on the new production schedule
- Speak with customer service on returning calls more promptly
- Coordinate a resolve to the Deerex Co billing problem

3. We prioritize by maintaining a "list" of these overall responsibilities combined with all the "tasks" and "to do" action items.

4. We continually write down all the things we have to do. If we depend on memory alone we and our relationships will be seriously disappointed regularly.

5. A third list will need to be maintained, with personal items that need to be done, that potentially will interfere with business scheduling, such as but not limited to:

- Set up dentist appointment for next Wednesday afternoon.
- Speak to your daughter Susie, regarding the chaperone request for the prom in April.
- Call BMW to schedule getting brakes looked at.
- Reach John B. @ DLG Securities to review the 401 k transfer documents required.

6. Recognize that there is not enough time in the day to get everything done, so prioritizing is a key step, to make sure we get the most important things done on time and communicate the balance.

7. The list of priorities allows us to begin the organization of our overall responsibilities and the day-to-day specific tasks we have to complete.

   When we can review the list(s) is one focused view we then can prioritize what needs to be accomplished first, second, third, to the 20th item on the list.

8. The list(s) need to be reviewed throughout the day and new items added, as they occur, and other items deleted as they are taken care of.

9. As a manager, you need to make sure your entire team is practicing this behavior, to the teams and their personal benefit. This is a leadership and coaching matter.

10. Organization is keeping every document in its place, files maintained, a neat and clean working office, desk, and surface.

    You need to be organized so you know where everything is, when you need it.

11. Depending upon your seniority, scope of your responsibilities, the company's culture, etc., this is where an assistant can provide support in keeping you organized.

12. Delegating is also a "time management" solution. Delegating is another leadership and mentoring behavior. It allows you to train others while at the same time moving subordinated tasks to others, while you focus on the more important priorities.

What will happen many times is that a manager gets too caught up in the minutia and the minor details (sometimes referred to as micro-managing), and this then does not allow them to deal with the important issues, as they run out of time in dealing with the minor areas of concern.

Delegating requires a clear and discernable communication on expectations and actions required. Include deadlines and all areas of what you need to get done, who needs to be communicated to, and whatever nuances are relevant.

Delegating is also an effective way of building and managing a team. It also affords camaraderie to take hold and a sense of loyalty to you and the other team members.

TIME MANAGEMENT

White Paper
October 2018
National Institute for World Trade

Executives who develop skill sets in managing their time will do a lot better in handling their overall responsibilities successfully.

In today's business environment, executives are busy with an array of responsibilities and a huge demand to consistently perform.

Most executives have multiple responsibilities making them overbearingly busy. Their ability to manage time becomes critical in managing their responsibilities well.

When time is not navigated successfully, the consequences are numerous:

- Dissatisfied staff, customers, vendors, and bosses
- Failure to perform as required

- Inability to meet expectations
- Operational and financial losses
- Loss of business, margin, and staff

On the other side of the equation, when time is managed successfully, the rewards are grand:

- Satisfied customers, staff, suppliers, and bosses
- Opportunity to "move up the ladder"
- Keeping everyone "happy and moving forward" more smoothly
- More business and higher margins
- An easier managed business model

REDUCTION IN STRESS

When problems occur and time is constrained, we become stressed. When stress becomes a common occurrence and grows in severity the potential consequences become critical:

- We tend to make hasty decisions which are not well thought out and could be mistakes.
- We emulate a nervousness, which could send out the wrong signal to those around us leading to their becoming nervous, upset, and dysfunctional.
- Stress can cause bad decision, bad actions, and less than desirable results.
- The wrong signal is sent out leaving us potentially vulnerable in a relationship, a negotiation, or in a leadership posture.

This all leads us to the conclusion that excessive stress has mostly negative consequences, and we need to get it under control.

A leading cause of stress is not managing time correctly. The obvious conclusion is that if we manage time better, we then can operate in a less stressful environment, which will allow us to be more successful in whatever we are attempting to accomplish.

Stress has a positive consequence as well. It causes us to produce cortisol. In balance, this hormone allows various defensive mechanisms of the mind and body to heavily influence thoughts and actions.

As an example, stress may come from fear. We are for a walk in the woods and come across a bear. Fear allows us to pump adrenaline, to make us run faster. The stress of that moment and the production of key hormones allow the mind to think quickly and the body to move faster.

All that results in not being harmed by the bear.

Fortunately in everyday life, we don't often come across bears. But in business, we do sometimes perceive "bears" and the stress becomes overbearing and creates chaos and all sorts of negative consequences.

Too much stress, too often can lead to more serious medical issues as well as depression.

We must get stress under control.

So mastering time management is one of the tools we can utilize to manage stress concerns.

Additionally, stress comes from excessive fear, making a problem larger than it is, and being over fearful of consequence taken way out of proportion to reality.

Stress can be better controlled by how we think through the everyday challenges of living and managing business responsibilities.

Some suggestions:

- We must work within ourselves and have reasonable expectations.
- We need to have people to talk to and be able to express our concerns and have them help us sort our perceptions from reality
- Sometimes this will require specialized help from therapists, counselors, and psychiatrists.
- We must learn to recognize that problems and failures are part of the business model. They both must be minimized and brought under reasonable control, but they are both part of the deal, when we chose to live and also when we chose to be in business
- We must gain control and influence over what causes us to be fearful. This typically is better understanding "consequences' and putting that into the overall perspective and balance of our lives and our business responsibilities.
- We must learn our stress indicators and be proactive in managing before the stress becomes consequential. Professional resources such as internet, books, seminars, and therapy all are excellent options in understanding and managing stress indicators.

Stress is managed in two ways our mindset and actions and better managing time, which is further outlined below.

MANAGING TIME BETTER

The big question then becomes how we manage time better. In answering that question, we need to look at a number of variables that surround the topic of "time management".

They are:

- Organizational skill sets
- Prioritization skill sets
- Delegation skill sets
- Establishing goals, boundaries, and sound time management practices

ORGANIZATIONAL SKILL SETS

If you are not organized well, you will never manage time well. Keeping yourself organized is a critical aspect of managing time well.

Organizing well means:

- Understanding what is expected of you
- A comprehensive list in some format of all you have on your plate
- Making sure you are communicating to all vested interests what you have on your plate

PRIORITIZATION SKILL SETS

Prioritizing ties directly into organizing, as it takes all that you have on your plate and structuring an order of priority.

Then time frames for action and completion are accomplished.

This then engages a "strategy" that will make sure you accomplish all that you need in a timely fashion.

Because we are busy, we never get everything done, so we need to make sure we are communicating what does not get done with readjusted time frames for completion.

Keep in mind that every day, problems will present themselves that will take us out of our preplanned day.

This means that priorities are a "work in process" that needs to be tweaked consistently and communicated outbound timely and responsibly.

DELEGATION SKILL SETS

Delegating is both an art and science following some of these guidelines:

- Understand what can be delegated and what cannot.
- Understand that who to and what is delegated must be well thought out.
- Delegation is also a "mentoring and coaching" task that allows you to mentor staff in how business should be handled.

It is very important to understand that when you delegate, you are shifting a transactional responsibility to someone else. This does not mean you are giving up responsibility to make sure what you delegated is eventually completed satisfactorily.

This means you still have "ownership" of the delegated task to the person of whom you delegated to, competes the task.

Delegation requires a system to "track and trace" individual delegated tasks, to make sure they are all done timely and responsibly. Microsoft Office, various bolt-on technology options, and simplified Excel spreadsheets can all assist in this regard.

Irrespective of the system you utilize having some "accountability and responsibility" practice in place is what is important.

Delegation has some of the following benefits:

- Allows you to move some minor tasks to subordinates to offer you more time and more important responsibilities
- A source for mentoring and coaching as well as evaluating performance of team members on how they approach this work and perform or not
- A demonstration to your senior colleagues of how well you manage your responsibilities in delegating and in time management
- It allows you to measure the performance of others and allows them to go through various learning curves that will eventually make them better employees and managers

Effective delegators understand that there are certain responsibilities that cannot be delegated and that must be carried out by themselves. Knowing what can be delegated and what cannot is a very prized capability.

Delegating the wrong tasks can prove to be negatively consequential and bring on a resentment of all concerned with the choices and actions you have delegated rather than have assumed.

At the end of the day "delegating" is really a core competency of both good management and leadership.

Some leaders look at delegating as a burden, rather than an opportunity. This is being shortsighted. Delegation is a natural occurrence both in life and in business and sets the stage for others to follow and grow.

I have found over the years many executives who will not delegate or who don't delegate well have certain fears or paranoias about being replaced by someone who is up and coming.

This is a fallacy and must be overcome.

Those who delegate must not delegate carelessly. Meaning they think though carefully as to what can get delegated and to who, based upon experience, capability, and their current workload.

It is well ok to push personnel to take on more, but one must be careful not to push so hard it becomes overbearing and leads to dismay. Personal and staff must be ready to be delegated to. The manager can best delegate by:

- Making sure the person is ready for the delegated task
- Expectations and deliverables are concise and clear
- There is an acknowledgment and acceptance of responsibility
- Comprehensive and exact instructions are provided
- Timelines are established and agreed to
- All "stakeholders" are identified
- Communication responsibilities are established

Delegating can be an important asset to any busy executive to make him or her more successful in the execution of their overall responsibilities.

ESTABLISHING GOALS, BOUNDARIES, AND SOUND TIME MANAGEMENT PRACTICES IN "DELEGATING"

When thinking out delegation as a management tactic, you must first make sure you have established goals as to what you are attempting to accomplish.

Boundaries must also be established. What we mean by boundaries these are guidelines, protocols, and business practices that set both high and lower water marks for what can and cannot be delegated.

This can be established by business unit, division, or vertical by individual, by scope of authority and along with company policies.

Boundaries help regulate delegating authorities and assure no one crosses the line into unauthorized delegating. Another example of this would be relative to financial and accounting controls within an organization, where "signing authority" has set limitations.

Or within the legal and contract requirements as to has signing authority and to what limits??

Tied into boundaries is also establishing sound time management practices. What we mean here is to structure guidelines for staff and employees to follow regarding task and project completion.

Example of a sound time management practice policy:

XYZ Corporation, NYC 2018

- **All tasks and projects will have clearly defined deliverables, expectations, and time frames for completion.**
- **No task or project can be delegated or received without establishing boundaries of authority.**
- **All stakeholders will be clearly recognized and the relevance to the task or project identified.**
- **Lines of timely and responsible communication will be established at the point of delegation and maintained throughout the life of the task or project delegated.**
- **A clear line of reporting problems and issues timely to management is required.**

One of the important benchmarks within a company that makes "time management" an overall priority of a "Best Practice" in business management will also structure how delegating is best managed with an organization and have protocols and guidelines in place for their executive team to use as a reference guideline.

This prevents delegating from being overutilized and being a problem in the business model of the organization.

Problem Resolution

In the day-to-day running of any business problems will arise. They will need to be dealt with and brought to a successful closure.

This is a typical responsibility for managers to handle. You may not need to do the grunt work but to assure the problem gets resolved.

The steps we utilize to manage through problems are as follows:

The seven steps outlined above are a pathway to mitigate issues, resolve problem, and keep customers happy.

When a problem first arises, we must do a *quick assessment*, so we will know what we need to do. This quick assessment will typically have a limitation on information flow and all the facts necessary for a more thorough examination of what happened.

The quick assessment will allow you to take the first steps of resolution "stop the bleeding".

This action will hopefully begin the process of mitigating the issue at hand.

Once the initial actions are taken, you can then conduct a more detailed and *comprehensive assessment* of the problem. This will require interviews, meetings, file reviews, information intake, etc. For the purpose of understanding exactly what happened and setting up responsibility and accountability in the problem and the resolve.

This secondary assessment will lead to an *Action Plan* to make sure the issue does not happen again, resolve the immediate concern, and make sure everyone involved knows what happened and how you will move forward.

This is a time the manager must walk a very fine line of being both very positive and optimistic but making sure everyone also feels a sense of concern and resolve.

When problems arise, keep in mind that everyone is watching you what you will say, how you will react, and what steps will you take, etc. This is where you are **mentoring** your subordinates and colleagues and showing them a methodology on problem resolution.

Trust allows a much easier pathway to resolution.

Another critical aspect of problem resolution is **communications** to all parties impacted where you are in the resolution of the problem. Communicating timely, accurately, and transparently is a fundamental issue of establishing trust with everyone involved.

Trust allows a much easier pathway to resolution which is a proven staple of how a good relationship will be a mitigating factor in any problem that develops in the normal day-to-day activities of business relationships.

At this point, **closure** will occur in bringing the problem to resolution. This must be communicated, and a **follow-up** dialog is pursued to make sure all impacted parties are aligned with the resolution.

CASE STUDY IN PROBLEM RESOLUTION

You have a new salesperson working for you who has landed their first large account. In the transition of that account into your organization, the first container load of product being shipped to them from your plant in China is delayed at sea.

The late delivery is causing several problems:

First shipment out of the box is a problem and there is a loss of confidence right away.

They need the product for anticipated assembly processes that will have at their Columbus Facility. Your product not arriving on time will delay processing and damage their sales and customer service requirements.

The original supplier is lurking in the shadows looking to come back in, with a supply of products ready to ship.

Your new salesperson is panicking and also fearing loss of the new client.

You immediately speak with the client along with your new salesperson to determine their level of concern and need.

The inbound container load had 40 pallets of their purchase onboard originally scheduled to arrive next week. The delay will add on another 10 days to the delivery schedule.

To mitigate the situation, you offer to air freight two pallets to them now, which they will have in 3 days, which will hold them over till the original shipment arrives. You agree to pay for the cost of the expedited shipping.

The client agrees to this and acknowledges that this is a reasonable resolution.

The shipment gets airfreighted and arrives as planned in the 3 days expected.

Your follow-up with the client who is satisfied that the problem that occurred was out of everyone's control and that as a new vendor you clearly and quickly resolved the problem.

Their confidence in you has increased, and your new salesperson is now much more relaxed as he or she has seen you provide support and resolve.

For the long term, you maintain a four-pallet supply of this client's product in your warehouse for any anticipated problems which may occur in the future, as a longer-term risk and preventive measure. The client is made aware of this, and their overall comfort level with their new vendor has been significantly enhanced.

Coaching and Mentoring

One of the most important areas of management is the ability to successfully coach and mentor your sales team and all the colleagues and subordinates that you interface with, in your business responsibilities.

Successful managers who are also respected as coaches and mentors have the loyalty of their staff and have a much easier time at managing the challenges of leadership in influencing, directing, and commanding.

Synonyms for this area are:

Leader Trainer Boss
　adviser · guide · confidant · confidante · coun-
selor · consultant · therapist · master · spiritual
leader · rav · rebbe · guru · swami · maharishi · acharya

The art of coaching and mentoring has an end result of influencing behavior of others. You are showing, demonstrating, and leading them into another way of looking at something or offering them a potentially better way of handling an area of responsibility.

But at the end of the day the goal is to impact better behavior. When this is done in a professional, articulate, and caring fashion we refer to this as "coaching or mentoring".

Negotiation

Negotiation is another important skill set that is required in sales. The sales manager must be a good negotiator in his or her own right but also must be in a position to coach and mentor negotiation skill sets to their sales team.

There are several key methods in teaching, coaching, and mentoring sales and operational colleagues and staff:

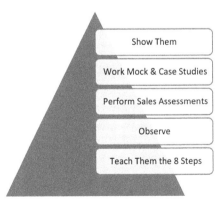

Mentoring Pyramid for Negotiation Skill Set Development

Show Them

An excellent step in negotiation coaching is to "show them". Meaning let them observe you in "ACTION" preferably on a real business situation, where there is clearly a challenge and you are confident you can bring it to a resolve.

Patience is an important aspect of negotiation. Showing them how to be patient is very relevant.

Additionally, pick a case where you know the negotiation is going to be difficult requiring several steps, changes in strategy, and over a longer period. This once brought to a successful close will generate a confidence in your capabilities both in negotiation prowess and in leadership.

Work Mock and Case Studies

Sit with your group of reports and work with them in various case studies and mock reviews discussing how you would approach the negotiation strategy on a specific scenario.

You can even review specific situations that have come up in your regular business flow. You can review each situation and discuss the pros and cons of what was done and maybe outline other ways a negotiation process may have been broached.

You can develop several cases each one getting progressively more difficult and make these a routine at the meetings and training sessions you hold for the team.

This can also be worked on an individual basis, where that personalization may be required or there is a "special need" with a particular person.

Perform Sales Assessments

On a regular basis, each success and each unsuccessful sale should be reviewed to determine what has been done right and wrong with the larger idea that improvement in the negotiation process can be best achieved by scrutiny in both directions what worked and what didn't?

This can be considered "Monday Quarter Backing" but when done with *the idea of constructive criticism and not the pointing of fingers* it works!

Continual scrutiny, assessment, and analysis will only lead to better results. You are also leading personnel to believe three important factors:

- There is always room for improvement.
- There is no one way to approach any strategy.

- There is a definite benefit to continually self-review, assess, and tweak in most situations.

You are leading the team to self-analysis and continual improvement.

This can be considered "Monday Quarter Backing" but when done with the idea of constructive criticism and not the pointing of fingers it works!

Observe

Listen-in on their phone calls. Go on sales calls with them. Observe every aspect of how they handle themselves which all impacts the negotiation process.

The observation will teach you what you need to work on with them.

It is important in this specific process to identify what they do right first, before getting into the constructive criticism side.

The observation process also has an additional benefit of holding the team and the individuals to a high standard of responsibility and accountability in their sales position. They need to know you are watching and observing.

Teach Them the Eight Steps

There are eight steps to follow in being a successful negotiator:

We cannot emphasize enough the strategic importance that relationship needs to be there with potential clients in order to increase the odds of successfully closing deals.

Relationship establishes trust, transparency, and a more open exchange of needs and information flow.

A quality relationship with a potential client raises the bar of opportunity significantly and increases the odds of closing a deal to everyone's mutual benefit.

Establish Goals

What are you attempting to achieve with the negotiation? That question is important because "it will then identify what your goals are".

Once the goals are established, you can construct a strategy that will deliver against those goals.

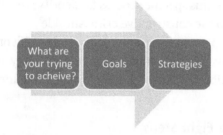

Goals will also assist you in "keeping your eye on the ball". It allows you to be focused on what actions you are taking, as they have to be targeted on what you are ultimately trying to achieve.

Mine

The concept of "Mining" is digging and collecting information that will be critical to having a successful negotiation.

Information is "gold"! It provides data, resources, and information flow that allows you to better assess, analyze, and evaluate your opportunity and then design a specific strategy.

Mining allows you the best opportunity to negotiate with leverage as information may contain secrets and concepts not previously identified that can be utilized to your advantage.

Strategize

A successful negotiation is approached by thinking through an "approach". This approach is better characterized as a "strategy".

The strategy develops a plan of attack on how you will approach the party on the other side of the table to be able to ultimately derive a favorable closure to what you are trying to achieve.

The strategy takes in all the relevant information gained from the "mining" process and combines that with the desired goals allowing the creation of how best to approach the negotiation with the best opportunity for success.

Send in Salvos

In the military "salvos: are weapon discharges into an area suspected of containing enemy positions. The salvos will ferret out the enemy and better define exactly where they are located and their proximate strength and capability.

The military sends in the salvos to learn better detail about the enemy, so they can plan or approach their strategy more successfully.

In commercial business, salvos could be questions, interrogations, meetings, and information gained by describing your position, outlining what you plan to do, and review expected results.

These forward actions (salvos) illicit a response from the other side of the negotiation. That response will allow you to gain insight into their mindset, position, negotiating stance, etc.

The salvo creates an information gain that better allows you to negotiate from strength.

Meet

In-person meetings are a valuable tool to utilize for a number of reasons and benefits:

Relationship Building

Better Opportunity to Figure Out the Otherside's Position

Advancing the Cause

When "eyeball to eyeball" occurs and you are sitting down together, the door is opened for developing a better relationship.

Phone, conference calls, and emails allow an exchange of communications, but it is difficult to allow a build of the relationship and bond between people. Electronic communications can serve as a "wall".

Face to face allows a relationship to build.

The meeting will also afford you the best opportunity to establish eye contact, read body language, and be in a more persuasive scenario.

Your negotiation is seeking a favorable closure. Meetings create a better pathway to advancing your cause to a favorable closure. It cuts out time, and the personal contact makes for more timely decisions.

It is harder for people to be negative or confrontational "face to face" which then increases the odds for the opposite effect to occur.

Tweak

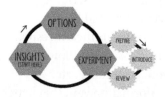

A negotiation that moves forward over time gains new information, new challenges, and new issues possibly even new players.

This then opens the door for the planned strategy with a need to be modified, tweaked, or changed to accommodate the new situation.

This requires insight, flexibility, and also creativity. Tweaking ultimately allows changes to be made to make your position stronger and more compelling.

Close

Eventually, the negotiation has to terminate and closure be brought forward.

The act of closure is a process. The order has to be obtained, final terms negotiated, and implementation steps created.

Closure brings the negotiation hopefully to a successful conclusion. However, the negotiation may not be successful. Then closure means walking away keeping future options open, a professional exit, and maintaining quality relationships.

Also keep in mind that closure is usually a second part referred to as "implementation" making what you just negotiated happen.

Implementation must go well to make the negotiation process close successfully.

Sub-Skill Sets: Legal, Financial, Operations, Insurance, and Human Resources

Sales and business development managers need to have a basic and even sometimes a more comprehensive understanding of a number of additional key operating venues in their company:

Finance

Human Resources

Legal

Operations

Insurance

Finance

Finance is important in sales and business development as everything will relate to a financial bottom line at some point in any business situation.

Sales managers need to understand issues such as:

- ROI (return on investment)
- Margins
- Payment and receivable terms
- Profit and loss
- Balance sheets

These basic financial considerations will tend to impact every decision involved in sales and business development management.

Human Resources

Sales and business development will always interface with human resources (HR) for both hiring and firing of personnel needs.

Additionally, HR will set controls in place for compensation, commission structures, deployment of personnel, and skill set training needs.

Sales management has a critical resource in HR that can assist in:

- Finding great sales and business development candidates
- Providing support in any personnel issues that may arise
- Providing guidance on compensation structure
- Accessing training and coaching tools

HR is often an undervalued asset when building a company and one that you will need to develop a basic understanding of.

Legal

Sales and business development are negotiating terms of trade, contracts, and resolving disputes all the time.

Internally or if outsourced, legal is another important area that you will have to gain basic knowledge about and be able to manage through the paperwork, documentation, and administrative responsibilities.

In many businesses, trade regulations will come into play that you will have to be able to comprehend and work through. Legal support and your ability to understand basic legal doctrines will be valuable allies to any successful sales or business development initiative.

You do not need to become a "lawyer", but you must be able to work with them, and the more you understand about what and how they do will be beneficial.

Operations

Operations in any business could mean …

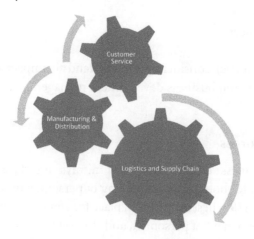

To be more successful in sales and business development management will require your basic understanding of all the above areas.

These areas will have a regular interface. That interface will be achieved with greater success when your ability to understand how they operate and impact sales and client relationships.

You will have a responsibility to influence these areas to deliver a better product or service to your clients. That will happen much more easily when you have a good grasp of what and how they do what they do.

Insurance

One of the most important areas that sales and business development managers need to gain knowledge of is commercial insurance and the subject of risk management.

Areas such as, but not limited to:

- Liability
- Property
- Workers Compensation
- Professional Liability
- Etc.

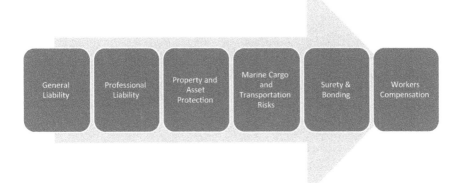

All these coverages outlined above interface with client and vendor relationships. The sales manager must learn the basics of these insurances and the role they play with client and vendor business dealings.

In concert with this is the area of risk management that has three steps of evolution:

- Identifying where risk lies in a business deal
- Understanding the impact of that risk to all parties with vested interests
- Creating a strategy to manage that risk successfully to everyone's mutual benefit who are party to the transaction or relationship

Risk Strategy

Once the three steps above are accomplished, you must develop a methodology in managing the risk. You have three options:

The three options are assumption, mitigation, or transference. A company can first choose to assume the risk. That means if anything happens they own the consequences.

Second, they can take steps to mitigate any potential losses. In risk management, this is referred to as *"Loss Control"*. Examples might be fire protection systems, alarms, security systems, better packaging, exercising more diligence, etc.

Transfer is where you move the risk to a third party such as an insurance or surety company. For a premium and agreed underwriting terms the insurance company will assume the risks involved in the transaction, such as but not limited to:

All these areas outlined above are potential risks that may enter into a negotiated agreement between two or more parties that sales and business development managers have to recognize and ultimately deal with.

This requires a basic skill set of understanding risk, its implications, and opportunities to successfully manage.

Insurance will always become a necessary evil in all business models. Therefore, it needs to be understood and managed.

Managing Off-Site and Foreign Sales and Business Development Personnel

Sales and business development personnel have a tendency to work from home. And having sales personnel located in overseas markets, though they may come to an office really work away from you.

Additionally, you may have sales personnel working from various offices, but again they are away from you.

It is both an art and science that needs to be accomplished to successfully manage off-site and distant sales personnel.

It is also a major challenge with lots of hurdles, e.g.:

- Personnel working off-site often feel disconnected from the organization.
- You rely heavily on their **"good will"** to legitimize how they spend their working hours.
- Collaboration with impacted internal organizational personnel is marginalized.
- You may be less available to provide necessary support.

Some recommendations in dealing successfully with those challenges for off-site and remote sales and business development personnel:

1. Keep personnel who work off-site engaged with the organization have them work on team-based projects, take on collaborative initiatives, and visit the home office, where management is located on a regular basis maybe quarterly?
2. Set up accountability and responsibility systems to make sure they are staying on track.
   - Excel spreadsheets on prospect and client activity
   - Daily activity reports
   - Weekly activity reports
   - Daily dialogs
3. Make sure the personnel are steadily interfacing and collaborating with internal personnel.
   This can be reflected in the daily reports.
4. Meet with and be proactive in going out on sales calls and business development meetings with all off-site sales personnel.
5. Speak to them daily. Make them feel as though they are important, needed, contributing, and involved.
   Almost "as if their office was next to yours".

In all companies here and abroad more and more are allowing all employees to work off-site and/or from home.

This is good for cost reduction measures and for employee well-being.

We need to learn to manage these employees successfully. Following the steps outlined above is a good start in that direction of exercising leadership and management prowess.

Sales and Business Development Managing the Related Areas Internally

Sales and business development managers at the end of the day are leading an entire team within a company to a successful conclusion satisfied clients and growth opportunities.

In order to accomplish this feat successfully the sales and business development team needs to address a few areas within a company to make sure they are able to achieve success.

These areas depending upon the company's business model are:

Sourcing Purchasing Manufacturing Inventory Distribution/Supply Chain Customer Service Finance R&D

All these above areas are critical to growing a business and maintaining existing clients along with sustainable and profitable operations.

Sourcing

The company needs to have an aggressive sourcing department to make sure manufacturing has what it needs to manufacture timely and comprehensively along with the most "state-of-the-art" materials, components, and ingredients to be innovative and desirous.

Purchasing

The purchasing team works closely with sourcing but adds the benefit of vendor management to assure competitive acquisition costs and sustainable vendor relationships. This aids sales in making sure goods and services can be delivered on time, quality controlled, and competitively priced.

Manufacturing

The manufacturing team makes sure the client receives what it ordered, in proper working or performing condition, and available when needed.

Inventory

Inventory maintains adequate levels of product, capabilities, and service needs to meet customer demand. The sales team can have a huge impact on managing proper inventory levels, which will always have enough product, but not too much to increase carrying costs to the demise of his or her company.

Distribution/Supply Chain/Logistics

The distribution, logistics, and supply chain functions interface directly with most clients in delivering the product, capability, or service to the client competitively, on-time, and in good working condition. This extension of sales is a critical element of the overall sales process.

Customer Service

Many in business development and sales consider "customer service" a direct extension of the sale and in numerous company structures customer service is part of sales and not a distinct operation.

The customer service team is heavily influenced by sales to deliver the services, responsiveness, and capabilities that were promised to the prospects that have now made them into clients.

Customer service is the "sustainability" team of any organization, and many will call it the "lifeblood" of client relationships.

Sales and business development executives typically work "hand in hand" with the customer service team nurturing successful client interface.

Finance

Sales and business development teams need to rely heavily on finance to:

- Offer competitive and contemporary payment options.
- Be sensitive to client needs.
- Maintain a cooperative approach rather than a contentious disposition.

At the end of the day some will say "it's always all about the money".

R&D

In many business models, the success of the sales team will rely heavily on the innovations, alterations, and transformations that R&D can bring to the sales process to make the company's products, capabilities, and services different, with value addition and competitiveness.

> The important message made above is that sales and business development executives must also manage an array of other company functions in order to succeed in the overall sales process.
> The ability to do that job well, consistently, and collaboratively can ultimately be the determining factor of sales success.

THE PROFILE OF THE VERY BEST SALESMAN

Sales are a very hard part of any company's business model. It is clearly a difficult task to get someone to:

- Change their mind
- Make a decision
- Direct them to your pathway
- But your product
- Utilize your service
- Leave their incumbent
- Take responsibility

It takes a unique sort of individual to sell and also do it consistently and successfully.

It takes a lot of energy, and one must learn to deal with continuous rejection.

And many times, the salesperson has to sell something that is:

- Priced too high
- Does not work too well
- The competitor's product is much better
- Is no longer contemporary
- Has a poor track record
- Specific product
- Or is just plain ugly

Sales drives the business model and therefore is a necessary component of sustainability, profitability, and meeting growth expectations.

In some companies, sales management is complicated because sales also has to take care of marketing customer service responsibilities. These additional two workloads distract from direct sales activity brining a slowdown of closure rates.

The best salesperson has to:

- Create opportunities
- Vet prospectus
- Present a marketing strategy
- Develop market share
- Service clients
- Deal with client problems
- Collect monies due
- Cold call
- Follow-up on leads
- Close more deals

There are an array of tasks, responsibilities, actions, and steps that the salesman needs to accomplish to be at their best. And they must do a multitude of tasks and skill sets well to be successful.

They must become a "jack of all trades" with a number of skill sets and capabilities across the board to be a successful salesperson.

In any given daytime, salesperson wears a different "hat". Technician, engineer, customer service, account receivables, marketing, report writing, problem resolution and then maybe 5 minutes left over for new business development and sales activity.

The salesperson is called upon tirelessly and continuously, pulled in numerous directions, expected to "jump through hoops", and make sales calls in between all of that.

Great salespeople can generally do pretty well in regard to compensation and perks. But this is usually very well deserved.

While personnel lodged in various company silos build resentments towards sales personnel some justified, most not so, the salesperson charges forward typically getting the job done on behalf of the company and themselves thus deserving the compensation package warranted for great salespeople.

One should not confuse working hard with working smart, and the great salesperson usually after years of experience has learned how to work smart and with the least amount of energy expended.

A key ingredient of successful salespeople is "flexibility and pliability". This is equated with being able to adjust the business sales model that answers the call of the client. A unique ability to adjust, tailor, and modify positions and showing a high degree of accommodation in order to close a deal.

This will often take a high degree of persistence, collaborative outreach, raising the bar of expectation and creative juices to make things happen to get the deal done and closed.

Many internal silo personnel will see disruption and quickly become fatigued when sales personnel call for change and flexibility to get deals closed.

This is where persistence kicks in and the salesperson moves forward despite all the "noise" and "conflict" internally. They charge forward, make things happen, and produce results.

This all equates to successful sales personnel and their differentiation from everyone else in the organization.

This forces the salesperson to become an excellent collaborator. They must bring various silos of a company together customer service, manufacturing, distribution, shipping, legal, finance, and senior management all on the same page to get the job done.

This requires persuasive negotiation through the company's maze of tunnels, walls, torpedoes, and land mines.

The great salesperson knows how to navigate through these challenges and is undaunted by the difficulties and the pursuit of achieving desired goals.

The great salesperson has high expectations, lofty goals, and is motivated for successful conclusions.

The motivation is developed by a need:

- To succeed
- Be a high achiever
- Earn a good living
- Move up the ladder of the corporate structure
- Gain more influence and power
- Obtain more perks
- Feed an appetite

Building a "Team" is an important skill set for personnel engaged in sales and sales management. This becomes increasingly important when we approach the international arena as the complexities are greater requiring input and collaboration from an effort of a team and numerous areas of expertise.

DEVELOPING AND MANAGING TEAM INITIATIVES

TEAM BUILDING

An effective tool in managing successfully is the ability to work within team structures.

This affords:

- Collaboration
- Camaraderie
- Effective delegation
- Mentoring effectiveness
- Crossing company silos
- Better results

Collaboration

When we take into consideration how others feel and value their input an appreciation is accomplished which allows for staff to feel more ingrained into the organization.

Additionally, their input may allow for wider and varied input which can create a path to more workable and doable solutions.

Project management is often better accomplished through team initiatives. This becomes a collaborative process allowing for a better path to higher achievement.

Collaboration in the decision-making phase will also afford a better opportunity for successful implementation as you are obtaining everyone's "buy-in" during the assessment and analysis process that usually takes place in any team project.

Camaraderie

When a team successfully works together bonds are formed, friendships are established, and colleague ties are fostered.

This creates a work environment where the impossible can be accomplished.

The military has known and leveraged this concept for over 3,000+ years develop camaraderie between the troops and you create a force to be reckoned with.

Camaraderie creates an environment where interpersonal relationships are matured into smooth running machines that make for the most effective and productive work forces.

Camaraderie creates the environment where team members watch each other's back and they care for one another. This atmosphere becomes conducive to working collaboratively at the highest levels producing and meeting desired goals and expectations.

Effective Delegation

The team takes on tasks and responsibilities as delegated by the project manager and the collaborative process.

This creates a dispersion of responsibilities among the collective team. This delegating allows for the best opportunity for the project to both gain momentum and move forward successfully.

Effective delegation also allows for the best use of individual skill sets and capabilities among the team members.

It should also create a cooperative spirit where the team accepts the delegated responsibilities and tasks with a "can do" attitude and positive approach to getting the job done well.

Delegating also creates an opportunity for senior management to observe how team members accept responsibility and ultimately perform.

Additionally, you can also observe how well each team member "plays in the sand box".

Effective delegation also makes the best use of limited resources among personnel who are already typically engaged at multiple levels within the organization.

Mentoring Effectiveness

Managers are given an opportunity to participate and demonstrate their prowess in mentoring staff members in:

- Collaborative ethics
- Building effective working relationships
- Participating effectively in "team-based activities"
- Taking responsibility in a project and bringing it to successful closure

Managers can show leadership skills in motivating a team initiative and taking charge of direction and forward movement.

Typically, problems and disruptions will interfere with project scheduling so leadership can demonstrate problem resolution skill sets and how best to negotiate problems to favorable resolution.

Crossing Company Silos

Any team initiative and/or project will typically cross-company silos. This will typically cause some issues as silo managers are "protective of their turf".

Silos also present different internal cultural concerns and many times have alternate agendas to other operational units.

This dynamic of "silo territory" is a challenge that often needs to be navigated carefully and even creatively.

It will challenge the team members to manage this challenge, which will be a good lesson for future benefit.

Better Results

The ultimate goal of any team or project effort is to make change, favorable impact, or bring an initiative to favorable closure.

The team concept for all the reasons outlined above creates the best structure and opportunity to make better collaborative decisions leading to "better results".

A better process will usually produce better results.

CHOOSING TEAM MEMBERS

Choosing team members can be a challenge. The implications of making good or poor choices will have both favorable and not-so-favorable consequences.

Here are some guidelines:

- Introverts will kill a team. Look for extroverts.
- The "ability" to get along and be a team player are important traits.
- Prior "team" experience is beneficial.
- Personnel with skill sets in communications, negotiations, obtaining compromise and consensus, and in working at collaborative alliances all prove beneficial.
- Personnel who know how to be organized and prioritized well will be beneficial.
- Bring teams together with personnel that have skill sets and behavior that bring diversity and an ability to meld.
- Make sure the team member has the time necessary to make a quality contribution and has complete authorization from their manager.
- Make sure team members understand and budget for serious time commitments.

Choosing team members following these basic guidelines will present the best opportunity to have success with the initiative or project.

MANAGING THE TEAM

While a team may work independently, as a senior manager you must "watch-dog" the effort to make sure it is successful and stays on track.

Here are some suggestions:

1. Establish a clear and concise set of goals, expectations, and deliverables. Utilize the "SMART" process having goals which are: Specific, Measurable, Attainable, Relevant, and Trackable.
2. Set reasonable time frames.
3. Set up a system for weekly reports on progress.
4. Establish a "point person", "leadership", and "ownership".
5. Allow independence, but make sure they are on "track", "on-schedule", and moving forward at an acceptable pace.
6. Make sure they are communicating progress or setbacks to impacted parties, stakeholders, and senior management.
7. Make sure you are made aware timely and comprehensively of any serious setbacks or problems.
8. Create an atmosphere with the team of openness, straight forward dialog, and transparency.
9. And in closing, make sure the project closes out, whether successful or not. Don't let it "die on the vine" be proactive and open in bringing closure.

COMMERCIAL EXAMPLE

Google defines what makes a "team".

The first step in answering this question of "what makes an effective team?" is to ask "what is a team?" More than an existential thought exercise, actually figuring out the memberships, relationships, and responsibilities of individuals all working together is tough but critical to cracking team effectiveness.

The term team can take on a wide array of meanings. Many definitions and frameworks exist, depending on task interdependence, organizational status, and team tenure. At the most fundamental level, the researchers sought to distinguish a "work group" from a "team":

- Work groups are characterized by the least amount of interdependence. They are based on organizational or managerial hierarchy. Work groups may meet periodically to hear and share information.

- Teams are highly interdependent – they plan work, solve problems, make decisions, and review progress in service of a specific project. Team members need one another to get work done.

Organizational charts only tell part of the story, so the Google research team focused on groups with truly interdependent working relationships, as determined by the teams themselves. The teams studied in Project Aristotle ranged from 3 to 50 individuals (with a median of nine members).

GOOGLE DEFINES "EFFECTIVENESS"

Once they understood what constituted a team at Google, the researchers had to determine how to quantitatively measure effectiveness. They looked at lines of code written, bugs fixed, customer satisfaction, and more. But Google's leaders, who had initially pushed for objective effectiveness measures, realized that every suggested measure could be inherently flawed – more lines of code aren't necessarily a good thing and more bugs fixed means more bugs were initially created.

Instead, the team decided to use a combination of qualitative assessments and quantitative measures. For qualitative assessments, the researchers captured input from three different perspectives – executives, team leads, and team members. While they all were asked to rate teams on similar scales, when asked to explain their ratings, their answers showed that each was focused on different aspects when assessing team effectiveness.

Executives were most concerned with results (e.g., sales numbers or product launches), but team members said that team culture was the most important measure of team effectiveness. Fittingly, the team lead's concept of effectiveness spanned both the big picture and the individuals' concerns saying that ownership, vision, and goals were the most important measures.

So the researchers measured team effectiveness in four different ways:

1. Executive evaluation of the team
2. Team leader evaluation of the team

3. Team member evaluation of the team
4. Sales performance against quarterly quota

The qualitative evaluations helped capture a nuanced look at results and culture but had inherent subjectivity. On the other hand, the quantitative metrics provided concrete team measures but lacked situational considerations. These four measures in combination, however, allowed researchers to home in on the comprehensive definition.

Conformity is the jailer of freedom and the enemy of growth.
John F. Kennedy, 35th President of the United States of America

5

Sales Management 101

The greatest thing in this world is not so much where we stand as in what direction we are moving.

Johann Wolfgang von Goethe, Writer/Statesman

Sales management must be a combined initiative of art and science. The science is clear concise quantitative data that surrounds the sales process. The more difficult component is qualitative. This chapter looks at both areas and provides advice on how best to master both skill sets.

HOW SALES PERSONNEL ARE "VIEWED" BY OTHER PERSONNEL IN YOUR COMPANY?

It is very important for any person to "see the forest through the trees" and to "have a realistic idea on how others view their being". It is for that reason this section of the *Sales Management* book is now discussed.

As a general statement, sales personnel in most organizations are:

- Not well liked
- Not well respected
- Viewed as not necessary "cogs in the wheel"
- Not taken seriously
- People who don't pay attention to detail
- People who move around a lot but get very little done
- People who cut corners
- Not to be trusted

- Selfish
- Arrogant and condescending

Now, many of these character traits are true, some embellished a bit and others absolutely perfect descriptions.

But we also know that there are a handful of sales personnel who have none of these traits and are outstanding corporate citizens at every level and in every way.

But more experienced management personnel and business executives would clearly outline many of these traits to hold water.

So are these good or bad attributes. The answer is not black and white … it is gray. It is gray because some are traits that "to an extent" could be valuable in sales doing what they need to do … sell!

The key phrase "to an extent" is the critical aspect to understand. Being selfish as an example, for a salesperson could prove valuable as a motivating trait but only to an extent. Because if the selfishness crosses the line of being obnoxious or being insensitive or impartial … then that makes them horrible traits.

Selfishness to an extent could be a positive characteristic or trait.

Another trait which to an extent has value is … "not paying attention to detail". This is controversial. In one instance you want sales personnel to focus on selling and spending time in that arena. Paying attention to detail takes a lot of time. The quandary that gets created is if sales personnel focus on all the detail … they have less time to chase and close deals.

There is a "balanced approach" that must be obtained. But having said that … I think sales management should free up sales personnel away from too heavy a load of detail and administrative work and put pressure on to sell.

The author has found hiring sales support and administrative personnel to handle this work is a more balanced approach and really frees the sales talent to "hunt".

Additionally:

- Sales personnel "appear" to have special privileges and muck about as prima donnas.
- Sales personnel travel a lot and are often out of the office, who many believe are then not working and become jealous of that external freedom.
- Sales personnel make a lot of money for doing very little.

These additional factors causing internal strife towards sales personnel are not well founded and are a perception that creates all sorts of unnecessary angst.

Sales and senior management should communicate and manage well and aggressively to avoid this type of stereotyping.

Though it is true that salespeople do not like operations and administrative responsibilities, typically.

True salespeople who are "Hunters" are not going to pay attention to operational details nor should they be elected to.

True "Hunters" are a scare commodity, and their expertise is in meeting people and creating business development opportunities. Their skill sets are being gregarious, extroverted, and in being in the right place at the right time and knowing just what, when, and how to say things … that create opportunity.

They should not have to fill out paperwork, complete applications, fill out reports, etc. …

- It is a waste of their valuable time … you want them out selling not administering. Administer with support and administrative personnel.
- They will be "reluctant campers", resistant to paperwork, and therefore, they will always be late, you will have to follow-up, and when done, it will be short changed material.
- Hunting is a specialized skill set and talent. I think it is akin to higher end trial attorneys … of which both need to be treated special, out of administration, and allowed to focus on what they do best … hunt and kill! (Figuratively speaking ☺)

So why do I point out that sales personnel need to understand this perception of them?

It is important for an array of reasons:

1. Perception is reality when it comes to how people make judgments and decisions. If they perceive negative traits and character flaws … that will determine how they will react, interface, and impact their relationship with you in a diminished or bad way.
2. Many of these traits … arrogance, condescension, not well respected, etc., are certainly not virtues from any perspective, and these are examples of traits that must be modified, corrected, and changed as soon as possible.

3. Change will take behavior modification, which is one of the hardest aspects of people's behaviors to deal with.
4. Change is necessary to "smooth out" internal personnel relations.
5. Change starts with a clear understanding of a realistic and forth-right view of how others perceive you and understanding that bad behavior and traits have negative consequences and good behavior and traits have positive and enhanced opportunities.
6. Smoothing out relations will make you a more effective salesperson and allow for a more collaborative process in handling and managing clients' needs.
7. Bad behavior may only be tolerated in the short term. Good behavior has a better opportunity for longer term sustainability and increased sales and greater margins.

Corrective behavior of sales personnel is a very serious matter. It is a skill set all by itself and requires a lot of diligence and creative processes:

- Quality leadership by management creates the best opportunity to correct behavior. Said in another way … "lead others to change" moves personnel into silos of corrective behavior.
- Leadership demonstrates better character traits through their own actions and behaviors.
- Leadership identifies a pathway with incentives for good behavior and consequences for bad behavior.
- Ingrained negative behavior may take some very creative approaches to cause successful change:
  - Intense diligence
  - Serious perseverance
  - Immediate feedback on actions, changes, and consequences
  - Far reaching approaches to cause change

CASE STUDY … THE RIGHT WAY

JLN Engineering, located in the Midwest, sold high-end construction services for building stadiums, event and amusement parks, and outdoor theaters. All their sales personnel (six) reported into a VP of sales (Bob). All were engineers by education and training.

They were supported by a team of Customer Service Managers who helped prepare bids, handle customer needs, and provide client support, when they were out on the road, which was often.

Five of the six sales team got along famously with the customer service team, with the exception of one (Jack), who struggled with several of the Customer Service Account Managers.

Bob made several attempts to work with Jack in smoothing out Bob's interaction with the Customer Service members, but with little success. Bob worked hard to identify CS Membership who were more tolerant and might be able to work with Jack.

But these initiatives failed over time. Jack was the youngest member of the sales team and the least experienced but had managed to produce a very large account early in his tenure with JLN Engineering. The account produced a lot of revenue for JLN and had a high profile in the organization. But the client was demanding, difficult, and required a lot of attention.

This put stress on Jack and some of the account managers when matters became hectic or problems surfaced.

When stress levels rose … Jack became demanding, impatient, unreasonable, rude, and to some extent … unforgiving.

Jack's handling of the client and his responsibilities caused an array of issues in the Customer Service Group.

This led to one of the customer service team, who was a valued member of the team, to leave the company, citing Jack's "attitude and demeanor" as her reasons.

The HR Manager and Bob's boss required an immediate resolution of the problem, even if it meant Jack's termination.

Bob knew that he had to try and save jack and that meant driving Jack to a serious dose of behavior modification.

Bob clearly understood he would have to exercise serious diligence and be creative in finding a solution.

He first met with jack, put him on notice of the seriousness of the matter, and advised he was going to come up with some suggestions and ideas on how this situation, which was not tolerable, was going to change.

He requested that Jack begin thinking about what he could do to begin to modify behavior to tone down his aggressive demeanor towards the customer service team.

He told Jack that he was a valued employee, a great salesperson, and that he was committed to finding a pathway on how best to move forward.

Bob also spent considerable time explaining why the situation was serious, concerning, and intolerable. But left matters on a positive reinforcement of believing a resolve would be forthcoming.

Bob decided he had to figure out what triggered Jack's bad behavior and move towards finding on implementing a solution.

He did not want to lose Jack as he believed Jack could easily develop into one of their top salespersons.

Bob structured a strategy:

- Find out more about jack on a personal level to determine if there was anything in his history or background that would incite such behavior.
- Meet with the other sales team members to obtain their input.
- Meet with the customer service team members to receive their input.
- Meet with HR to determine what he could and could not do.
- Put all the data together and come up with a strategy to resolve the problem. It would include corrective behavior.

The strategy that Bob structured was as follows:

- Meet with Jack again and make sure he understands and accepts the level of concern.
- Obtain Jack's commitment to do what he has to do … to resolve the issues.
- Commit himself and the resources of the firm to work towards a favorable resolution.
- Set a time frame of 90 days to start to see results.
- He placed Jack within the customer service team for 2 weeks with the hope that Jack would be more sensitive to their needs if he understood what they were dealing with each day. It would also help him develop better relationships with the people he was struggling with.
- He met with Jack a number of times, and through some intimate and deep dialog determined that stress triggered a lot of his bad behavior.

    Bob found a local consulting company that acts as support to executives who require support in what they do. He found an experienced consultant within that organization that had workshops in stress management and provided customized counseling for those managers in need. He had Jack meet the consultant, and they agreed to meet two times a week over the next 60 days.

The consultant determined after several sessions that Jack became stressed believing that when he got busy not everything was going to get done and he would lose his most valued client ... leading to his failure and eventual termination.

The consultant worked on several fronts with Jack:

- Time management
- Effective delegation techniques
- Relaxation exercises to reduce stress
- Developing a better mindset to deal with pressure

The consultant tied in his work with Bob, as Jack's manager and mentor, teaching Bob how do be a better manager and leader in this type of personnel issue.

- Bob created a number of off-set social events ... a dinner and an evening hockey game for both the sales and customer service teams to socialize with one another ... causing bonding and better relationships both as a team and in favor of Jack's situation.
- Bob also realized that this specific client was more demanding and problematic than any other clients and created a special support team for Jack to delegate to when the situation warranted.

Move ahead to the 90-day mark.

Bob's management initiatives worked, as follows:

1. Jack became more sensitive to and more aligned with customer service. Having spent 2 weeks "walking in their shoes" paid off dramatically as he was now much more understanding of what they had to deal with daily, and at the end of the day ... how important they were to his team and more importantly ... to be more respectful of them as individuals, friends, and colleagues.
2. Gaining support during peak client demand was a "Godsend" and eliminated a lot of panic and stress.
3. His work with the consultant, and supported by Bob's leadership, allowed Jack to better manage his time, delegate more effectively, and to communicate more responsibly without causing stress levels to rise.

   He had to still learn to better control his own fears and build confidence ... but that will be a work-in-process to be accomplished over time.

4. The social activities created better harmony between the sales and customer service teams which helped not only all team members but also Jack.

In conclusion, Bob utilized numerous resources, got creative, and manufactured a successful solution to getting Jack to change his behavior. It did require professional assistance, which is ok ... as that is why they exist and can be very valuable in theses more difficult circumstances.

Jack still needed continued professional support, and Bob will have to stay on top of matters more diligently, but the corrective path forward has been accomplished hopefully providing sustainable changes to avoid having to deal with this problem again.

Behavior change is a complicated and difficult process requiring skill set, experience, resource utilization, and lots of good management and luck.

CASE STUDY ... THE WRONG WAY

Arc Enterprises located in a business suburb of Philadelphia manufactures specialized medical equipment for dental surgeons all over the world.

There is a Director of Sales (Jenna) who has five sales personnel covering both domestic and foreign markets. The sales team are experienced, all coming from various aspects of the medical industry.

Their sale is direct to trade practitioners and is an expensive purchase that requires a much focused sales process. The sales team is highly paid, they travel over 60% of the time, and have mastered telecommunications to keep in touch with the office and transmit orders and client instructions.

Interaction with the home office is mostly accomplished electronically. The team rarely sees one another with the exception of an annual sales team meeting in January of every year.

Brian has been with the sales team for 3 years and is a good salesman somewhere in the "middle of the pack" in overall sales volume. He came out of the fetal field as he went to school to be a dentist, but in his last year, which he never finished, dropped out for personal reasons and took this job.

He is somewhat arrogant and condescending in his approach internally, and though most communications are electronic ... seems to "piss-off" someone in the company everyday with an attitude that "his shit don't stink" and "yes, I am better and more important than you" approach.

Recently, his attitude has become increasingly unbearable by the operations team who process the orders, arrange shipping, and dialog with the customers, once a sale is made.

The operations team has now dropped the ball a few times on Brian's accounts ... probably not intentionally, but certainly not as a result of caring about him and his accounts.

Brian's behavior has to be acknowledged by him in order to create a pathway to resolution of the problem. He must take ownership and agree to make the necessary behavioral changes to keep his job.

MEASURING RESULTS: MANAGING BY "INPUT VERSUS OUTPUT"

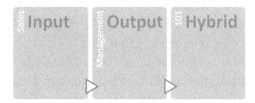

When we manage sales personnel, we have three finite options when measuring results:

INPUT

When we ask sales personnel to see ten new appointments a week, and they do ... that is an example of measuring them by input.

Their "input" was the initiative to see and accomplish the ten appointments ... success!

But maybe not? The effort was made but what about the results?

The whole point of the ten appointments was to create opportunities and close deals, not see ten companies.

Seeing the ten companies is a step in what typically might need to be done to create opportunities and close deals but in itself ... it has not achieved that goal.

Another salesperson may only see two companies that week, so it missed its mark. But if that person closed both of those deals … it is in a much better position than the one who saw ten but closed no deals.

The point being that measuring by input may work for a new salesperson or trainee but certainly not for one who is seasoned or has matured.

The goal is to produce. Measuring by input does not evidence result. Yes, input may be a step towards results … but not necessarily a direct correlation. There are numerous variables that could enter that equation.

The conclusion is that measuring by input has limitations, usually set for the inexperienced, unseasoned salesperson.

OUTPUT

A preferred measuring method is by output. The sales or business development person is given an agreed goal. The important measure is … meeting that, not meeting that, or exceeding that goal.

How they get there is relevant but at the end of the day not that important. One salesperson may need to see ten accounts a week to obtain the desired goal. Another person could see three accounts a week and achieve their goal.

The first person may need more leads in the pipeline. The second person may need less.

The first person may have difficulty "closing". The second person may be a great "closer".

There are numerous reasons for the difference, but at the end of the day … the judgment of sales success is measured by the results. The assumption is … that if the desired results have been achieved … then the process to get there is justified.

While many sales operations work in this manner … it is fraught with risk.

You must make sure that the process to achieve the desired results is legal, ethical, and in no way would harm or be of concern to your organization, as well as your clients.

This would mean that you must have some degree of management oversight when you utilize the method of measure … as results only.

Oversight is both a best practice and a diligent procedure to protect all vested interests from any potential issue.

HYBRID

In the hybrid model, you are both utilizing input and output as the measure of a salesperson's success.

It combines the benefits of managing both by input and output. In our experience, the hybrid method works best for seasoned and very experienced tenured sales personnel.

You would not be overly micro-managing day-to-day activity, but you would be aware of scheduling and basic weekly reports on prospect and client visits and undertakings.

And at the same time keeping close tabs on the actual numbers being produced measured against expectations in that agreed time period.

MANAGING AN INSIDE SALES TEAM

The challenges are both huge and different from on-site sales and business development where the sales model is based on "inside sales".

Inside sales has two big advantages:

Minimized Sales Expense

Maximized Control over the Sales Effort

The sales manager in overseeing inside sales has a lower cost in sales personnel, as they do not leave the office, have little to zero production costs, minimized client entertainment, and are generally paid much less than outside sales personnel.

Additionally, the sales manager has an opportunity for developing very tight QC (quality control) standards …

- As the sales team sits right there in the office
- They can be heard and seen
- Calls monitored
- Sales scripts followed

The author would argue that inside sales is:

1. Not as effective as outside sales
2. Only successful in certain verticals
3. Produces less robust results
4. Can only be utilized in smaller, consumer-type markets on lower value products and services

But having said all of that, there are many companies who have been very successful in their inside sales programs.

INSIDE SALES CASE STUDY #1

Bobson Delicacies is a family-owned business, spanning 25 years, into the second generation, based in Parsippany, NJ.

Their products were mainly gift and holiday gift baskets that contained candies and fruits. Customized baskets contained an array of other goods more in line with their customers' businesses.

As an example, they had a client that created scale models of building developments. So in their baskets were miniature replicas of some of their buildings, as paper weight giveaways.

Their sales are just over $65 million annually. They have two outside sales personnel and eight inside sales personnel.

In annualized new business, the two outside sales personnel account for just over 2.2 million, with a margin of 22%.

The eight inside sales team produces almost 14 million, with a margin of 16%.

The outside team approaches larger clients, provides a more personalized approach, and can gain higher margins.

The inside sales team provides a less robust customer service offering and is much more price driven … hence the lower margin.

At Bobson, many of the leads go to outside sales representatives from the inside sales team.

The inside sales team are also "telemarketing specialists" and often come across companies that would be better suited for a more customized and personalized approach.

The inside sales team earns a referral fee on leads that turn into business for Bobson.

When the author studied this company's sales strategy, that was clearly working very successfully, as revenue projections for this company were doubling gross sales volume over the next 5–6 years. The author observed a number of very keen marketing and sales approaches that were quite unique.

Many of their sales initiatives contained business models which:

- They paid to a market research company that was able to gather data on companies that had previously made gift basket purchases or inquiries.
- That effort above produced over a thousand leads a year.
- They would send promotional samples to those companies identified, without ever reaching out or qualifying first.

  They would then wait a few days after the sample had arrived to determine how well it was received.

  They received positive feedback from 65% of the prospects and was able to move 80% of that amount into a future sale by the inside sales group.

  Ninety percent of that total created an ongoing client relationship.
- Bobson products were all high-end candies and fruits originating from the finest chocolate houses of Europe and fruit directly from growers all over the world.

All their products were fresh, delicious, and of the highest quality.

The feedback they always received from the recipients was … "this was the best basket of candy and fruit we have ever received", "most fresh and delicious", and "very unique and delightful".

- Another creative approach was to put a survey card in each basket. This requested the recipient to respond to a few basic questions over a web portal access.

This gained them insight and an email address. They offered the recipient a 50% off on their first purchase. The response and purchase rate exceeded 32%.

- All the sales personnel received aggressive bonus on new sales and a smaller cut on renewed activity. This promoted new business activity, as senior management was convinced, rightfully so … that the products' quality sold itself with existing customers.

In this model, inside sales worked very successfully and that led into outside sales referrals.

INSIDE SALES CASE STUDY #2

Lily Designs engineers and creates beautiful landscapes and gardens for higher end homes in several northeast cities for these past 10 years. They originally had only an inside sales structure where sales were flat for the first few years of operation.

Once they moved to outside sales, their business development began to increase double digit.

If you dissected the nature of their sale:

- Higher end homes ... dealing with the wealthy
- Not very price sensitive
- Sales were made when the homeowner met with the sales representative and was visually shown what could happen to their gardens and landscaping
- The sale was made principally on the homeowner connecting with the sales representative and believing in their designs and creativity.

  Additionally, they developed an approach to sales that typically closed on 70% of all opportunities:
- They developed software that transferred their current backyard to the computer screen and the sales representative, while on the first call could magically make some changes on the screen that would take the homeowner to what a finished product could look like.

  It was both creative and very convincing.
- All the sales representatives were trained landscape engineers or technicians
- They would commit to a return date with several design options for them to view and consider. The homeowners were always mostly impressed
- The design options could easily be viewed, tweaked, and modified as the homeowner and engineer sat together, many times outside in the yard ... where creativity, customization, and visualization could be of great value to closing a deal.

- Lily Designs also developed a strong capability in water features (pools, waterfalls, streams, ponds, koi pools, etc.).
- The sale was made by the "hands-on" approach on-site at the homeowner's lair sitting in their backyard.

In this case study, we demonstrated that inside sales does not always work well in certain business models.

In this business model ... the hands-on and on-site approach was a major factor in this company differentiating its capabilities to the homeowner ... which drove sales success.

As the company grew, its inside sales group was eventually transferred into telemarketers creating sales leads for the landscape and design sales representatives to follow-up on.

RECOMMENDATIONS FOR INSIDE SALES

Inside sales can work well in the following circumstances:

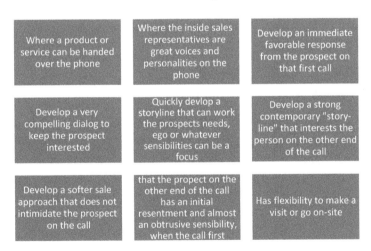

Inside sales is not the author's most favored sales business model, mainly because it minimizes or eliminates the direct "face-to-face" interface between the salesperson and the prospect/client.

But we know in certain circumstances it has its place as a marketing, sales, and customer service interface.

Though the world of business and particularly with the millennials has adapted significant online selling and buying experiences ... mostly business to consumer (AKA Amazon, eBay, Alibaba, and Wayfair) ... business to business sales are still dominated by individual sales personnel on the road visiting clients and selling "face to face".

How long this will last as a dominant business to business sales model is anyone's best guess, but the author believes it will be a long time coming for it to end as a main means of companies selling its products and services from a business to another business.

> The visual of the salesman on the road making first, second, and service calls at the clients' offices will not dissipate soon.
>
> While technology has and will continue to play a larger role in client relationships and the overall sales process ... there is no substitution for the intimacy established and successful working relationships that happen between the seller and the buyer.
>
> They have been in place for over 300 years and will probably be around for the next 300 years.

MENTORING YOUNGER AND INEXPERIENCED SALES TALENT

There is a huge challenge facing all sales and business development managers in mentoring the inexperienced and unseasoned sales team members.

There are some companies who will not hire "newbies" and will only hire experienced sales staff. You often hear ... "let someone else try them ... then I'll get them when they are peaking to produce".

Some companies dislike and do not prefer to hire seasoned sales personnel and you often hear ... "they have too much baggage, too many bad habits, and if they are available, something must be wrong".

There are both truths and untruths in both scenarios. But the fact is that most companies will hire unseasoned sales personnel with the hope they can train them in a certain process and create a loyal employee in the same breath.

Either way ... there are challenges we face to mentor the unseasoned salesperson.

Some of these challenges are:

- Lack of business acumen
- Lack of specific sales experience
- Unmotivated
- Entitled
- Difficulty in goal setting
- Poor execution
- Untested negotiation skill sets
- Not sure they want to follow, lead, or get out of the way!
- Defining mentoring
- Millennials pose their own set of issues and have become a huge challenge for more senior managers and companies to navigate successful solutions

The key to managing millennials are as follows:

- Customization is critical
- Must create new solutions
- More altruistic
- High on utilization of technology (possibly too much so)
- Understand the difference from everyone else
- Social issues have greater relevance
- Having more of a balance between work and time-off
- Learning and training are very important
- Money is not everything
- Team involvement over independent approaches
- Need feedback continuously
- Moves quickly in career advancement and decisions
- Flexibility is critical
- Do not get upset by their need of "entitlement" … that is mostly the older generations fault and can be easily managed through quality and comprehensive communicating, mentoring, and patience
- Take smaller steps first, keep the topics narrow, and provide timely updates and guidance
- Be patient!

LACK OF BUSINESS ACUMEN

There is no replacement for experience, but you can train them. What many companies are doing with unseasoned business personnel is putting them through 60- to 120-day programs at their point of hire. Some programs can run as long as 1–2 years depending upon the business model.

They are training them in numerous areas such as but not limited to:

- Business communicating … writing, speaking, and presenting
- Business ethics
- Business manners
- Business regulations
- Basic human resource information
- Managing conflict
- Basic leadership and management skill sets
- Business social behavior

In these areas are the basics of business behavior that some learn as they are in high school, college, trade schools, or through early employment settings.

Many managers today complain that the newly arriving personnel in business have little of any of the above traits, experience, or business practice savvy.

So, training right from their starting point is an excellent option in accomplishing the enhancement of these needed attributes.

Additionally, when they are trained by you or outsourced entities, you can influence "customization" and even "specialization" that would be unique to your culture, mission, and operating agendas.

Lack of Specific Sales Experience

This is a difficult area to resolve. What we have done to move sales personnel along more expeditiously is to assign them a senior mentor utilizing an older more experienced salesperson, that:

- They can shadow for some agreed time period and be introduced to sales from an already established expert providing some serious and intimate mentoring.

This person who is doing the mentoring should receive some form of benefit or compensation for the effort and to assist motivating them to a robust mentoring experience.

- Create an aggressive training program in all the necessary skill sets over a 1- to 2-year period in areas such as prospecting, marketing, customer service, writing proposals, mining and fact finding, relationship building, utilization of technology, and in closing deals.
- Feed them to the "LIONS". Meaning, get them out there selling. Maybe not to the most important opportunities, but out there where they can "cut their teeth" by doing, losing, winning, and experiencing.

    It may be somewhat of a painful experience for them and you, but if you are patient, tolerant, and understanding … there will be mutual benefit.

Unmotivated

Many older managers complain that the new world millennials are difficult to private, and in my own experiences … is a true expression of concern.

We have found that in motivating the inexperienced millennial you have to exercise:

- Flexibility in your approach
- Find creative ways to compensate and incentivize in areas important to them, which might fall away from more traditional incentive programs.

    In this regard, you have to find out areas that might be more important to them … than just straight financial compensation, such as but not limited to areas like:
    - Time off
    - Car allowances
    - Savings programs
    - Paid perks
- Motivation has also to be de-incentives, as well … Loss of base pay, no access to privileges, perks and bonuses, fewer leads, etc.

Generally, a combination of all factors nice will lead to motivated sales personnel.

Entitled

Entitlement is mostly the older generations' issue. Learn to be patient. Be communicative. Mentor and offer comprehensive explanations and examples to get over this issue.

Difficulty in Goal Setting

You will need to provide guidance in setting up goals for your younger sales personnel. These initial goals should be somewhat easier to achieve and follow. Once established and time has passed … the goal setting can be expanded, be more comprehensive and push for greater achievements.

Always keep in mind to point out … goals get you where you want to be.

Poor Execution

Goal setting or strategizing desired results are important, but we really need to determine specific tactics on executing what we need to do … to make the desired goals happen.

Untested Negotiation Skill Sets

You should believe that unseasoned sales personnel lack the necessary skill sets for good negotiation results. This is an area that requires training, mentoring, coaching, and a lot of support.

Your sales personnel will look to you for guidance here and expect you to show, lead, and tutor them in all aspects of negotiation and achieving "wins "in their column.

Not Sure They Want to Follow, Lead, or Get Out of the Way!

This area will require a lot of patience and understanding. And it will need to be highly customized to the individual salesperson.

You will need to be a "leader" here and show them the basics of determining when they need to follow, when they need to lead … or just when they need to get out of the way.

This can be a frustrating area for younger, less-seasoned sales talent, and your leadership here will be well served.

Defining Mentoring

Other descriptions of mentoring are … coaching, managing, leading, training, assisting, teaching, instructing, edifying, educating, championing, and sponsoring.

They all at the end of the day … mean to move someone along is their capabilities, skill sets, and motivation.

All good leaders and managers are good mentors. It is an unselfish act that will pay back in "spades".

Weekly Sales Management Reports

A good management tool is to have personnel complete weekly updates to their activity. This process is more important for less-seasoned sales personnel. Keep in mind that people generally rise to the level you hold them accountable.

This report is an excellent method for sales accountability and a document to keep all vested parties aware of the teams and the individual sales results.

Below is an example of a sales weekly report:

WEEKLY SALES MANAGEMENT SUMMARY REPORT

Salesperson _____Cook_____   Two pages
Week Ending _____8/24/12_____
Yearly Goals: Freight ____$425,000____% Achieved ____65%____
Consulting _____$145,000_____% Achieved _____110%_____

ACCOUNTS CLOSED

Name	Area Sold	Annualized Revenue
Polan Rolph Lash	Foreign Trade Zone (FTZ) review	$27,500
Industrial Products	Import freight	$2,200.000
Nickel Labs	Facilities review	$29,000

FIRST PAGE ACCOUNTS WORKING

Name	Area Being Worked on	Status
Kyocgena	Freight	Awaiting final request for additional info
Empire NCE	Clearances from Canada	Awaiting answer on proposal
U.S. Non-Wanen	Import freight	$750,000

ASSOCIATIONS

Name	Status
LIEXA	Working on Fall seminar
ISM	Working on Fall seminar in NY and on national conference in April 2013

WHAT WORK WEEK LOOKED LIKE?

Monday: Traveled Sunday night to Atlanta ... five sales call Monday and Tuesday, outlined on trip report
Tuesday: As above
Wednesday: In office in AM, golfed with Joe in the afternoon
Thursday: Handled proposals, follow-up calls, and called new AMA leads from Neil
Friday: In NYC on three sales calls, on trip report.

ACTION PLAN ... LOOKING AHEAD

Heading next week to NAS Conference in Chicago. Then following week back to DC on follow-up sales calls from last month.
Expect to close all pending deals by September 15. And add five new leads to the first page.
Going to Negotiation Class at the end of September in NYC with TMA.

AREAS OF CONCERN?

RFP for Tahearst is not looking good
CS problem on Sall Corporation

Establishing KPIs (Key Performance Indicators) for Sales Personnel Is Also Important as Outlined Below:

Advanced Sales Management … Sales Personnel KPIs May 2018 T. Cook
Sales Personnel Evaluation Criteria:
Performance Metrics:

Visits:	Numbers	Goal	% of Goal
Renewal:			
New:			
Penetration:			

Team Player:			
Internal Support:			
Demand Planning Assistance:			

On-Time Performance:			
Addressing Areas of Improvement:			
Internal Committee Participation:			

Marketing:			
Customer Service:			

6

Discerning Marketing, Sales, and Customer Service

No company can afford not to move forward. It may be at the top of the heap today but at the bottom of the heap tomorrow, if it doesn't.

James Cash Penney, Founder, JC Penney

The three critical factors in any organization's business development model, which is the integration of marketing, sales, and customer service, designed to obtain and maintain clients both in the short and long term.

This chapter looks at all three key factors and lays out a plan of attack for the most successful business development programs.

UNDERSTANDING THE SIMILARITIES, DIFFERENCES, AND THE COLLABORATION NEEDS IN BUSINESS DEVELOPMENT STRATEGIES AND STRUCTURE

The order in which we study business development is first marketing, followed by sales, and then customer service.

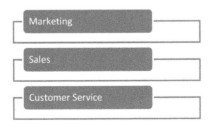

We study in this order quite simply as follows:

> Marketing gets us in the door, sales closes the deal, and customer service maintains the client.

MARKETING GETS US IN THE DOOR

Opportunities are first created by a marketing strategy that would include the following:

Value Add

Competition drives companies to offer more than the basic product or service that clients see value in.

Examples:

These examples all outlined above are one we are all aware of and many of us find real value in these "value-added" perks in our vendor/supplier/retailer relationships.

More and more customers are demanding "value add" in their purchasing decisions, and as the world becomes more highly competitive … companies are scrambling, racing, and innovating value adds every day.

This creates a "win-win" … the customer obtains greater value for their spend, and the vendor obtains or keeps clients satisfied … thereby retaining their business loyalty.

Product or Service Differentiation

Part of "value add" but somewhat different is the concept of "product and service differentiation".

Defining Differentiation

In business, economics, and marketing, product or service differentiation is the **process of distinguishing a product or service from competitors, to make it of greater value to a particular target market segment. This involves differentiating it from competitors' products as well as internally with its own products.

Examples of Differentiation

Volvo Defining Vehicle Safety

Holland Amercian Lines Defining Elegance

Rolex Defining Sophistication

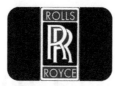
Royles Royce Defining Style

I believe that differentiation can also be explained as how organizations define themselves. As the definition clearly states differentiation from the competition.

This can also be included in "branding", which can be explained as your brand is your promise to your customer. It tells them what they can expect from your products and services, and it differentiates your offering from your competition. Your brand is derived from who you are, who you want to be, and how you create perception of all above.

Mottos, mantra, and slogans are also defining how companies differentiate themselves from their competition.

Examples:

A diamond is forever.	DeBeers
A mind is a terrible thing to waste...	United Negro College Fund
Be all that you can be.	United States Army
Connecting People.	Nokia
Good to the last drop.	Maxwell House coffee
Eat Mor Chikin!	Chick-fil-A
Have You Met Life Today?	Metropolitan Life

The new millennium redefined how companies differentiate, and creative slogans is a growing contemporary tool, proven over the ages to be effective and allowing new business development goals to be met.

Advertising

Wikipedia defines advertising:

Advertising (or advertising) is a form of marketing communication used to promote or sell something, usually a business's product or service. In Latin, ad vertere means "to turn toward". The purpose of advertising may also be to reassure employees or shareholders that a company is viable or successful.

Advertising is part of the overall marketing strategy that usually allows for huge prospect contact to be made through public access resources: radio, TV, print, etc.

Advertising allows a message to be sent that is seeking a prospect response … "wonder", "amazement", "happiness", "sadness", "hey, I want that product", "maybe I need to contact them", and "Yea, I am hungry now".

The ultimate goal is to influence behavior and lead people to make a choice in your favor.

While there are many goals and expectations of advertising … there are three main deliverables:

Advertising utilizes slogans that can be defined as short phrases used in marketing campaigns to generate publicity and unify a company's marketing strategy. The phrases may be used to attract attention to a distinctive product feature or reinforce a company's brand.

Advertising can have many benefits. The benefits achieved are a result of this focused approach in a companies' spend to motivate its prospect and client base to its favor.

Outreach

As outlined above "advertising" is one form of outreach. It is focused and typically utilizes a media option.

Outreach, in general, can utilize several venues to achieve business development success. There may be a local event where the attendees are potential prospects and clients. You might have personnel show up to make a form of contact which translates eventually to opportunities.

Industry trade shows are a form of "outreach" that can often create numerous opportunities and be very beneficial to an overall marketing strategy.

Working with foundations, volunteering, charity, and non-profit ventures are also ways to create outreach opportunities.

Supporting local educational, sports, and small business activities is also another way to create "outreach".

Outreach can be a very important component of the overall marketing strategy as it creates:

- A "buzz" about your product or service
- Assesses the relevance and validity of your product and marketing strategy
- Can be utilized as a "sampling or testing" of what you are looking to accomplish on a smaller scale
- Shows interest in the local communities, which as an altruistic activity, creates support and product interest, all by itself
- Can assist in evaluating advertising and sales activities

Product Placement

Product placement has become an important tool in marketing campaigns to introduce products to potential markets and creating a desire for that product from the world.

Mercedes Benz was very successful in introducing its new line of SUVs in several of the Jurassic Park movies. Many authorities on the subject of product placement extolled the success of this marketing strategy of Mercedes Benz ... also validated by Mercedes Executives through interviews and media releases.

The most common method of product placement is having your company's product utilized in the making of a movie through still shots, action scenes, discussed or utilized in the script, or somewhere placed where it is very visible and pronounced to the audience.

As we enter the third semester of the New Millennium ... product placement is increasingly becoming a major method of how companies advertise, promote, and outreach their products and services to wide audience segments.

Products or services observed by the public in a movie ... creates a certain degree of credibility and endorsement from the movie, the stars and the producers ... opening the door to increased sales.

There is no reason to not expect that product placement will continue to grow and marketing executives and movie producers becoming more creative in making the process more cost-effective and successful for all interests involved.

Product placement is also utilized in name recognition among entertainers, sports figures, and personalities who wear logos, slogans, and labels advertising their clients' products and services as they are seen on TV, stage, or other media outlets.

I am also seeing product placement in several professional venues such as but not limited to trade magazines, white papers, business books, webinars, and conference settings.

At the end of the day, the opportunities with product placement as a marketing strategy are endless, and we are only seeing the "tip of the iceberg".

Media Options

There are several media options for companies to utilize in their marketing strategies:

Print   Radio   TV

Social Media

While there are numerous media options ... these four represent over 90% of the options available to reach business and general public potential buyers and users.

Social media is now being heavily utilized and in a number of business verticals is a huge success.

Most companies fund a multi-pronged approach leverages their opportunity for quality outreach in their marketing initiatives.

Anticipating Market Conditions

Studying the history of the following areas will help in anticipating market conditions in the future:

- History of the economy in similar sets of circumstances
- Prior transactional records in your industry vertical and within your business model
- Professional resources that are available that utilize quantitative data combined with proven algorithms that can create predictors of futuristic trends

Quantitative Data is an excellent resource in deciding on future strategies …

- Information flow from reliable sources, clients, vendors, channel partners, those with vested interests who may be impacted by the future planning results

Overall Marketing Strategy

Once the strategy is developed, the message must be sent to a targeted audience of potential prospects.

The message can be sent in a number of methods:

Direct Sales

The marketing approach that ties directly into sales personnel is where the message is carried by the salesperson directly to the prospect.

It has a historical track record with proven results and usually is a faster method of success or failure being identified than the other three options.

Direct sales means that the sales personnel are also carrying the message that creates the opportunity.

Typically, the salesperson will also be attempting to close a deal once the message is sent and received.

This makes this approach creating a "dual role" ... marketing and sales ... back to back.

The good news that in this approach, you receive immediate feedback on the result of the marketing initiative.

The bad news is that you may lose out, if unsuccessful in marketing, sales probably has no or little opportunity to close a deal.

Marketing typically is designed to work independently of sales. This kind creates the opportunity by promotion of a benefit or differentiation.

Before any time is wasted on a sales effort, following a marketing campaign ... there are various "acid tests" that are available to "test the waters" and somewhat gauge the opportunity of being able to close a deal.

Marketing coming first has that very defined benefit, with little downside.

Social Media

Since 2010, social media has exploded as a source for companies to market their products and services.

Companies such as but not limited to:

Facebook, Twitter, and Linked-In ... are three of dozens of social media platforms that have begun to make money on marketing through their operating portals and as we enter 2020 ... this will continue to grow and expand.

One problem associated with social media marketing is it is difficult to "target". But that fact is changing as the social media operators are beginning to and are going through a strict learning curve where they are quickly becoming educated on how to better "target" opportunities for their clients.

This initiative is led by "technology and innovation" and has grasped the younger generations by storm. I personally believe that the "millennials" have become totally dependent and entwined with social media as their primary means of information flow, communications, and decision-making in their purchasing habits.

Commercially, everyday social media becomes more important. Commerce to commerce is growing as well, but more traditional means of outreach still dominate ... business to business.

Advertising

Advertising is still a very strong component of sales and business development through a number of primary mediums:

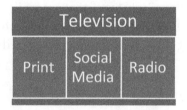

All these four primary advertising modes are strong in particular verticals, depending upon the industry. Many companies continually utilize all four modes leveraging their outreach hoping all or several will get their point across.

Advertising will always have a return on investment (ROI), but sometimes when done for branding, name recognition, or product placement ... it may not be quick to measure and take a longer time to determine its effectiveness.

Telemarketing

Telemarketing is a controversial method of advertising and prospect outreach. Mainly because it is sometimes considered intrusive and annoying to the recipients.

The government has begun to regulate telemarketing to impact the intrusive nature. "Robo-calling" which technology has mastered allows hundreds of thousands of calls to be made simultaneously and in succession with electronically recorded messages.

Most persons both at home and in business find that method very disconcerting … hence all new regulations.

Having said that, it still remains an effective tool.

SALES MANAGEMENT TIED INTO MARKETING AND CUSTOMER SERVICE

At the front end of the pipeline is marketing. While the middle part is sales, which closes the deals and brings the prospect into a client mode.

Also said as … while marketing creates the opportunity, sales closes the deal.

Sales works off a pipeline of opportunity that marketing evaluates, creates, and then feeds:

- At the front end or top of the pipeline is the array of companies we are looking to sell our products and services. Shown above as "Suspects: 100".

  In most situations, one might state that all companies or individuals are "suspects" at first. That may or may not be true, depending upon your perspective.

  As communications and relationships are moved forward, a vetting process occurs which lessens the number of companies considered.
- Once the vetting process has occurred … the pipeline will narrow and the number of opportunities are reduced, but we are getting closer to an opportunity becoming a client.

The vetting process in the initial stages is kind of like qualifying the list of names to determine which ones may be serious opportunities as a result of:

- Size?
- Spend?
- Volume?
- In your wheelhouse or not?
- Opportunity to successfully close?
- The vetting process continues to determine who are the best qualified leads and opportunities. Expressed above as "Qualified: 50".

This method allows you to **focus** your energies and efforts on those opportunities, that have now been vetted and determined to more likely be able to successfully close.

This process moves the opportunity down the pipeline and affords you the business of prioritizing any actions, steps, or initiatives you need to take to ultimately close the deal.

In larger businesses at this stage, senior management may want to become involved to leverage the opportunity to assess next steps or close the deal.

- The end of the pipeline moves prospects in one of two directions:

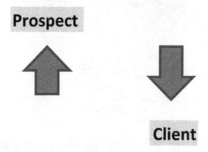

The original suspect at the end of the pipeline is either becoming a client or back to being a prospect.

If you managed the vetting process responsibly, sensibly, and diligently ... the pipeline line theory, strategy, and process should produce a success rate exceeding 20%. Any amounts north of that mark are spectacular results.

Closing the deal in sales will typically also include an implementation or onboarding process which takes what everyone agreed to ... and makes it happen.

CUSTOMER SERVICE

Customer service is made up of five key elements:

The Five Critical Elements of a Successful … Customer Service Capability!!!

ONBOARDING AND TRANSITION

Once a new account is sold, it has to move from the "sales process" into the "caretaking process".

This very critical stage becomes a complete extension of the sale and may still win or lose the client at this very tenuous point. Keep in mind that the client is probably somewhat sheepish at this time and watching carefully over the transition process.

The key words are …. HANDLE WITH TENDER LOVING CARE.

This onboarding plan is best managed by creating a plan of attack, that is outlined with a time frame on an Excel spreadsheet.

The Excel document needs to identify the actions (tasks), who has ownership, status, and timing. See the example below:

	Montgomery Onboarding Plan		
Action	**Person**	**Status and Open Steps**	**Timing**
Finalize Contract	Liz	Draft completed under legal review	by 6/15
Set up 1st transition meeting with account team and client	Sam + Ellen	Tentative Date set for 6/10	by 6/20
Set up new account management interviews	Dick	Waiting to hear back from Sue in Human Resources	ASAP
Create the onboarding SOPs	Liz + Tom	Draft finalized, sent to Bob and George for their review and approval	by 7/1

The Action Plan will help the client to begin to feel comfortable that they made the right decision and they can see a **full court press** on their behalf, from their new vendor.

Tight communications with follow-up and making sure that the transition runs as smooth as possible … will go a long way in taking the first steps with a new client.

CREATING COMFORT LEVELS

The quality of the transition process assists in quickly developing a client that becomes comfortable and at ease.

When I go see existing clients and ask how we are doing in servicing their needs … the common responses I hear:

"Kelly is great … whenever I get into trouble, she is there to bail me out."

"Diane is always available, responsive, and easy to deal with … we wish all our vendors were like you."

"Mark knows his business and is showing us really well how to build our global sourcing model … we love you guys."

All of those kind words demonstrate that the client feels comfortable. They would be hard pressed to move away from us. Additionally, service like that … minimizes the impact of price.

This opens the door to further establish trust and a great working relationship.

ESTABLISHING RELATIONSHIP AND TRUST

Trust is one of the most important aspects that come out of good working relationships between clients and their vendors.

When things are going right … it is not as important … but when things go wrong … it is very important. It will get you through those tough times as trust relates to confidence and confidence translates to getting through issues successfully.

Keep in mind that it can take months and years to build trust … but it can be lost with just one bad act, action, statement, or circumstance.

Your clients chose you and they want you to succeed in the relationship. It works for everyone's mutual interests. Keep open and honest dialogue. Address problems head on. You will find most clients willing to cooperate, be collaborative, and work as a team … when approached responsibly, comprehensively, timely, and responsibly.

To best establish trust …

- Be straight forward, no nonsense and responsibly direct
- Exude responsible confidence
- Do what you say you will do when you need to
- Make promises, keep them
- Exceed expectations
- Be responsibly honest

DELIVERING

At the end of the day … you must **"DELIVER"**.

Meaning your promises made … must be kept. Price, service, capabilities, performance, and results all must be there.

Customer service must be intimately aware of what promises were made by sales and make sure they are kept. Too often, there is a disconnect between sales and customer service.

The two must be aligned. Sales should not over or under commit. And customer service must honor all obligations.

It is senior management role to make sure the alignment exists between sales and customer service because if not, the customer experience will be unfavorable.

As previously mentioned, the onboarding process should create the alignment and everyone being on the same page on what the deliverables are and how best to make them happen.

That will best assure satisfied clients.

CREATING SUSTAINABILITY

The cost of customer acquisition is expensive. Often in the first year of a client relationship, a provider may lose money. But the intent is to make it up over the course of a longer tenure.

That is an acceptable and reliable strategy but only as long as sustainability of the relationship matures.

The best steps to make that happen are as follows:

PREVENTING COMPLACENCY

Complacency is one of the most frequent killers of great relationships that end up going south real fast.

In most of my sales management training sessions, I preach to those responsible for client relationships ... not to let complacency set in. What you took years to build will be washed away as if a Tsunami passed through.

TRUST

Trust is the most important aspect or quality relationships and is a vital element of successful customer service.

You need to be believed and if you are trusted ... believing comes easier.

Trust gets you through the difficult times and offers a platform for problem resolution and ease of convening business transactions.

CONTINUALLY ADDING VALUE

To create sustainability, you must be continually developing the ways to add value and differentiation.

Complacency kills relationships and must be managed through the process of continually adding value in customer service.

BENCHMARK PRICE

You need to always be aware of how your pricing matches up against the competition straight-up and also comparing "apples to apples".

Believe that your clients are always watching pricing and you do not want to be in apposition of upsetting your client who finds out that your pricing is way above market averages. Benchmarking, reviewing, and scrutinizing are the important sales responsibility to mutually protect your client and your interests.

7

Negotiation in Business Development

To be successful, you have to have your heart in your business, and your business in your heart.

Thomas Watson, Sr., Former CEO, IBM

Negotiation is a critical skill set that sales executives need to master in the responsibilities in business development. While many of the characteristics of sales negotiation are both domestic and international ... the astute marketing and salesperson knows when best to distinguish between domestic and international, sensitive to cultural concerns, and knows how to best leverage in either scenario, which is what is covered in this chapter.

WHY STUDY NEGOTIATION?

Negotiation is a skill set ... few **"master"**. Those that do are more successful than those that don't.

We study negotiation, because that skill set opens the door to having the best opportunity for ourselves and our company to achieve our mutually synched goals.

Negotiation is both an art and a science. People with high degrees of emotional intelligence (EI) are traditionally matured negotiators and get through life and business issues more easily, because of that innate ability to negotiate.

Sales and business development executives must be able to develop and master negotiation skill sets, in order to best represent their company in growth and expansion.

The skill sets of negotiation are:

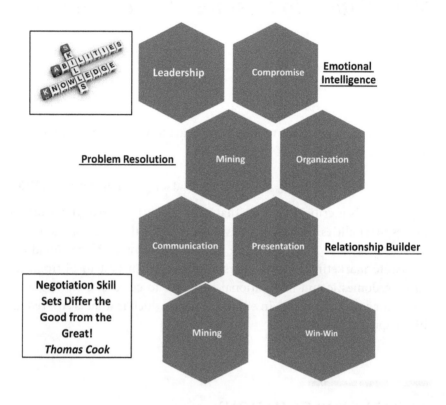

KEY SKILL SETS REFINED

Leadership

Negotiation is influencing another party to move in a direction that meets what you need to accomplish.

When you demonstrate "leadership" … influencing people is a much easier task.

The basic nature of human beings is to follow. But they will only follow those who exude leadership qualities.

Qualities such as but not limited to:

All leaders need to make sure these characteristics are part of their nature. If not, then must make them a part of how they handle and communicate their responsibilities as it becomes part of their personal.

Leaders with high degrees of EI will find these traits easier to manage. Some executives will require behavior modification, which is not easy and requires commitment and persistence.

Emotional Intelligence

Defined

Noun

Noun: **Emotional intelligence (EI, EQ, EIQ)**

1. The capacity to be aware of, control, and express one's emotions and to handle interpersonal relationships judiciously and empathetically.

   Emotional intelligence is the key to both personal and professional success

   Or

   EI, also known as **emotional quotient** (**EQ**) and **emotional intelligence quotient** (**EIQ**), is the capability of individuals to recognize their own emotions and those of others, discern between different feelings and label them appropriately, use emotional information to guide thinking and behavior, and manage and/or adjust emotions to adapt to environments or achieve one's goal(s).

Those executives in business development that have high degrees of EQ are in the best position to negotiate better and achieve better results.

In the art of decision-making, qualitative traits work well and when these tie into EQ ... this makes a formula for a powerful negotiator.

The negotiator can measure the other party's feelings, emotions, and sensibilities and anticipate what to expect. This allows them to prepare what to say which will influence their behavior and their decision-making.

The dominance and importance of EI

The author wrote a book in 2010 *The Art of Mastering Sales Management* CRC Press of the Taylor & Francis Publishing Group.

An excerpt from that book on EI follows:

EMOTIONAL INTELLIGENCE

EI (emotional quotient, EQ) is a relatively new discussion point in corporate America coming from a group of progressive corporate cultural icons who have studied the subject in great depth. Some attribute the discussion to Adele Lynn, Robert Cooper, Ayman Sawaf, Bob Kelly, and Dan Coleman. They all identify EQ as the dimension of intelligence responsible for our ability to manage ourselves and our relationships with others.

EQ is the distinguishing factor that determines whether we make lemonade when life hands us lemons or whether we spend our life in bitterness. EQ is the distinguishing factor that enables us to have wholesome, warm relationships or cold, distant ones. EQ is the distinguishing factor between finding and living our lives' passions or just existing.

In the business world, I believe that EQ is the major factor of differentiation between mediocre managers and leaders and great ones. In the business world, however, so much of our emphasis has been placed on intellect. It has all been on IQ and the analytical, factual, and measured reasoning power that IQ represents. Make no mistake; intellect has proven invaluable to drive success in business and life. Financial decisions based on analytical details, sound strategies based on facts and data, and processes and procedures based on review and analysis are all critically important.

To get to the next level of business, we combine IQ and EQ to raise the bar of all our skill sets and merge them into a persona and actions that exude confidence and prowess, causing our own inspiration as well as providing a reason for others to follow.

In life, IQ would be akin to the athlete who practices all the time, is in the best shape and physical condition, continually studies all the plays, but is time and time again unable to deliver wins. It is also the actor who can sing, dance, and act; who works real hard; and who knows all the lines but is never pursued by the directors as he or she totally lacks "stage presence". It is also the beautiful woman who has the looks, the figure, the intelligence, all the perceived talent, and who is constantly being pursued but who has difficulty in relationships and goes through life alone. It is also the businessman whose father started the business, who has all the schooling, the training, and did all the right things but who never rise to his father's place.

In all these examples, the formula for success was there, but it just did not happen. We all know numerous situations like this in our business and personal lives. They all seem to get to "third base" but cannot get "home". And even in our own circumstances, we have probably had times when we felt like these examples. Some use the phrase, "not seeing the forest through the trees"; or "the ship has sailed, but it does not know where it is going"; or "there are many animals to herd, but no pastures to show them".

In business, I found that these people lose out because they are unable to connect the dots. They have good intentions, all the fundamentals, but lack the ability to make it all bear fruit.

Consider the case of a very intelligent CEO from an Ivy League school. He has 20 years of training, has worked his way up the ladder, and has always been successful. He seems to go through life and business without a care kind of the golden child. He finally has his first major challenge, where all can be won or lost, and he loses. He is unable to muster the troops and lead the team through turbulent waters or navigate them to resolution. It seems he has all the talents but is unable to bring it all together and make it happen.

Most highly regarded leaders have EQ. They are commanding, intelligent, intuitive, and most of all can get others to follow. Few people have the skill sets and a high degree of EQ.

As this concept of EQ develops into more of a science and its traits and characteristics are identified, sales managers will look to raise the bar of their capabilities and, ultimately, their performance.

Some EQ considerations:

- Understanding that the job is not just thinking and doing but to get others to think and do
- Seeing yourself realistically and getting others to be more honest with themselves and with the world
- Getting others to be their very best
- Learning the relationship between thinking and acting, imagining and creating, believing and living
- Recognizing that everything is connected directly and indirectly
- Being able to connect the dots to conclusion and remembering that everything eventually needs closure and that the timing of this is critical
- Understanding that articulation often separates the good from the best
- Recognizing that perception is very often reality and knowing when it is not
- Learning how and why people behave the way they do; studying human nature
- Seeing the big picture and also paying attention to vital details
- Learning to focus
- Recognizing that health is everything – physical and emotional
- Learning to command, yet be respectful
- Listening well

- Understanding that business is business and that personal is personal; learning to know when they are the same and when they are different
- Being street smart
- Recognizing when to be patient and when not to be
- Being more responsible, less fair
- Showing common sense, intuition, and realistic perspective, and a forthright demeanor, all of which are virtues
- Being honest, considerate, direct, and no nonsense
- Being traditional, contemporary, and futuristic
- Always influencing in a positive way
- Realizing that stimuli influence mindset (beliefs), which causes thoughts, which influences behavior, which causes actions that influence results. (We generally choose our stimuli, the beginning of how we perceive and, ultimately, influence the world.)
- Not sweating the small stuff
- Approaching every day with a positive can-do mindset
- Compromising everything, except your values
- Creating "win-win" scenarios
- Reducing your emotional highs and lows to more of a steady demeanor
- Taking well-thought-out risks
- Knowing when to exercise passion, and compassion
- Knowing when to delegate, mentor, and lead
- Always being grateful and living every moment and day as a gift

There has been both a seasoned and recent debate whether all these considerations are innate or whether they can be learned. For sure, they can be learned to some extent. For those who have the benefit of these innate gifts, they can certainly be enhanced and bettered.

To some, many of these EQ skills come naturally. For others, they have to be learned, practiced, and highlighted in everyday consciousness and action. For these EQ skills to work in building the character of a person, they must be practiced consistently and in all aspects of a person's business behavior and life persona.

The listed EQ considerations, when practiced with all the skill sets outlined in this book, will create a formula that will maximize your opportunities for ultimate success in sale, sales management, and in life.

THOUGHTS TO SELL BY...

Gratitude unlocks the fullness of life. It turns what we have into enough, and more. It turns denial into acceptance, chaos to order, confusion to clarity. It can turn a meal into a feast, a house into a home, a stranger into a friend.

Melody Beattie

As we enter a period in the second half of the second decade of the new millennium, business has substantially changed from the 20th century. There is an increasing demand on all business executives to perform, particularly those engaged in sales and business development.

Developing and mastering the skill of EI in this very competitive and demanding business world we now live in has become increasingly vital.

It is very clear that those business executives with higher degrees of EI are in a much more leveraged position in:

- Developing quality relationships
- Understanding people's behavior
- Influencing people more easily
- Leading people to more favorable decisions

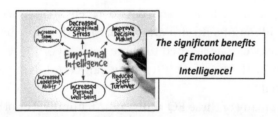

- Resolving more problems more easily
- Negotiating deals with greater ease

- Knowing when to be aggressive, when to be patient, and when to be both
- Being more successful in managing people overall

We need to hone our skills in EI. A question often asked of me is as follows:

CAN EMOTIONAL INTELLIGENCE BE DEVELOPED?

The theory of **EI** is popular because it implies that EQ can be **developed**. This is not universally accepted, but research has supported the idea that **EI** competencies can be significantly improved over time.

The author believes some people have it, some don't, and others have some of it, to some extent.

In either case, we should always try and improve in this area, be cognizant of what it is, and continually make progress in this area of people skills.

The mindset of the negotiator must be to think "win-win". What we mean by this is that the best opportunity to have a successful negotiation is to have as a goal that both sides will benefit from the conclusion of the negotiation.

It shows an empathy for the other side and creates a more balanced approach that both sides will compromise and gain in the negotiation.

This requires the negotiator to strategically think through his or her tactics to know what they want to achieve and how best to approach that compromise and gain scenario and then establishing the infamous "win-win".

Relationship Builder

One of the most important aspects of successful negotiators … is their ability to bridge the gap of people by developing quality relationships.

Relationships make both parties:

- Have confidence in one another
- Establish trust
- Minimize difference so they can be bridged

Quality relationships also help bridge problems when they arise. No relationship … very little success of problem resolution.

Have a good relationship and the door is opened to work at the problem, the willingness to resolve is present, and the issue will be dissipated.

Many negotiators focus on the issue, the talking points, and his or her position. This is at the risk of the other party thinking that you are self-ishly focused and not being empathetic.

Working on relationship issues will be a better tactic to manage what you are trying to accomplish.

Win-Win

The concept of creating a "win-win" in negotiations is as old as is modern man. You want to enter every negotiation with a mindset of "winning" but one where both sides and/or all parties come out winning.

This concept is a distinguishing factor of "mindset" that then creates the best path forward where at the end of the negotiation, all parties walk-away as they have made some gain. Perhaps with compromise … but with gain.

A "win-win" approach will also establish "trust" between the negotia-tors as the other side will perceive you are trying to create mutuality in benefit for both sides.

You want the person on the other side of the table … to feel and sense that you are not one sided and are working towards something that pro-vides mutual benefit.

Compromise

Most negotiations will result in a resolution where the parties involved both gain what they want and compromise to some extent what they com-pletely wanted.

As long as the compromises are balanced, transparent, and agreed to … they tend to be part of a totally successful negotiation initiative.

Compromise on everything … except your "values" …

Thomas Cook

Compromise is both an attribute and a great tool to own. All successful negotiators know that the value of a good compromise can bring to help resolve a problem or negotiate a favorable solution.

Communication

Communicating timely and responsibly by all the vested parties and sides to a negotiation is another important element to creating the best opportunity for a successful negotiation.

It demonstrates a good sense of responsibility and keeps everyone both informed and on the same page.

Additionally, you generally have a need to move the negotiation along an agreed process ... good communications allow that to happen better.

Communication can be accomplished by:

- Personal meetings
- Conference calls
- Emails
- Webinars
- Other agreed methods

Choose the method that works for all the vested interests and assure that the messaging gets through.

Mining

Mining is the gathering of facts and data that can be utilized in the negotiation that can offer leverage and advantage to your cause and for a successful close.

This takes:

- The development of resources
- Time and initiative
- Expenditures
- Outreach
- Utilization of both internal and external contacts

The benefits will outweigh the costs and typically prove valuable as a tool in raising the bar of your position in the negotiation that will bring a favorable resolution.

Organization

You will be in a stronger position in the negotiation process if you organize:

- Your strategy
- Your thoughts
- Your leverage points
- Complete a SWOT (strengths, weaknesses, opportunities, and threats) analysis
- Your material
- Document your process in writing

Taking the time and effort to get organized will pay you back in a number of ways ... the most important one ... in creating the best opportunity to succeed in the negotiation at hand.

Presentation

An example of a powerful presentation and communication outline in the subject matter of negotiation is profiled as follows:

DRAFT PRESENTATION FOR NEGOTIATION
BUSINESS SKILL SETS: INTERNATIONAL FOCUSED

WHY STUDY NEGOTIATION

- More responsible and favored results
- Lead people to make better, more favored decisions
- Protect you and your company
- In supply chain/purchasing/domestic/international business ... a critical skill to define success
- Personally ... big benefits!!!
- Transaction by transaction and long term

NEGOTIATION ... KEY ISSUES

What is a "negotiation" attempting to accomplish?

- Change?
- Influencing?

- Behavior Modification?
- Going your way?
- Information flow?
- Make a better or more favored decision!!!
- Trust!!!!!!!!!

A successful negotiation is more likely to be won ... even before it starts ... if ... "Preparation" is managed diligently!!!!!!!!!

"PREPARATION" IS MANAGED DILIGENTLY!!!!!!!!!

- Information gain
- Mining and benchmarking
- Gaining insight
- Thinking through to ... the person on the "other side of the table"
- Strategically planning
- Successful tactics

WHAT ARE OUR PRIMARY RESPONSIBILITIES?

- List...
- How does this relate to negotiation?

If we "Negotiate" better ... we increase our chance of successful business management in every area of responsibility and personally!!!

TRUMP ... ART OF THE DEAL
EVERYTHING IS WINNABLE! IS IT?

Negotiating can sometimes be explained as two or more parties reaching a consensus and compromise!

Case Study

You are the Purchasing Manager for a printing company in New York City and have a total spend on paper products of 5.5 million. You have a favored vendor for 6 years but have encountered a number of problems with poor performance for on-time delivery schedules.

You decided to run a request for proposal (RFP) and the other two companies which have been impressive are offering (conceptually) what appears to be better pricing and a service portfolio reducing the delivery issues.

Both are looking to obtain current pricing so they can compete effectively.

How do you handle that negotiation?

NEGOTIATION

Is it innate or can it be learned?
How much is science and/or art?

- The "Science" part ...
  - Buying a car
  - Negotiating compesnsation.
- The "Art" part ...
  - Sensibility
  - Gut feeling
  - Experience

BETTER DECISION-MAKING

Qualitative versus quantitatively

How does this "work-in" to negotiation skill set?

DISCUSS THE FOLLOWING "TRAITS AND BUSINESS PROCESS" IN NEGOTIATION

- Transparency?
  - Open, honest, straight forward?
  - No nonsense?
- Professional
  - Being "nice", "courteous"
  - Realistic?
  - Suspicious?

Importance of "Trust" and "Relationship".

DISCUSS THE IMPORTANCE OF "TRUST" AND "RELATIONSHIP"

- Trust
- Relationship
- What can we do to build trust and relationship?
  - Trust is earned, respect is given, and loyalty is demonstrated. Betrayal of any one of those is to lose all three.

Establishing "TRUST" is the most important influencing factor that makes successful negotiators.
And vice versa ...

MOTIVATION

- In business
  - Career
  - Security
  - Money

INTERNATIONAL BUSINESS

It requires a differentiation of methodology incorporating ... political, economic, and cultural allowances.

IN PURCHASING ... WHAT DO WE PRIMARILY NEGOTIATE?

- Price
- Risk
- Services and capabilities
- Value add
- Contracts
- Single versus multiple sourcing
- Suppliers versus internal

GLOBAL NEGOTIATION

- Deals with ...
  - General negotiation skill sets
  - Negotiating domestically versus internationally

BIGGEST DIFFERENCES BETWEEN DOMESTIC VERSUS INTERNATIONAL ...

- Consequences when a mistake is made
- Cultural issues
- Mind-set of a "contract or an agreement"
- Commitment to mine and exercise patience

BASIC STRATEGY

- Win-Win negotiation theory
- Outcome for both sides or numerous parties and benefits
- Internationally ... just maybe more complex

THE PSYCHOLOGY OF NEGOTIATION IN BUSINESS

- Change behavior
- Impact decision-making
- Persuade
- Change mind-set
- Move in a different direction
- Convince
- Create

On a "softer" note ... "Influence"

THE PSYCHOLOGY OF NEGOTIATION IN BUSINESS

- Win-Win-Win
- Compromise
- Timing ... process
- Lifespan
- In steps ... timing?
- Pieces
- Short term versus long term
- Patience is a virtue
- Potential consequences ... of winning or losing?

THE PSYCHOLOGY OF NEGOTIATION IN BUSINESS

Which "animal" are you … and which one are they?

- Owl
- Rooster
- Eagle
- Dove

INTERNAL NEGOTIATION CONSIDERATIONS: YOU

- Up
- Down
- In
- Out

NEGOTIATION EXAMPLE

You are the Purchasing Manager for a New York-based credit card company, and you will be managing an RFP initiative within your organization for a managed printing service.

You have six divisional managers who are making this purchase independently who are all Eagles or Roosters. They believe their business model within their control has unique issues and giving "push-back" to allowing purchasing to provide a centralized acquisition of these services.

Your boss … the CFO wants to see savings and business process improvements.

So how do you handle? **Create a win-win scenario.**

SOME THOUGHTS

- Quantify price anticipation
- Determine other issues or benefits/value added
- Send "tests"
- Don't get "lost" in the detail or minutia
- Determine decision makers … meet if possible
- As an example, longer term commitments, bundling, purchasing options … may add to price-lowering opportunity

- Importance of knowledge, wherewithal, and specific awareness of the issues
- Bring to closure … example as it relates to an RFP!

PROJECT MANAGEMENT AND NEGOTIATION

The entire process of project management is a negotiation over time to achieve a result or to obtain or gain something.

Case Study

As a Purchasing Director, you have successfully negotiated a deal with a new supplier of hardware and software with a small IT vendor.

You had conducted an RFP, and this company, though smaller and newer than the other RFP participants, including the incumbent, offered a seriously more robust offering and at the best price, by far!

You had your business owners engaged in the RFP process, and the decision was very much unanimous.

As you approach the Statement of Work and Master Services Agreement (SOW and MSA) stage, you are seeing a serious reluctance to include risk management in the wording.

The apprehensions are impacting your ability to close the deal? How do you negotiate a solution and keep both parties satisfied or happy?

STRATEGY VERSUS TACTICS

Goals … strategies … tactics … action plans … accountability and responsibility systems.

Goal Setting:

S mart
M easureable
A ttainable
R elevant
T rackable
Twelve steps in successful negotiation

1. Understanding what you are looking to accomplish … goals!
2. Gaining senior management support

3. Creating a team approach
4. Mining
5. Setting the stage
6. Executing initial strategy … timing?
7. Outlining what will be necessary to earn an agreement
8. Tactics/execution/problem resolution
9. Closing the d
10. Implementation
11. In on-going negotiations that will repeat … evaluate and set the stage for next year
12. Follow-up (win or lose)

1. Understanding what you are looking to accomplish …
   - What you have determined
   - What others have determined
   - If goals … SMART?
   - Parameters and timing
   - This effort will be successful if we accomplish ….?
   - EI reigns supreme!
2. <u>Gaining senior management support …</u>
   - Why?
   - How to obtain?
   - How to utilize?
   - Risks and rewards … take notice!
   - Keep them appraised
   - Leadership to help get the deal done!
3. <u>Creating a team approach (TOM – You didn't have a slide on this point)</u>
4. <u>Mining … knowledge can be the most critical element of any negotiation …</u>
   - Resources
   - Spending and investing time … everyday!
   - Building a "Rolodex"
   - See vendor options
   - Internet
   - Networking … trade shows, industry events
5. <u>Setting the stage …</u>

Bringing a plan together ... first in your head, second with your management, then with a written outline
- Relationship building
- Initial information gathering
- Determine decision makers.

6. <u>Executing initial strategy</u>
- Short-term goals versus long-term goals
- Meetings ... business and social
- Establishing relationship and "trust"
- Qualifying
- Commit ... then honor!
- Ask questions ... probing ... "SWOT analysis"
- Time frames are potentially established
- Next steps ... intellectual confrontation on what to expect ... action plan is created
- Prioritize issues, needs, and wants ... "must haves versus maybes?"

7. <u>Outline what will be necessary to earn an agreement</u>
- Ask, ask again and again ... be creative in your approach
- Obtain an understanding and maybe even an agreement
- Establish actions and next steps
- Set up next meeting or action time frame
- Beginning of the "close".

The framework or foundation is established, which everything will rest upon ... in the negotiation initiative!!

8. <u>Tactics/execution/problem resolution</u>
- Straight forward ... no nonsense
- Make sure you are heard
- Persistence, pushy, aggressive, forward
- Set stage for close ... the close should happen naturally!

9. <u>Closing the deal</u>
- Should happen "naturally" and without asking
- Closing questions ... indirect approach
- Direct approach
- Prior agreements in writing

- Action plan ... creating comfort level and continued sensibility that a correct decision was made
- RFP proposals ... go back to the proposal!

10. <u>Implementation</u>
    - Deal not successful until implemented
    - Should be part of all understandings and agreements
    - Big area for failure in new relationships

11. <u>On-going negotiations:</u>
    - That repeat or renew
    - Strategy and execution

12. <u>Follow-up (win or lose)</u>
    Maybe the most important step(s) = in new customer care or in what was accomplished!

Workshop Review

You are an LIC-based insurance company Purchasing Manager. You have a favored IT vendor with a spend of 2.5 million. They have been engaged by your company for 5 years and the business owners in your company have developed a very tight and good relationship with this vendor.

It is a critical area of spend and vendor relationship.

Company policy dictates an RFP every 2 years. In your initial outreach, you have determined some more robust options and with lower costing.

When you broach a potential change to the internal business owners, there is a lot of "push-back".

Go through the steps:

Challenges, who are you negotiating with?

Outline what will be necessary to earn an agreement.

Prepare a discussion outline of how you would approach this step in the negotiation process.

Workshop Review #2

You are a New York-based financial services company, Purchasing Manager.

Senior management is requiring you to cut costs by 15% on two contracts with two long-term suppliers/vendors ... one a building maintenance company and the other an office equipment provider.

Both are great vendors/suppliers with good service and price and a tenured relationship with your company preceding even your arrival.

How do you approach the negotiations?

Workshop Review

Straight forward, no nonsense, honest, to the point ... grip it, and rip it!

Approach to relationship and negotiation????

Relationship Building

Accomplish more with good relationships
eCommerce????
Good means quality and honesty/transparency
Gets you through the difficult times
Allow more honesty

Emotional Issues

- Anger
- Dissatisfaction
- Trust or lack of
- Trying to make everyone "happy"
- Which hat to wear?
- Control and balance ... is the critical element

SWOT Analysis

S trengths
  W eaknesses
  O pportunites
  T hreats
  Some thoughts ... SWOT
  S ... price, valued added
  W ... incumbent may have relationship
  O ... capture business

T ... one-time chance, do you know what you need to do, how you are perceived, current strength of existing relationships (change issue)

Leading to ... strategies ... then tactics.

Tactics/Execution/Problem Resolution

- You want the close to come naturally
- You want to identify and counter all issues
- You want to place yourself in the best position to be able to close the deal

Sidebar: Problem Resolution (Crisis Management)

- Stop bleeding
- Information gather (intensely)
- Meet and conference call with all concerned parties
- Obtain options
- Create a strategy
- Execute
- Tweak
- Review and follow-up

Closing the Deal

- Get a feel of where they are at?
- Ask open-ended questions?
- Ask soft questions? (suggestions)
- Timing is critical
- Bring closure

Follow-Up (Win or Lose)

- Win or lose......follow-up is critical
  - Lose – Sets the stage for a future opportunity
  - Win – Demonstrates concern, assures success, proactive problem resolution

What Motivates the Other Side of the Table?

- Price
- Service

- Timeliness
- Value added
- Personal issues (Maslow)

International

- Complications
- Mind-set
- Challenge
  When things go wrong!
  Cultural issues ... China, Latin America, Middle East
  One shoe fits all ... nada!
  Strategies are very diverse and customized

International Contracts Export Sales and Import Purchase Orders

- Terms of sale
- Terms of payment
- Freight
- Insurance
- Title
- Revenue recognition
- Marking, packing, and labeling
- Permits and registrations
- Intellectual property rights
- Disputes

Incoterms®

Incoterms® are:
  Point in time and trade ...
  Responsibility
  Liability
  Transfer   seller <-> buyer
              Importer <-> exporter
              Costs and risks – that's it!

Incoterms® ... Negotiating a Better Price or Reducing Risks

Examples:
Landed costs and risks
Export >>> trade compliance

Ex works
Delivered Duty Paid
Import >>> landed costs
Ex works versus free on board

Negotiation Character Traits?

Outline ten character traits that will help a person more successfully close deal.

Negotiation Character Traits

1. Honesty
2. Sincerity
3. Caring
4. Product and industry knowledge
5. Problem solver
6. Responsive
7. Quality communicator
8. Leadership
9. Charisma
10. Serious, but not too much so
11. Funny, but not too much so (sense of humor)
12. Make them feel good
13. Cater to their ego, needs, and wishes
14. Learn how they listen and learn
15. Think on your feet
16. Credible
17. Authority figure
18. Do what you say you will
19. Be persistent

Negotiation Questions

Identify ten questions you can ask to obtain a sense of where a vendor is at, in a negotiation ... without being offensive or too obtrusive.

Negotiation Questions

1. What is your primary strategy on price?
2. What examples can you give me to evidence your price reduction strategies?

3. What "value add" and "differentiation" do you bring to the table?
4. How do you access risk and how do you assist your clients in reducing risk?
5. How do you manage your Tier One suppliers, to assure product and or service flow?
6. Due diligence:
   - Can we have three referrals of existing clients and one client you recently lost?
   - P&L and balance sheet?
   - Can we meet the actual servicing team?
7. What size client would we be in your office?
8. How do you handle off-hours accessibility?
9. How do you pass on savings you may have achieved in your acquisition of product or service that lowers your costing model?
10. What areas of concern or challenges do you have in your business model?

Workshop

You are a vendor and Sourcing Manager for an NJ-based pharmaceutical company. You manage numerous contracts for outsourced third-party manufacturing.

You have been requested by your R&D group to help negotiate with a third-party contract laboratory in Princeton. They provide a unique service, and it appears there is little or no competition, in this particular area, according to your technicians and scientists.

Relative to other similar work, how do you assure competitive pricing when benchmarking is limited?

The value of the contract is small, less than $250,000, but the work being done is critical to a much larger related project.

Create a negotiation strategy.

Some Thoughts …

- Do we believe what we were told?
- Do we "turn over more stones"?
- Like or similar deals or circumstances?

Some Additional Thoughts ...

Contract negotiation strategy:
- Wear your lawyer hat
- Upfront disclosure
- Promises made ... promises delivered
- Include the proposal
- Set the stage in the process
- Deliverables
- Prices
- Risks
- Template

RFP Management
- What are you trying to achieve?
- Deliverables?
- Process ...
- Science versus art?
- Identify options?
- Qualify options?
- Price equation ...
- Value versus price
- Steps ...
- Training seminar on managing RFPs

Supplier Agreements (SLA)

How do we manage, hold accountable, and gain greatest value ... while paying competitively???

Lack of Technical Expertise

When I work in a field that is technical ... how do I not step on technicians' toes and how best to manage my negotiation responsibilities???

Intonation
- Repeating points
- Soft tone versus firm
- Different language
- Order of topics in a discussion

EI ... Emotional Intelligence Better Negotiations

Summary
- Negotiation skills can be learned ... "learning/training is a process"
- Develop a "win-win" mentality, identify with your other side
- Patience is a virtue ... overall and transactional!
- Create a strategy, develop tactics.
- Learn to manage up, down, in and out.
- Goals, expectations need to be SMART!
- Execute with consistency, persistence, and structure.

Problem Resolution

In order to resolve most problems, one typically must "negotiate" towards a solution. It will require a strategy and an execution that includes a compromise between all the impacted parties.

Most personnel with problem-solving skill sets are also great negotiators. They understand the assessment process in evaluating the details surrounding a problem and know the steps necessary to bring the problem to a favorable close.

Negotiation as an Art and Science

Negotiation is considered by most professionals to be both an art and a science ... meaning that there are both technical and esoteric skill sets that are needed to make someone a good negotiator.

The "art" of the negotiation process ties directly into the dialog in this book where we discuss "emotional intelligence". EI is the esoteric side that brings some innate abilities of an individual to bring "feel and sensibilities" into the negotiation process ... which sometimes can prove to be the deciding factor in any negotiation.

The "science" part will typically relate to hard data that can be mined to obtain information valuable in creating a negotiation strategy. Additionally, it will include facts, principles, and details that come from very specific verifiable sources that can be leveraged in the negotiation process.

Great negotiators bring together both the art and the science to successfully negotiate.

Negotiating International Agreements
Negotiating an Agreement with a Foreign Representative

When your company has found a prospective representative that meets its requirements, the next step is to negotiate a foreign sales agreement. Export Assistance Centers provide advice to firms contemplating that step. The International Chamber of Commerce also provides useful guidelines.

Here is an important information to consider when negotiating an agreement with a foreign representative

Your company should provide foreign representatives with information on:

- *Pricing structure*
- *Product profit potential*
- *Terms of payment*
- *Product regulation*
- *Competitors*
- *Firm support*
- *Sales aids*
- *Promotional material*
- *Advertising*
- *Sales training*
- *Service training*
- *Ability to deliver on schedule*

The agreement may contain provisions that specify the actions of the foreign representative, including the following:

- *Not having business dealings with competing firms (because of antitrust laws, this provision may cause problems in some European countries)*
- *Not revealing any confidential information in a way that would prove injurious, detrimental, or competitive to your firm*
- *Not entering into agreements with other parties that would be binding to your firm*
- *Referring all inquiries received from outside the designated sales territory to your firm for action*

These are some of the legal questions to consider:

- *How far in advance must the representative be notified of your intention to terminate the agreement? Three months satisfy the requirements of many countries, but a registered letter may be needed to establish when the notice was served.*
- *What is "just cause" for terminating a representative? Specifying causes for termination in the written contract usually strengthens your position.*
- *Which country's laws (or which international conventions) govern a contract dispute? Laws in the representative's country may forbid the representative company from waiving its nation's legal jurisdiction.*
- *What compensation is due to the representative on dismissal? Depending on the length of the relationship, the added value of the market that the representative created for you, and whether termination is for just cause as defined by the foreign country, you may be required to compensate the representative for losses.*
- *What must the representative give up if dismissed? The contract should specify the return of property, including patents, trademarks, name registrations, and customer records.*
- *Should the representative be referred to as an agent? In some countries, the word agent implies power of attorney. The contract needs to specify whether the representative is a legal agent with power of attorney.*
- *In what language should the contract be drafted? In most cases, the contract should be in both English and the official language of the foreign country. Foreign representatives often request exclusivity for marketing in a country or region. It is recommended that you not grant exclusivity until the foreign representative has proven his or her capabilities or that it be granted for a limited, defined period of time, such as 1 year, with the possibility of renewal. The territory covered by exclusivity may also need to be defined, although some countries' laws may prohibit that type of limitation.*

Important steps:

Accountability

Agreements should be able to hold foreign representatives accountable. Consider including performance requirements, such as a minimum sales volume and an expected rate of increase.

Ending an agreement

In drafting the agreement, you must pay special attention to safeguarding your company's interests in case the representative proves less than satisfactory. It is vital to include an escape clause in the agreement that allows you to end the relationship safely and cleanly if the representative does not fulfill expectations.

Some contracts specify that either party may terminate the agreement with written advance notice of 30, 60, or 90 days.

The contract may also spell out exactly what constitutes "just cause" for ending the agreement (e.g., failure to meet specified performance levels). Other contracts specify a certain term for the agreement (usually 1 year) but arrange for automatic annual renewal unless either party gives written notice of its intention not to renew.

In all cases, escape clauses and other provisions to safeguard your company may be limited by the laws of the country in which the representative is located so be sure to check with local expertise, such as a lawyer or other legal professional.

For this reason, you should learn as much as you can about the legal requirements of the representative's country and obtain qualified legal counsel in preparing the contract.

Legal jurisdiction

The agreement with the foreign representative should define what laws apply to the agreement. Even if you choose U.S. law or that of a third country, the laws of the representative's country may take precedence.

Many suppliers define the United Nations Convention on Contracts for the International Sale of Goods (CISG, or the Vienna Convention) as the source of resolution for contract disputes or they defer to a ruling by the International Court of Arbitration of the International Chamber of Commerce.

Arbitration can often provide an excellent alternative to the legal system.

For more information, refer to the International Chamber of Commerce arbitration page.

Prepared by the International Trade Administration.

With its network of 108 offices across the United States and in more than 75 countries, the International Trade Administration of the U.S. Department of Commerce utilizes its global presence and international marketing expertise to help U.S. companies sell their products and services worldwide. Locate the trade specialist in the United States nearest you by visiting http://export.gov/usoffices.

The Department of Commerce is an excellent resource for international sales personnel.

8

Best Practices in Sales, Sales Management, and Business Development

The most successful sales and business development structures contain absolute defined "Best Practice" Guidelines within their operation and make sure these are part of the culture established within the sales organization.

We have identified ten steps that senior management should structure to accomplish a "Best Practice" structure in their business development models.

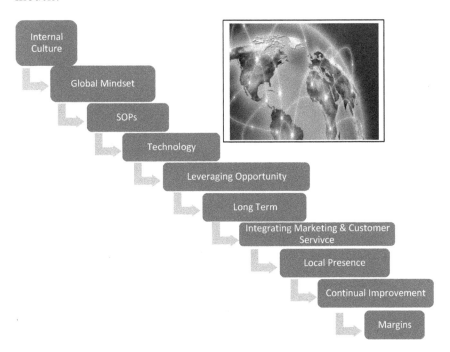

Internal Culture

Global Mindset

SOPs

Technology

Leveraging Opportunity

Long Term

Integrating Marketing & Customer Servivce

Local Presence

Continual Improvement

Margins

INTERNAL CULTURE

Establishing an internal culture in sales and business development is a first step in making sure of high levels of performance and success.

The culture emanates from a ... mission focus ... that becomes the mantra of how sales navigates the challenges of developing business on an international scale.

As examples:

BLUE TIGER INTERNATIONAL

The sales team will:

Work hard and creatively to provide a value proposition to all companies that continually exceed expectations.

DRAGONFLY GLOBAL

The business development team will:

Sales drive this company forward, and this team will do all possible to earn the respect of prospects turning them into clients by offering competitive pricing, great customer service, and value for their spend.

NATIONAL INSTITUTE FOR WORLD TRADE

Sales will:

Offer great value, customer service, responsiveness, and responsible account management to our clients' continual benefit.

These three examples emulate a mind-set on how their sales team will pursue and interface with prospects and clients.

Notice the word "value", which is utilized in different forms ... but creating an important sensibility with the prospects and clients.

This "internal culture": becomes a motto to lead conversations and leadership in some of the following areas:

Prospecting ➡ Pricing ➡ Creative Approaches ➡ Differentiation ➡ Persistence ➡ Client Focus and Value Add

In sales ... think about how important ... continual prospecting, competitive pricing, creative approaches, differentiation, persistence, and client focus/value add ... are all to the overall success of any sales or business development initiative.

GLOBAL MIND-SET

The international salesperson needs to develop a mind-set on a much larger and comprehensive scale that incorporates all of the global community as his or her market.

When this mind-set occurs, you are developing a pathway that is truly global in nature. It encompasses culture, politics, economics, and geography on a much larger and diverse base.

It opens up a much larger market of opportunity.

That thought process reduces risk and maximizes opportunity for your organization.

STANDARD OPERATING PROCEDURES

Standard operating procedures (SOPs) become the cornerstone of compliance, process, and strategy. They glue everything everyone is supposed to do into a document(s) that evidence knowledge, adherence, and practice within the walls of a corporation.

It is a management tool to prove that a company is doing what it is supposed to do.

It ties in personnel as to who, what, and how they are responsible for certain things and occurrences within any organization.

SOPs at the end of the day are the best method to evidence compliance. When tied into an audit trail ... is the nirvana of management doing the right thing.

TECHNOLOGY

Technology every year increases in relevance and importance in every aspect of business and more particularly in overall sales management.

Companies that pay attention to technology as a competitive tool, value add, and differentiator do better than those that don't.

Today if you are not at the forefront of technology and its application in your business model ... and if you are not dead or dying ... you will soon be.

Technology drives most businesses today, and sales personnel need to be at the front-end of this capability in your organization in order to tout it to the prospects in turning them into clients.

LEVERAGING OPPORTUNITY

Opportunity must be sought out, and on an international scale ... the reach must be robust, huge, and complex.

Once opportunity is identified, it must be leveraged.

Internationally, opportunity:

- Can be found in overseas markets not often approached by other companies, such as in third world countries and developing nations
- In certain areas of European and Asian markets that are often not approached by other established international companies
- By differentiating your value adds to offer competitive advantage.

CASE STUDY IN LEVERAGING OPPORTUNITY

A U.S. based dog food company started to export products to a number of traditional markets in Europe and Asia. While some sales occurred, they soon found out that they had a lot of U.S. based competition.

As they explored alternative markets, they were provided numerous opportunities in the Middle East and Africa. In evaluating the risks associated with many of these countries, payment of receivables became a predominant concern.

When they approached their export consultant, Blue Tiger International (bluetigeriintl.com), they were advised that there were several programs available where they could insure their foreign receivables in these countries. They would still need to be diligent in assuring credit worthiness, but this would seriously reduce the risks involved in selling to these countries.

After a year of successful sales to Saudi Arabia, Nigeria, South Africa … they began to market to other countries in the region. Two years later, sales grew to 4.6 million annually.

They learned that a huge differentiator in these countries was their willingness to extend credit for 30–60 days. They found the insurance in place covering the receivable to be a big leverage in their ability to extend payment terms.

They still have a robust credit application and scrutiny process but are now being approached by other dog food importers and distributors in Africa and now some calls from South America.

At the end of the day, this company has leveraged credit insurance to be a differentiator in developing foreign sales.

LONG TERM

It can take a long time to be successful in entering into sales in overseas markets. Patience, persistence, and inevitability will lead to foreign sales.

Therefore, you must be committed to longer periods of time to show success. Global markets have options coming at them from all over the world.

It may take you time to observe, learn, and then develop successful marketing and business development strategies in any particular foreign market.

Building the appropriate time, costing, and resource development in overseas markets are all part of the deal as you expand internationally.

INTEGRATED MARKETING AND CUSTOMER SERVICE

Marketing and customer service, the two areas we discussed in Chapter 6, must be customized by client and country in foreign sales and very much integrated into the overall selling process.

American businesses are well known for their prowess in both marketing and customer service. Many experts around the globe prize American customer service as best in the works, bar none.

Sales personnel must think through how the marketing and customer service will tie into their prospecting and eventual proposal offerings.

LOCAL PRESENCE

Having a local presence in certain markets can be an important element of being successful in that market. Culture, language, and dominant vertical nuances in certain countries may be better served through local presence ... "boots on the ground".

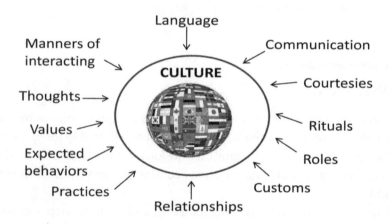

The author having built several international businesses has learned that having a local presence in more cases than not ... will be the key determining factor of succeeding in that market.

You cannot place a higher value than not ... on leveraging language and culture, when you have someone who speaks the language and understands the culture locally ... it creates leverage.

Our situation always improved tenfold once we had local representation. You still have to be involved and visit often ... but the odds of creating and sustaining customers in any foreign market will be in direct proportion by a local presence.

CONTINUAL IMPROVEMENT

This has been stated in this book numerous times. Continual improvement in how you sell, service, and offer value ... creates the best path forward to sustainable relationships that can carry on for the long term.

Internationally, continual improvement is more difficult and challenging. You have to bring in language, culture, economic, demographic, and regulations and a local level before making any decisions.

MARGINS

We always need to be conscientious of what margins are domestically and internationally and be adjusting our costing models to make sure we are both competitive and having the desired margins we require in our business strategies.

ADDITIONAL FACTORS IN BEST PRACTICES

When Sales and Business Development Go South!!

There will be times in any company's tenure that sales will slide and dip.

Understanding that this occurrence is likely to happen at various points in time ... the key is not to beat yourself up but to focus on turning the situation around, as quickly as possible.

We have developed a multi-step process in turning the situation around quickly and even grow sales with greater robust initiatives.

Step 1 ... Assessment

The first step is to evaluate the reasoning why sales have dipped. This process needs to have the following traits:

- Move forward quickly, comprehensively, and thoroughly.
- Dig deep, mine, and assess all "nooks and crannies".

- Be straight forward, honest, and direct in the evaluation and assessment process.
- Eliminate "egos, personalities, silos, fiefdoms", and other internal obstacles in allowing the assessment to move forward.
- Be very transparent.

The above tactics will create the best opportunity for evaluating sales downward spiral. Keep in mind that another purpose of this process is as follows:

- If sales are slipping ... is customer service failing as well ... you do not want to lose any existing clients, so an evaluation of this area should happen simultaneously and any concerns discovered ... managed to favorable conclusion.
- You should look to anything found in the initial assessment and secure corrective actions, as they are known, so you can stabilize the sales and business development decline.

Every company will have numerous and unique reasons for a sales dip. In our experience, the following list constitutes what we have found in a consistent pattern in a lot of the organizations we consult with:

- Complacency. The bottom line is that you have become complacent in your sales efforts and you will need to ignite the sales team.
- Loss of key sales personnel. The bottom line is that you lost valued sales personnel and they have yet to be replaced or their replacements are taking a longer time than expected to secure opportunities.

  Additionally, losing personnel can have a disastrous and endemic impact on organizations when the loss is not managed well, quickly, and comprehensively. It can stifle sales in a big way.

  Not handling loss of personnel both internally and externally ... can cause a "pattern of decline and making the hole bigger" ... and the situation will potentially worsen over time.

  It is best to "jump on the matter" quickly and decisively. It will offer mitigation and eventually resolve.
- Change in pricing. Your organization put through some rate increases and the clients are not responding well. Perhaps the delivery process needs to be evaluated. Or maybe better communications explaining the changes. Or maybe the pricing increases are unwarranted and you may need to reverse them or modify to be more competitive.

- Change in operations. You might have made a change in your operations, customer service, or business processes that are not being received well from your prospects.

  This may require an intense review of what changes you have made to re-justify. You may need to better communicate the changes. Or you may need to take some changes backward and re-work the changes to keep the prospects happy.

- Your approach. Many companies have changed their approach to sales and business development, and those changes are not working. Or existing approaches have become stale or not contemporary.

  As a side note, for those of us who are more seasoned … selling to millennials takes another entirely different approach. Their expectations and concepts of relationship and communications can be very different.

  Utilization of digital technology, social media, and other related communication channels is more successful to millennials than more traditional means that those over 40 might be utilizing.

- Flexibility. Successful selling and business development practices often mean showing and demonstrating flexibility. Flexibility means:

  - Adapting to the individual business needs and requirements of our prospects
  - Being willing to change our approach to better suit the selling requirements
  - Ability to quickly change to market conditions. Some very large companies lose market share and production opportunities who are too slow to change or even too arrogant to acknowledge the need to change
  - Being "nimble" can be a great characteristic of business development management.

    Lack of flexibility is a critical aspect of sales decline and needs to be evaluated considered and acted upon.

Step 2 … Engage Senior Management

Generally, senior management will be aware of any decline in business development or sales. But they need to be aware of what your assessment has determined and more importantly what you are doing about it.

In public companies, this would be a Sarbanes–Oxley principle and in private entities ... a "Best Practice".

Action plans and strategies developed to manage the issues will typically cross company silos. This will require a collaborative structure. Senior management being now informed and engaged will help breakdown the silo walls and help in the strategies and actions working within all levels and silos and fiefdoms of the organization.

Additionally, many initiatives will have expenses associated with them, which will need senior management approval and allocation of that cost.

Step 3 ... Create a Strategy and Action Plan

Following the assessment and discussion with senior management, typically occurring simultaneously or very close together ... is now deciding what steps you are going to take to "right the ship".

A strategy needs to be developed which falls in line with what was discovered with the assessment in providing mitigation and resolution.

This strategy needs to be converted to an Excel spreadsheet, such as we have outlined below:

> The strategy becomes the plan to resolve the decline in new sales and business development. It must be converted to specific actions which the Excel spreadsheet outlines.
>
> It also sets up lines of responsibility and accountability to individual persons and actions.
>
> It keeps everyone on the same page who is a stakeholder in sales, business development, and senior management.

The action plan/Excel spreadsheet:

- Needs to be updated regularly
- Tweaked and modified as circumstances warrant
- Communicated to all impacted and engaged parties
- Begin at some agreed point to prove valuable in resolving the sales decline
- And at some point, be brought to successful closure

Step 4 ... Re-Assess Steps and Actions Taken

At some point both in the near and long-term, you must re-assess that the measures you put forward are working and will provide sustainable sales and business development.

They may be working as is ... but maybe need some modification, adjustments, or tweaking to move the needle to obtain greater levels of success.

Change is always a work-in-process ... growing, maturing, and developing as circumstances warrant.

This is again where flexibility arises and becomes an important aspect of managing sales and business development responsibilities.

Step 5 ... Build a Sustainable Sales Model

You have come through a rough patch. You worked hard to provide a successful resolution.

Now you must develop a model which will hold up for the long term. Sustainability means tenure for the ages. A noble goal for sure but it allows a company to grow, prosper, and create a win-win for the stockholders and employees.

Areas to consider in a sustainable sales and business development model:

1. Keep visiting that what you are doing is working.
2. Learn to self-evaluate and take constructive criticism.
3. Always observe the competition.
4. Be creative, innovative, and always thinking "out of the box".
5. Take cautious, well thought out risks.
6. Be bold, aggressive, and fearless.
7. Be proactive in making adjustments before concerns turn into critical mistakes.
8. Lead the team to do all of the above ... every day and never become complacent.

Best Practices in eCommerce Sales

Current sales models for almost all companies have eCommerce as all or part of their business development models. We need to establish guidelines for "Best Practices" so we are leveraging these international opportunities in the eCommerce vertical.

In the United States, eCommerce is growing by 20% annually and in some international markets is growing by over 50%.

eCommerce (B2C) is growing because:

- It makes it easy and simple to order merchandise.
- It can lower the cost of purchasing ... no need to go out to a retail store.
- The world of online millennials finds this option aligned with their utilization of mobile devices, a preferable option.
- It allows people to focus on other tasks and responsibilities with the efficiencies gained by eCommerce product acquisition.
- It expands the reach into a greater variety of products, markets, and online retailers offering a larger expanse of product options and choices.

Best practice for eCommerce in international markets

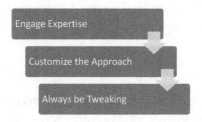

Engage Expertise

The entire subject matter of eCommerce requires experience. Internationally, it requires expert experience because the challenges are huge.

Companies need to hire or engage the expertise it takes to build an eCommerce platform globally.

Personnel, consultants, and experts with specific international eCommerce experience and skill sets are a fundamental requirement.

Customize the Approach

You are likely to ship to multiple countries around the world. Each one is unique. Language, culture, economics, and regulations will all have a huge impact.

You must customize your approach to meet all these variables which could be very extensive from one country to another.

Always Be Tweaking

Innovation, creativity, and adaptation are strong virtues of eCommerce success in export markets. Competition is fierce, and by some strong player … a.k.a. … Amazon … Alibaba … Shopify … are three good examples of very large players you could be up against.

Your success will be determined by your structure and willingness to adapt and be flexible to change. Your eCommerce platform will continually need to be tweaked to offer:

- Ease of access and utilization
- Differentiation
- Value add
- Creative approaches
- Functionality

eCommerce opens the door to the world, where 95% of the consumer market lies and over 80% of the commercial market awaits.

CASE STUDY IN SELLING INTERNATIONAL FREIGHT SERVICES

Growth Strategies

Raising the Bar of Sales Management:

In Organic Sales of … Air Freight, Logistics, and Supply Chain

Thomas Cook, Managing Director, Blue Tiger International

In 2016, companies looking to expand and grow have two primary options. One is to become involved with M&A activity where opportunities are purchased.

The other option and central to this article is the expansion by building your company and developing your growth "organically".

Most companies that are successful in freight, logistics, and supply chain that are aggressively looking to expand and grow their business will work both options simultaneously with a focus on one or the other.

This article will focus on growth organically.

The challenges in organic sales management are numerous, such as but not limited to the following:

- This author boldly states that in the service provider sector of the transportation vertical and particularly in the air freight business ... quality sales personnel are one of the hardest hires to make??
- To discern who really is the prospect is difficult as not every company has freight or air freight needs??
- Price is a very significant factor in decision-making process of many corporate supply chain executives??
- No one likes to spend their freight dollars on air freight when other less expensive modes of transit are a less expensive option??
- Many sales personnel are great at selling freight business. What really makes one a "great" salesperson is one that protects the necessary margins to make decent profits??
- Organic growth, and particularly when compared to M&A growth strategies, is a slower process to mature and the return on investment (ROI) may take longer to make senior management happy.

All these challenges can be managed successfully through the proper management of sales, business development, and opportunity leveraging.

The author has been involved in sales management for over 30 years. He has tried a number of ways, methods, and sales processes to grow the businesses he has been involved with. Some initiatives have worked, some have failed, and both to certain degrees.

But in the past 15 years, he has been very successful at helping companies grow their business models organically being guided by following this outlined formula.

The formula has five primary areas of engagement. These areas of engagement are the focus and platform for a successful organic growth model to be utilized by and sector of the freight, logistics, or supply chain business.

The five cornerstones are:

- Creating a viable sales strategy
- Hiring quality personnel
- Building a sales pipeline of opportunity
- Creating an inventory of prospects
- Closing more deals

The author says ... learn these cornerstones, master them, and organic sales can be very successful.

Creating a Viable Sales Strategy

The sales strategy becomes the blueprint for a plan of attack. The quality and realistic approach of that plan will determine the success of the organic sales initiative.

The steps in the planning process are as follows:

- Where do we want to be? How big do we want to grow? How realistic are these goals?

  Do these goals pass the SMART test? Are the goals specific, measurable, attainable, realistic, and trackable?
- Do a SWOT analysis ... strengths, weaknesses, opportunities, and threats.

  What you are doing here is an assessment of your current operations. You are asking questions like ...
  - What types and size clients are in our portfolio ... is there a "trend" or reason we have these clients?
  - What verticals are we in and why? What verticals should we be in?
  - What are the strengths and weaknesses of our existing sales staff? Do they need to be trained further ... in what skill sets? Will they ever be successful sales personnel?

  The sales strategy once ready to establish will include:
    - Growth goals
    - Specific action plan to achieve the goals
    - Accountability structure from stakeholders to senior management
    - Timing and milestones
    - Contingency plans
    - Once the strategy is in plzace, we move to the personnel who will make it happen.

Hiring Quality Personnel

The first hire, promotion, or internal designation to be made is who is in charge of sales.

A major mistake many companies make is to take their top salesperson and make him or her the sales manager.

Believing that the skill sets to sell well ... equate to managing well? This is very often a big misnomer.

The head of the sales snake ... has to both sell and manage and more importantly have the capacity to make the new sales strategy in organic growth ... be successful!

Some companies look internally to operations personnel. Another potential mistake. You need a person who can sell. I would agree that an operations person, with all that experience, if they also have sales skills, could be a great option ... but finding that combination is extremely rare.

When we look outside our company, we are met with primarily two choices ... the seasoned candidate or the newbie.

The seasoned candidate may bring some baggage and will more likely cost more. But they often can bring books of business, so their ROI is more immediate.

The newbie has the advantage of no baggage or preconceived notions. But they may require more attention, training, and time for that ROI.

In either case, your choice needs to mirror what your strategy requires.

Attributes of quality sales personnel include some of the following traits:

> High energy, persistent, flexible, good negotiator, accepts rejection well, likes socialization and people in general, understands the importance of compromise, won't allow objections, challenges, and walls interfere with finding a way to move forward, is likeable, is able to motivate others, learns the technical side of what they are selling (in freight this means understanding freight operations), knows how to create opportunity/deliver compelling arguments/and close deals, protects company margin requirements, continually learns, and has a boatload emotional intelligence and street smarts!

Additionally:

- Make sure you have a robust sales compensation strategy that is not only contemporary but offers value add to the sales team which attracts more and better sales talent.
- Spend money to create the initial pipeline of opportunities. Invest in information, marketing, branding, memberships, and travel and

entertainment ... to allow the interface to start the building of prospects and relationships.

- Go after low-hanging fruit. Assess where you can obtain easier and quicker results.
- You can never replace experience ... seasoned sales talents are always a great option and typically provide faster and better results.
- Moving your company and your sales initiatives into global and international business opportunities will enhance your business profile and increase the number of serious prospects and a door to differentiation.
- The utilization of Customer Relationship Management systems and technology should be a serious consideration where and when sales become robust and cumbersome to manage manually.

Building a Sales Pipeline of Opportunity

The sales pipeline begins with establishing a flow of opportunities of companies to engage in a dialog with you.

Sales at the end of the day ... is sometimes considered a "numbers" game. Meaning that there has to be a certain number of opportunities that will lead into sales.

In my sales management strategy ... I believe there are three stages of the sales process as outlined in the pictorial.

The <u>first stage</u> is ... opportunities.
The second stage is ... prospects.
The third stage is closing deals.

Stages 2 and 3 are covered below in more detail.

The first stage of creating opportunities can be an infinitum number of companies. You can never have too many opportunities.

But an opportunity may not also be a "prospect". Because "opportunities" need to go through a vetting process to determine whether or not:

- You have something to specifically sell them
- Is the effort going to pay off?
- Is what they need and what you can deliver ... compatible?

- Are there values aligned with yours?
- How do they pay?
- Can you make your margin?
- Do you have the internal expertise necessary to handle the account well? (Side note … you do not want a new client to come in that you cannot service well. You will lose it horribly and the opportunity will be lost forever.)

The vetting process of opportunities will pay back in spades and in a quality sales management structure will prove to be a very valuable business process.

Creating a robust supply of opportunities can come in many forms. Cold calling is a common method, but a lot of time is wasted here.

Telemarketing, networking, attendance at industry events, buying vetted lists, and with certain verticals and their associations are better methods.

CREATING AN INVENTORY OF PROSPECTS

Here is where the real numbers game starts. Here is where you most likely need a certain number of prospects.

A prospect that has been vetted has the trademarks of an opportunity moved down the pipeline … closer to a deal that can be won!

A vetted opportunity which has turned into a "prospect" might look like this:

- You know who the "real" decision makers are in the company you are soliciting.
- You have established a working relationship with the necessary personnel at the prospects business (the higher up you can go will increase the likelihood of a favorable close).
- Your company has the right tools, services, and expertise to handle the client's needs.
- You are receiving all the necessary information to provide a responsible proposal.
- You can offer competitive pricing.

- Do not entertain RFPs that come in where you are just one of the participants and have not developed the necessary relationships with the prospect to leverage your opportunity.

Having passed that acid test ... now an "opportunity" is moved up in status to a "prospect".

In the numbers game ... I think you need a certain number of serious prospects in the pipeline to close a certain number of deals to eventually meet your strategy and your ultimate sales and growth goals.

Many factors will determine what this magic number is. The nature of your sale, the exclusivity of what you have to offer, the rareness of what you can do for the client, and your competitive pricing.

In the air freight and logistics business, for the average salesperson ... this might mean anywhere from a low of ten to as much as thirty companies who have been vetted and can be considered a serious prospect.

This number in the pipeline over the course of time and experience ... will equate to a track record of closed deals.

Management needs to know what these ratios are and hold their personnel accountable to achieve certain results.

Many companies would be very happy with closing ratios of 10%. Others have been successful in moving the numbers to 50% or higher.

Eventually, a number will be determined that fits your business model. I would stress here that the more quality of the vetting process ... will enhance the opportunity for a higher percentage closing ratio.

The higher the ratio ... means more closed deals against the sales strategy ... which is a wonderful occurrence.

Moving prospects into more closed deals also is an art all by itself outlined below.

Closing More Deals

Every salesperson and those in senior management would like to see more deals closed. What a great place to line in with a "Nirvana" of all our solicitations being successful. I think the last time we saw that was when Viagra first came out ... and was the only erectile dysfunction solution in tablet form!

Being a Pfizer salesperson, back then ... was probably a pretty good gig!

But reality smacks us in the face, and we all live with a ratio that falls in less than we would like.

But we can take steps to increase our odds of closing more deals and here are some thoughts to make that happen.

Price

Steer away from opportunities that are only driven by price. If they come to you for $.50 less a kilo today ... tomorrow they will leave you for $.50 less when the next salesperson comes along and offers a better price.

Offering a competitive price is a very different approach than offering the lowest price.

Don't allow your service to be a "commodity". If you do, you will become a market-driven product, and unless you can always produce the best price ... you will always be struggling to maintain your accounts and obtain new ones.

In the vetting price discuss with the opportunity how they go about making their purchasing decisions. Stay away from those that tell you price is the only or highly important factor in their decision-making process.

And you must be able to sell a price where your company's margin requirements are minimally met and hopefully surpassed. This will make you a great salesperson versus one that is mediocre.

NO one wants to lose an opportunity. But it is ok to walk away from opportunities that will not allow your company to earn a responsible living.

Learning when to move onto the next and the next better opportunity is part of the maturing process of quality sales personnel.

Customer Service

We all talk a good story and say we offer great service ... but do we really? And how do we know?

Many unhappy clients never complain first ... they just move on quietly one day.

Thoughts on a great customer service program in the logistics and air freight community of service providers:

- We need to continually assess how we are doing. Client surveys and outreach are good ways along with QBR (Quarterly Business Review) meetings where this subject gets discussed directly and openly.
- Are our customer service representatives out seeing our larger and more important clients?

"Face to face" with operations personnel is a great way to "bond and further develop" client relationships.

- Can our customer service team offer the scope of services, skill sets, and capabilities to satisfy the client's needs?
- Are our customer service representatives being trained with contemporary tools, skill sets, and education to ensure their performance?
- Are we adding value to the client relationship that differentiates us from the competition?
- Do we have the technology in place in our relationship with our clients that is contemporary and offers real value?

Specific Sales Strategy

- Does the salesperson have the necessary relationships with the prospect and are they senior enough to approach this size client or complexity of the deal?
- Are you offering a "compelling" story to the prospect? Did you qualify upfront what you needed to do to get the business and are you now there?

  Can you offer enough intelligence, serious rationale, and business process improvements to overcome the cost of air freight versus other modes of transit?
- How is your ability to negotiate overall? When is the last time you received training in negotiation skill sets?

  Have you mined and dug for information valuable about your prospect that will help close the deal?

  Are you offering leveraged points of engagement that differentiate you from the competition?

  Are you able to minimize the importance of being the "least expensive" with the balance of a higher value add and service portfolio?
- What is the quality of how you are presenting your story? Utilizing a PowerPoint … is it mind boggling or just ho hum? Who is making the presentation? Is your best foot moving forward?
- Do you have the resilience and stamina necessary to work on the prospect till it closes into a client?

Concluding Remarks

If we are serious about searching out our best options to grow our business, then we must bring organic sales into the picture to some extent.

Following the above recommendations and allowing ourselves to be challenged with all the questions being asked and thought out ... gives us the best opportunity to grow our businesses and increase margins and long-term sustainability.

The author, with contact information below, is always available to the AFA membership to answer questions and provide support and assistance.

White Paper

The National Institute for World Trade

Sales Management is a Collaborative Process

Successful sales management in an organization will generally require a "team effort" within any well-structured company.

That team's effort requires a collaborative process linking together all the necessary components both directly and indirectly involved in the "sale".

The diagram above depicts the centralized function of sales and the many interfaces it has internally within most organizations.

For the salesperson to successfully close the deal, they will require close collaboration with all these above-pictured silos in the organization.

Sales management handling several sales personnel is like the Team Manager coordinating this interface for the purpose of the following:

- Marketing creating opportunities
- Offer competitive structured and priced offerings

- Comprehensive customer service
- Competitive payment terms put forth by finance
- Internal legal support to move contracts forward easily and balanced in protecting both the company and clients' interests
- Warehousing, distribution, and shipping making deliveries happen when they need to
- R&D … making products unique, robust, and offering value add
- Senior management priding the necessary support and resources to make the sales process as effective as it can be
- Planning/thinking out future needs and anticipating correctly (most of the time)

This formula works best when all the "silos" are collaborating harmoniously, in synch and in support of one another. It is senior management's role to make sure that happens supported by the driving force of the organization … sales and sales management!!!!

In all my years as a sales management coach and being on the inside of hundreds of companies … small, big, and huge … the ones with the most robust sales initiatives are those that have tightly managed collaborative personnel and their silos working closely and well with each other.

It does not mean that there are no difference of opinion or alternate views on how things should be done … but what it does mean is that after all the debate and banter … one face is put forward and the "back room" rhetoric is unseen to the external world.

Responsible sales management leads the charge of this collaborative behavior. One saying … you get more with "honey" than "vinegar" and that may be true … but in sales management, you get more when you create an atmosphere of collaboration between your sales team and the balance of the organization.

In many organizations … sales talents are "bastard sons of the company", not well thought of and treated badly. In those companies … growth is minimized.

In organizations where sales personnel are "valued" and their place "validated" by their contributions places the company in the very best position to grow, have good margins, and create sustainability.

Sales will always "struggle" in most organizations as they can be thought of as "prima donnas" … and they may or may not be true … but is often a valid reality.

That struggle is usually well founded for many reasons:

- Some sales personnel can be arrogant and condescending internally while easing prospects and clients on a pedestal.
- It is perceived that salespeople are overpaid.
- Sales personnel don't work very hard.
- Sales personnel control their time.

For all or some of these reasons, sales personnel will struggle within an organization and that is ok, as long as the struggle is not heated, contentious, or interferes with progress.

Constructive differences can lead to better outcomes and very often sales personnel will have a very different perspective on how things should get done.

Sales personnel who may be somewhat selfish, very client focused always offering more than less, and are great at delegating the operational component to others in the organization ... will typically see things differently from other company personnel.

The saying, "until you walk in someone else's shoes" is valid. Over the years, I often have put operational personnel into temporary sales positions so they can get a sense of what it takes to be a successful salesperson ... most want back in operations 2 weeks later. They never contemplated how hard sales could be.

Additionally, I placed sales personnel in temporary operations and customer service positions so they can get a sense of what that work is like. They too want to quickly get back into sales, after that experience.

Collaborative efforts are best accomplished when personnel within an organization in various silos, with different responsibilities and varied interests ... obtain a sense of what it is like in the other areas ... will often provide better and more favored collaborative efforts with their fellow colleagues ... producing better results for the organization in whole.

Collaborative initiatives are best accomplished when the following is in place:

- Senior management being good role models in leading the charge
- Obtained when personnel get along with one another through mutual respect
- When teams are established that can work well together
- Everyone understands the "mission, expectations, and deliverables"

- Everyone understands their role on the team
- Everyone on the team has everyone's back

BEST PRACTICES IN CONTROLLING INTERNATIONAL SHIPPING IN FOREIGN SALES

Sales personnel need to make sure that the shipment part of the sale goes smoothly and without incident. The following white paper provides some very good guidance on making sure the logistics goes well.

WHITE PAPER ON INTERNATIONAL FREIGHT AND TRADE COMPLIANCE: "REDUCE RISK AND SPEND"

Author: Thomas A. Cook, Managing Director
  Blue Tiger International (www.bluetigerintl.com)

OVERVIEW

The CORPORATE membership is engaged in global trade. Importing, exporting, and distributing products and services worldwide.

The ability to move goods in the international arena will make or break a sale or even maintain a client relationship. **Risk Managers** need to participate in the risk strategies that are aligned with how the global supply chains are managed, within their organizations.

The ability to deliver products and services on a timely and loss-free basis is a critical component to the CORPORATE member.

This "white paper" created for the CORPORATE membership for their **CORPORATE Annual Conference**… addresses "Seven Steps" to follow to help reduce risk and cost in the area of international shipping, freight, and logistics.

THE SEVEN STEPS

The following seven steps originate from the author's 35- year experience in moving freight all around the world and in assisting corporations with risk management, global logistics, and programs in reducing global spend ... that are cost effective and reduce risk to themselves and their clients.

1. Choose the Best INCO Term
2. Insure the shipment
3. Choose the right freight forwarder and carrier
4. Track all shipments proactively
5. Understand the total "Landed Costs"
6. Be trade compliant!
7. Defend against cyber security risks

CHOOSE THE BEST INCO TERM

The INCO Term, established by the International Commerce Commission, is followed by all countries belonging to the United Nations for goods that pass through international borders.
There are 11 options in the 2020 edition.

Incoterms for Any Mode or Modes of Transport

- **EXW** – Ex works
- **FCA** – Free carrier
- **CPT** – Carriage paid to
- **CIP** – Carriage and insurance paid
- **DAP** – Delivered at place
- **DPU** – Delivered at place (new)
- **DDP** – Delivered duty paid

Incoterms for Sea and Inland Waterway Transport Only

- **FAS** – Free alongside ship
- **FOB** – Free on board
- **CFR** – Cost and freight
- **CIF** – Cost, insurance, and freight.

The INCO Term is a term of sale between a seller and a buyer that picks a point in time in the transaction where risk and cost are transferred from one party to the other.

It does not address other contractual concerns, such as payment method, title, and details of marine insurance.

What it really does is advise an exporter till what time and place in a transaction is it responsible for cost and risk to … and conversely where the importer picks up on.

Depending upon the INCO Term utilized … the risks and costs could be dramatically impactful for either the seller or the buyer.

We recommend that all operations, purchasing, and sales personnel in the CORPORATE membership learn at a very detailed level all they can about INCO Terms and more specifically how to best leverage the term to reduce risk and cost in their transaction.

The author is available to the membership at bringing in-house classes on INCO Terms to the CORPORATE membership and always available to assist CORPORATE members with any questions. (tomcook@bluetigerintl.com)

INSURE THE SHIPMENT

The typical importer and exporter never worry about loss or damage until it occurs.

And at that point, everyone from the forwarder to the carrier is blamed for the occurrence.

Freight will always get lost or damaged at some point in time, when you ship frequently and all over the world.

It is very important to make sure that you first identify through the purchase or sales contract who has risk of loss or damage. What INCO Term is being utilized? How payment is being made?

Once the risk is understood ... then marine cargo insurance should be acquired ... on an "All Risk" and "Warehouse to Warehouse" basis with a reputable international cargo insurance underwriting company.

Additionally, some loss control elements need to be considered to mirror the insurance policy that considers:

- That the freight is packed, marked, and labeled well
- A responsible forwarder and carrier is utilized
- Freight needs to pass through the system quickly ... delays at border pints open the door for loss and damage
- Freight needs to clear customs ... thoroughly, legally, following all import regulations, and timely ... all that will mitigate the potential for loss and damage.

CHOOSE THE RIGHT FREIGHT FORWARDER AND CARRIER

As an extension of your shipping personnel, the forwarder and carrier take responsibility to move your freight through the global system.

They need to do this:

- Timely
- Safely
- Cost effectively

Choosing the right company that is qualified experts in pet products' distribution becomes some very important criteria to make sure the shipment, the freight, and the logistics move your package to your customer's satisfaction.

Blue Tiger International with over 35 years' experience has developed some very key relationships with an array of freight forwarders and carriers and can assist you in making sure you have all the necessary information to make the best choices.

Other organizations such as the NCBFAA, AFA, and TIA ... all freight trade associations can produce members who specialize in this CORPORATE industry vertical.

TRACK ALL SHIPMENTS PROACTIVELY

Making sure the shipments arrive on time and in workable condition is the guarantee of customer satisfaction, long-term relationships, less headaches, and greater margins.

This can be a service your freight forwarder or carrier provides, but it needs to be clearly identified in that vein and it must be done proactively … through every step of an international shipment.
Depending upon distances involved, countries of export and import, choices of mode and carrier … some freight can travel 12,000 miles, through four to five carrier handoffs, via several customs authorities, and in several modes of transit.

All these convolutions can create exposure to loss, damage, or delay. All three concerns we want to avoid. They lead to loss of revenue, customer dissatisfaction, and lots of stress within your organization. To mitigate this concern, you need to structure a proactive system to "track and trace" all your international shipments through all the convolutions, handoffs, and modes of transit.

Many "track and trace" systems can be electronic and advise you through web portals, emails, and other electronic means on all your shipping activity.

The benefits of proactively in lieu of a "reactionary" mind-set will pay off in spades over the course of time and client relationships.

UNDERSTAND THE TOTAL "LANDED COSTS"

Landed costs are the total of all the accumulated expenses attached to a shipment moving internationally.

Many of these costs are outlined as follows:

- International freight
- Duties, taxes, and fees
- License charges
- Handling charges
- Domestic freight
- Clearance and handling charges
- Importers Security Filing fees
- Carrier surcharges

- Demurrage
- Storage and warehousing

LANDED COST CALCULATOR

FOB Value	826.25	Freight-INR	439333.15	CIF Value	64301.10	Assessable Value	65474.98		
FOB- INR	53006.56	C&F Value	63703.88	Loading or Handling	1173.88				
Shipmt Type(AF/SL/SF)	1			Air Shipment	LCL Shipment	FCL Shipment	Basic CD	10.0%	6547.50
(Enter 1for Air/2for Sea-LCL/3for Sea-FCL at B4)		Freight Charges	471002	NA	NA				
ExWorks Chgs in FOB(y/n)	0	CC fee	9422	NA	NA	CVD	10.0%	7202.25
(enter 1 for y,0 for n at B6)		DO Charges	750	NA	NA				
Freight Method	1	Other for FF*	0.0			Spl. Duty on CVD	3.0%	216.07
(Enter 1 for Calculation ,0 for Fixed)		Documentation	1050	100	100				
		Seal/Strapping	600	NA	NA	Spl Duty on CD, CVD & SPL. CVD	3.0%	418.97
No. Of Line Items	6	Examination	600	600	600				
Invoice Value	332.10	Demd Debit		150	150	S. ADD. DUTY	4.0%	3194.4
Currency	EUR	Load/Unl'g	600	NA	NA				
Exchange Rate	64.25	Transport*				Total Duty		17679.18	
Gross Weight in Kg	3841.50	Handling Chgs	1000	0	0				ACTUAL duty 351730
Freight Rate - F Cur	1.78	DO Collection	100	100	100	Landed Cost	All costs included	547318.53	
International Freight	6837.87	Duty P.O.		100	100				
Ex works Charges	494.15	Agency	1600	2600	3500				
Other Chgs on Way/Oil	0.00			NA	NA	Factor	on Invoice Value	25.0%	
Total Freight(cal)- F.C.	7332.02	Other*	840						
Total Freight(fixed)-F.C.	300.00	* These charges are to be put at actual , if there.							
Insurance	1.125			Clearing Charges	Freight Forwarder Chg	Local Freight			
Port Chgo loading%age	1.00			6290.00	481254	1650.00			
SVB Loading%age	1.00								
				GR/THC	19208				

DON'T ADD NEW LINE IN BETWEEN ROWS THE CELLS ARE CONTROLLED BY FORMULA'S

Foot Notes :

1) Enter the Shipment type - enter 1 for Air / 2 for Sea - LCL / 3 for Sea - FCL
When you enter the value in shipment type the values in the right side will get prominent with light green.
2) If you know the fount rate exclude charges highlighted in the right side you can enter in.

Sometimes the landed costs can exceed the value of the actual shipment.

In order to protect margins and profits … it is critical to make sure "transactional" that you completely understand what the "landed costs" are for your shipment … then you can make sure these costs are covered in the eventual client invoicing that will follow.

Remember no one likes surprises … particularly those that have an additional price tag attached to them.

BE TRADE COMPLIANT!

It is imperative that both importers and exporters operate their global supply chains trade compliantly.

This is following procedures and operational practice that accomplishes:

- Due diligence
- Reasonable care

- Supervision and control
- Engagement

This includes ...

- Understanding the regulations
- Building internal SOPs to comply with the regulations
- Train personnel on how to interpret and practice the SOPs and in a regulatory manner
- Engaged in government programs that provide evidence of managing secure and compliant global supply chains, such as CTPAT (Customs Trade Partnership against Terrorism)

CTPAT is a voluntary program of security created for importers into the United States managed by CBP (Customs Border and Protection) ... now open to include exporters from the United States.

Areas also included in trade compliance have to do with ... documentation, classification (Harmonized Tariff System of the United States/Schedule B numbers), valuation, record keeping, export license requirements, denied party listing ... to name a few of the operational concerns.

The penalties for non-compliance are fines, penalties, and potential loss of import or export privileges. More serious areas can include criminal prosecutions.

DEFEND AGAINST CYBER SECURITY RISKS

Cyber security refers to preventative methods used to protect information from being stolen, compromised, or attacked. It requires an understanding of potential information threats, such as viruses and other malicious code. Cyber security strategies include identity management, risk management, and incident management.

As corporations expand globally, develop international supply chains, and grow eCommerce sales ... the threats of cyber security are increased dramatically.

Many of the largest organizations in the world have had their firewalls breached which has created huge financial losses, reputation concerns, loss of business, and disrupted global supply chains.

The U.S. Government has proclaimed that cyber risks may be our greatest threat to our sovereignty along with commercial and personal exposures.

Corporations are mostly strengthening their Cyber Risk Defensive Postures which include:

- Threat assessments
- Personnel, resources, and structured programs focused on cyber risks
- Funding allocation to mitigate financial exposures
- Risk management programs in transferring the risks to third parties
- Developing loss control programs in managing cyber threats

SUMMARY

Importing and exporting successfully means paying attention to detail. These seven areas outlined above are a good foundation for creating a detailed and comprehensive approach to managing global supply chain responsibilities.

Our 35 years' plus of global supply chain experience has demonstrated that those companies that are diligent about how they manage the risks of: freight, logistics, and distribution of parts and equipment will create the best opportunity to:

- Protect margins and grow profits
- Increase customer satisfaction
- Decrease stress and problem areas in global markets
- Better the reputation, which converts to client retention and expansion
- Developing risk management strategies in mitigating global risks

THE AUTHOR

Thomas A. Cook

He is a 30-year seasoned veteran of global trade and Managing Director of Blue Tiger International, based in New York, LA, and West Palm Beach, Florida.

He is the author of 19 books on international business, two best business sellers. Graduate of NYS Maritime Academy with an undergraduate and graduate degree in marine transportation and business management.

Tom has a worldwide presence through over 300 agents in every major city along with an array of transportation providers and solutions.

Tom works with a number of associations, such as CORPORATE in providing "value add" to their membership services and enhancing their overall reach into risk management, supply chain operations, global sourcing, and in export sales management.

He can be reached at tomcook@bluetigerintl.com or 516-359-6232.

It's very easy to be different but very difficult to be better.

Jonathan Ive, Chief Design Officer, Apple

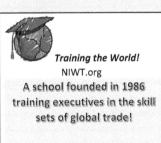

Training the World!
NIWT.org
A school founded in 1986 training executives in the skill sets of global trade!

Credits

Kelly Raia
International Chamber of Commerce
American Management Association
Air Forwarders Association
American Pet Products Association
Google
Department of Commerce
Apex Global Logistics
Sparx Logistics

Glossary of International Trade Terms for Global Sales and Business Development

TRADE TERMS GLOSSARY

Ad Valorem Tariff: A tariff calculated "according to value", or as a percentage of the value of goods cleared through customs; for example, 15% ad valorem means 15% of the value of the entered merchandise.

Air Waybill: A bill of lading covers both domestic and international flights transporting goods to a specified destination. It is a non-negotiable instrument of air transport that serves as a receipt for the shipper, indicating that the carrier has accepted the goods listed therein, and obligates the carrier to deliver the consignment to the destination airport as specified.

Anti-diversion Clause: This is a statement within the shipping documents to help ensure that U.S. exports go only to legally authorized destinations. The U.S. government generally requires a Destination Control Statement (DCS) on shipping documents. The DCS must be entered for items subject to the Export Administration Regulations (EAR) (items with potential military uses).

Antidumping Duty: A special duty imposed to offset the price effect of dumping that has been determined to be materially harmful to domestic producers. (See also dumping.)

APHIS Certificates: Before shipment, all agricultural products must be inspected by the US Department of Agriculture's "Animal and Plant Inspection Service", also known by the acronym APHIS. Fresh food, plants, and plant products (like lumber) must be checked for bug or bacterial infestation. And, if deemed safe, they are issued a "phytosanitary certificate". Without these certificates, your goods may not be allowed into the destination country.

ATA Carnet: (see Carnet)

Bill of Lading: A contract between the owner of the goods and the shipping carrier. For vessels, there are two types: a straight bill of lading, which is not negotiable, and a negotiable, and shipper's orders bill of lading. The latter can be bought, sold, or traded while the goods are in transit.

Bonded Goods: These are products stored in a secure warehouse. While there, the owners are not required to pay import duties, until the goods are sold. They may also be re-exported without paying duties.

Brokerage: Often refers to Customs House Broker, a third-party company that arranges for the customs clearance of inbound shipments.

Carnet: This is a standardized international customs document (also known as an Admission Temporary Admission (ATA) Carnet) that allows duty-free temporary admission of certain goods into the countries that are signatories to the ATA Convention. This allows commercial and professional travelers to take commercial samples, tools of the trade, advertising material, audiovisual, or other professional equipment into member countries temporarily, without paying customs duties and taxes. This is often done for goods displayed at international trade shows.

Cash in Advance (advance payment): This means the foreign customer must pay in advance for the exporter's products. It is the least risky form of payment for exporters. However, it is not a customer-friendly payment term and is most commonly used for new customers or for shipment to high risk destinations. (Note: credit card payments are not considered as cash-in-advance, since the charges can later be reversed by to overseas customer.)

Central America and Dominican Republic Free Trade Agreement (CAFTA-DR): A free trade agreement involving the U.S. DR and several Central American countries. Benefits include duty-free or reduced-duty access, better overall market access, treatment equal to local companies, and intellectual property protection.

Certificate of Conformity: A signed statement from the manufacturer attesting that a product meets certain technical standards. This is used by some countries to exclude poor quality or unsafe products.

Certificate of Free Sale: A signed statement from the producer or exporter attesting that a product has been commercially sold within the country of origin. It is considered a warrantee that the product is not an inferior export-only version.

Certificate of Origin: These are documents certifying that the goods originate in a specific country. Certificates of origin are usually validated by a semiofficial organization, such as a local chamber of commerce. Often, certificates of origin are required to receive preferential import terms under free trade agreements.

CFR (Cost and Freight): This Incoterm specifies that the seller contracts and pays the costs and freight to a named destination. CFR is only used for sea and inland waterway transportation. The buyer undertakes the risk of loss or damage once the goods are delivered to a carrier.

CIF (Costs, Insurance, and Freight): This Incoterm means that the sales price includes all costs, insurance, and freight for shipping the goods to a given point of import. CIF quotations do not include exporter payment of customs duties or taxes in the destination country.

CIP (Carriage and Insurance Paid To): Under this Incoterm, the seller must pay for shipment to the destination port, and procure cargo insurance to cover the buyer's risks of loss or damage to the goods during shipment. The seller contracts for insurance and pays the insurance premium. CIP is used for any mode of transportation.

Commercial Invoice: A commercial invoice is a bill from the seller to the buyer. Commercial invoices are often used by governments to determine the value of goods when assessing customs duties. They should provide basic information about the transaction, including a precise description of the goods, the address of the shipper and seller, and the delivery and payment terms.

Confirming House: A company based in the destination country that acts as the importer's agent, and which places "confirmed" orders with U.S. exporters. The confirming house also guarantees payment to the U.S. exporters.

Consignment: This implies delivery of merchandise to an overseas buyer or distributor, who agrees to sell it and only then pay the U.S. exporter. The seller (technically) retains ownership of the goods until they are sold, but also carries all of the financial burden and risk. This arrangement is only used when the U.S. exporter knows the customer and is confident of getting paid.

Consular Invoice: A shipping document that describes the goods being shipped, the quantity, consignor, consignee, and cost. It must be certified by a consular official of the foreign country who is stationed in the United States. It is used by that country's customs officials to verify the value and nature of the shipment.

Consumer Goods: Goods that directly satisfy human desires (as opposed to capital goods). An automobile used for pleasure is considered a consumer good. An automobile used by a business person to deliver wares is considered a capital good.

Countertrade: General expression meaning the sale or barter of goods on a reciprocal basis. There may also be multilateral transactions involved.

Countervailable Subsidy: Some foreign governments subsidize industries with financial assistance to benefit the production, manufacture, or exportation of goods. Subsidies can take many forms, such as direct cash payments, credits against taxes, and loans. When an unfair subsidy has been given, the value of these foreign subsidies may be "countervailed", through higher import duties.

Countervailing Duties (CVD): Specific duties imposed on imports to off-set the value of subsidies given to producers or exporters in the exporting country.

CPT (Carriage Paid To): This Incoterm means only shipping is paid to a named destination. This term may be used for all modes of transportation including intermodal. It does not include payment for insurance or tariffs.

Customs-Bonded Warehouse: Building or other secured areas in which dutiable goods may be stored, manipulated, or used in manufacturing operations without payment of duty. However, duties must be paid if the goods are sold into a destination country. This can be the country where the warehouse is located, or elsewhere.

Customs Declaration: A form prescribed or accepted by customs in the destination country which gives information they require on the shipment.

Customs Invoice: A document used to clear goods through customs entry that provides evidence of the value of the goods. In some cases, the commercial invoice may be used for this purpose.

D/A (Documents Against Acceptance): This is a payment method in which an exporter instructs a bank to hand over shipping and title documents to the importer only if he accepts the accompanying bill of exchange or draft by signing it.

D/C (Documentary Credit): This is a payment method (also called "letter of credit") where a bank (usually in the destination country) promises to pay for a shipment, provided that the exporter submits the required documents (such as a clean bill of lading, certificate of insurance, certificate of origin) within a specified time period. A letter of credit issued by a foreign bank is sometimes confirmed by a U.S. bank (highly recommended). This confirmation means that the U.S. bank (the confirming bank) adds its promise to pay to that of the foreign bank (the issuing bank). A letter of credit should be "irrevocable", which means it cannot be changed unless both parties agree to do so.

D/P (Documents Against Payment): Under this payment method, the exporter instructs the banks (collecting bank via remitting bank) to release the title rights and other shipping documents to the importer subject to payment.

DAP (Delivered at Place): Under this Incoterm, the seller has fulfilled his obligation to deliver when the goods are ready for unloading from the arriving carrier at the named destination. The seller bears all risks involved in bringing the goods to that destination. DAP may be used for any mode of transportation.

DAT (Delivered at Terminal): Under this Incoterm, the seller fulfills his obligation to deliver once the goods are unloaded at a named destination, and cleared for export. The seller bears all risks involved in bringing the goods to and unloading them at the destination. DAP may be used for any mode of transportation.

DDP (Delivered Duty Paid): Under this Incoterm, the seller is obligated to deliver the goods to a named place in the country of importation. The seller bears all risks and costs including import duties, taxes, delivery charges, and clears for importation. DDP may be used for any mode of transportation. Because the seller is responsible for clearing the goods through overseas customs (which can be problematic), this Incoterm is generally avoided by exporters, if at all possible.

De Minimis: This is a Latin term and is a shortened version of the expression "de minimis non curat lex", meaning "the law does not care about very small matters". It is often considered more efficient to waive very small amounts of duties and taxes rather than collect them.

Destination Control Statement (DCS): A Destination Control Statement is a legal statement required by the EAR and the International Traffic in Arms Regulations (ITAR) stating that the goods you are exporting are destined to the country indicated in all the shipping documents. It is a necessary legal boundary clarifying what happens to shipments, and it essentially states that the buyer isn't going to take the goods and forward them to another country.

Dock Receipt: This is a receipt issued by an ocean carrier to acknowledge receipt of a shipment at the carrier's dock or warehouse facilities.

Documentary Letter of Credit/Documentary Draft: This is a payment method (also called simply "letter of credit") where a bank (usually in the destination country) promises to pay for a shipment, provided that the exporter submits the required documents (such as a clean bill of lading, certificate of insurance, certificate of origin) within a specified time period. A letter of credit issued by a foreign bank is sometimes confirmed by a U.S. bank (highly recommended). This confirmation means that the U.S. bank (the confirming bank) adds its promise to pay to that of the foreign bank (the issuing bank). A letter of credit should be "irrevocable", which means it cannot be changed unless both parties agree to do so.

Dumping: Dumping is a term used when a country or company exports a product at a price that is lower in the foreign importing market than the price in the exporter's domestic market. Dumping is considered an actionable trade practice when it disrupts markets and injures producers of competitive products in the importing country. Article VI of the General Agreement on Tariffs and Trade (World Trade Organization) permits the imposition of special antidumping duties on goods equal to the difference between their export price and their normal value.

EAR: Export Administration Regulations (or "EAR") are overseen by the Commerce Department's Bureau of Industry and Security. They govern products that are considered potentially "dual-use". In other words, products may have both civilian and military applications. Any civilian products with potential military applications, like off-road vehicles, may be considered as "dual-use" items by the U.S. government.

Electronic Export Information (EEI): Formerly known as a Shipper's Export Declaration, this document is used to control exports and acts as a source document for official U.S. export statistics. EEI is required for all shipments, and their value, as classified under any single Schedule B or Harmonized Code number, is more than $2,500. EEI must also be submitted for all shipments requiring an export license or destined for countries restricted by the EAR, regardless of value.

Embargo: Partial or complete prohibition of commerce and trade with a particular country.

ETA (Estimated Time of Arrival): The projected date and time a shipment scheduled to arrive at its destination.

ETD (Estimated Time of Departure): The projected date and time a shipment scheduled to depart.

EXIM Bank (Export-Import Bank of the United States): This institution is the official export credit agency of the Federal Government. Operating as a wholly owned government corporation, the bank "assists in financing and facilitating U.S. exports of goods and services". It also offers both export financing and export credit insurance.

Export Control Classification Number (ECCN): These are five-character alpha-numeric designations used on the Commerce Control List (CCL) to identify dual-use (military/civilian) items for export control purposes. An ECCN categorizes items based on the type of product, including software or technology, and its respective technical parameters.

Export Credit Insurance: Export credit insurance is a product offered by private insurance companies and by governmental organizations (like EXIM Bank) to companies wishing to protect their foreign accounts receivable from loss due to default, insolvency, or bankruptcy. It can include a component of political risk insurance, which covers such things as currency issues, political unrest, expropriation, etc.

Export License: This is a government-issued document that authorizes the export of specific items (including technology), in specific quantities, to specific destinations. It may be required for all exports to some countries, or just for specific items going to other countries.

Export Management Company (EMC): A company that performs the functions that would be typically performed in-house by the export department or the international sales department of manufacturers and suppliers. EMCs develop personalized services promoting their clients' products to international buyers and distributors. They solicit and transact business in the names of the producers they represent or in their own name for a commission, salary, or retainer plus commission. EMCs usually specialize either by product or foreign market. They are often used by companies too small to employ in-house trade experts or which only export occasionally. Because of their specialization, the best EMCs know their products and the markets they serve very well and usually have well-established networks of foreign distributors already in place. This immediate access to foreign markets is one of the principal reasons for using an EMC because establishing a productive relationship with a foreign representative can be a slow and costly process.

Export Packing List: A list that itemizes the exported material in each package and indicates the type of package, such as a box, crate, drum, or carton. An export packing list is considerably more detailed and informative than a standard domestic packing list. It also shows the individual net, tare, and gross weights and measurements for each package (in both U.S. and metric systems).

Export Processing Zone (EPZ): A site in a foreign country established to encourage and facilitate international trade. EPZs include free trade zones, special economic zones, bonded warehouses, free ports, and customs zones. EPZs have evolved from initial assembly and simple processing activities to include high-tech and science parks, finance zones, logistics centers, and even tourist resorts.

Export Quotas: These are specific restrictions or ceilings imposed by an exporting country on the value or volume of certain exports designed, for example, to protect domestic producers and consumers from temporary shortages of the goods affected or to bolster their prices in world markets. Just as an example, the United States imposes quotas on imported sugar.

Export Subsidies: Government payments or other financially quantifiable benefits provided to domestic producers or exporters contingent on the export of their goods and services.

Export Trading Company (ETC): These are companies which act as independent distributors, creating transactions by linking domestic producers and foreign buyers. As opposed to representing a given manufacturer in a foreign market, the ETC determines what U.S. products are desired in a given market and then works with U.S. producers to satisfy the demand. ETCs can perform a sourcing function, searching for U.S. suppliers to fill specific foreign requests for U.S. products.

EXW (Ex Works): This Incoterm indicates that a seller fulfills his obligation when he makes the goods available to the buyer at his own premises or at another named place of delivery. The buyer bears all costs and risks involved in taking the goods to overseas delivery. EXW is used for any mode of transportation.

FAS (Free Alongside Ship): This Incoterm indicates that the seller fulfills his obligation to deliver when the goods have been placed alongside the vessel at the named port of shipment. The buyer bears all costs and risks of goods from that moment onward. FAS is used only for sea or inland water transportation.

FCA (Free Carrier): This Incoterm means that the U.S. exporter has fulfilled his obligation when the goods are cleared for export and delivered to the carrier or another person at the seller's premises or another named place. FCA is used for any mode of transportation.

FCL (Full Container Load): A full container load means a 40-foot container filled with goods from one consignor to one consignee.

FOB (Free on Board): This Incoterm means that the seller is obligated to deliver the goods onto the ship and cleared for export, at a named port of shipment (e.g., FOB Miami). The buyer bears all costs and risks from that point forward. FOB is used for sea and inland water transportation.

Foreign Agricultural Service (FAS): FAS is the U.S. Department of Agriculture's bureau for export market development, international trade agreements and negotiations, and the collection of export statistics and market information. It also administers the USDA's export credit guarantee and food aid programs and helps increase income and food availability in developing nations.

Foreign Corrupt Practices Act (FCPA): This act makes it unlawful for U.S. citizens or companies to bribe, offer, pay, or promise to pay money or anything of value to any foreign government official for the purpose of obtaining business. It is also unlawful to make a payment to any person while knowing that all or a portion of the payment will be offered, given, or promised, directly or indirectly, to any foreign official for the purposes of assisting the company in obtaining or retaining business. "Knowing" includes the concepts of "conscious disregard" and "willful blindness". The FCPA also covers foreign persons or companies that commit acts in furtherance of such bribery in the territory of the United States. Basically, if you bribe an overseas government official, you are in violation of U.S. law and subject to serious fines or imprisonment.

Free In: This is a pricing term that indicates the charterer of a vessel is responsible for the cost of loading goods onto the vessel.

Free in and Out: This pricing term indicates that the charterer of the vessel is responsible for the cost of loading and unloading goods from the vessel.

Free Trade Agreements: These are agreements that create stable and transparent trading between countries by reducing barriers to exports. They enable easier access to foreign markets and reduce the end cost of U.S. goods.

Freight Forwarder: A freight forwarder is an agent responsible for moving cargo to an overseas destination. The forwarder is essentially a travel agent for your goods. Competent freight forwarders are familiar with the import rules and regulations of foreign countries, the export regulations of the U.S. government, the methods of shipping, and the documents related to foreign trade. Their job is to provide the best and most economical export shipping. And, while they may prepare much of the shipping paperwork, you the exporter are ultimately responsible for the documentation process.

Goods and Services Tax (GST): These are taxes levied on goods or services purchased in the destination country, whether the goods are imported or not. They impact a product's end price overseas, and thus affect both the exporter and importer.

Gross Domestic Product (GDP): The total value of all goods and services produced by a country.

GSP (Generalized System of Preference): GSP is a framework under which developed countries give preferential tariff (a reduced or zero rate) treatment to manufactured goods from certain developing countries.

Harmonization: The process of making procedures or measures applied by different countries – especially those affecting international trade – more compatible. As an example, they might involve simultaneous tariff cuts to make tariff structures more uniform.

Harmonized System: This is an international numbering system published by the World Customs Organization that classifies all products shipped internationally. The six-digit HS code is used by customs and statistical authorities, traders, and carriers. Goods are grouped in Sections, Chapters, and Sub-chapters. IATA (International Air Transport Association): An international organization of airlines that promotes commercial air traffic.

ICC (International Chamber of Commerce): ICC is a non-government organization of over 12,000 chambers and their business communities worldwide. It represents the world business community at international levels, promotes world trade and investment, and provides a range of practical services to trade. It also governs the Incoterm coding platform, which is used worldwide to determine import customs duties.

IMDG Code (International Maritime Dangerous Goods Code): This is an international guideline for the safe water transportation of dangerous goods or hazardous materials, established by the International Maritime Organization. It contains advice on emergency procedures, packing of dangerous goods, labeling handling, etc. The guideline is recommended to governments for adoption or for use as the basis for national regulations.

Importer of Record (IOR): This is the person responsible for receiving the goods and shipment documents provided to customs. They are also responsible for all import duties and taxes, unless otherwise specified.

Incoterms®: Incoterms are a set of rules that clearly define the responsibilities of sellers and buyers for the shipment and delivery of goods internationally. They are published by the International Chamber of Commerce (ICC) and are widely used in international commercial transactions. The most recent version, Incoterms 2020, was launched in Fall of 2019 and became effective January 1, 2020. The most commonly used Incoterms are listed in this glossary.

Indirect Exporting: This means the domestic sale of goods by a U.S. producer to another company which then exports the product. Oftentimes, the sale is to another manufacturer who installs the item in something they make or assemble. As an example, a U.S. tire manufacturer may sell to a vehicle manufacturer who then exports the finished car or truck.

Inspection Certificate: This document is required by some purchasers and countries to attest to the specifications of the goods shipped. The inspection is usually performed by a credible third party.

Insurance Certificate: This document is prepared by the exporter or freight forwarder to provide evidence that insurance against loss or damage has been obtained for the goods.

International Buyer Program (IBP): This is an (excellent) U.S. Department of Commerce, ITA program that brings thousands of international buyers to the United States for business-to-business matchmaking with U.S. firms exhibiting at major industry trade shows. Every year, the IBP results in approximately a billion dollars in new business for U.S. companies, and increased international attendance for participating U.S. trade show organizers.

International Trade Administration (ITA): This is a bureau within the U.S. Department of Commerce which is responsible for export promotion programs. The U.S. Commercial Service (USCS) is part of the ITA and operates U.S. Export Assistance Centers (USEACs) nationwide and commercial posts overseas in more than 75 countries. (Among other things, the USCS has supported the operation of the Export-U website.)

ITAR Regulations: International Traffic in Arms Regulations (commonly referred to as ITAR) are administered by the State Department. They govern the export of all types of military weapons and technologies.

Joint Venture: This is an independent business formed cooperatively by two or more parent companies. This type of partnership is often used to avoid restrictions on foreign ownership in some countries and for longer-term arrangements that require joint product development, manufacturing, and marketing.

Landed Cost: Landed cost is the total price of a product or shipment once it has arrived at a buyer's doorstep. It includes the price of goods, shipping costs, insurance fees, customs duties, and any other charges incurred along the way.

L/C (Letter of Credit): This is a payment method where a bank (usually in the destination country) promises to pay for a shipment, if the exporter submits the required documents (such as a clean bill of lading, certificate of insurance, certificate of origin) within a specified time period. A letter of credit issued by a foreign bank is sometimes confirmed by a U.S. bank (highly recommended). This confirmation means that the U.S. bank (the confirming bank) adds its promise to pay. A letter of credit should be "irrevocable", which means it cannot be changed unless both parties agree to do so. Letters of credit are not used for all export payments because they can be expensive. They are most often used when the buyer and seller have not done business before, or for shipments to unfamiliar or risky destinations.

LCL (Less than Container Load): LCL implies a shipment smaller than a full container, where the container is shared by more than one exporter for cost savings. Freight forwarders often arrange to have LCL shipments "consolidated" in this manner.

Licensing: An arrangement under which a company sells the rights to use its products or services but retains some control. Although not usually considered to be a form of partnership, licensing can lead to partnerships.

Market Access: The ability of U.S. providers of goods and services to penetrate a foreign market. The extent to which the foreign market is accessible generally depends on the existence and extent of trade barriers.

Market Economy: The national economy of a country that relies on market forces to determine levels of production, consumption, investment, and savings without substantial government intervention.

MT (Mail Transfer): This is a bank transfer made by mail, especially airmail, as opposed to a telegraphic or cable transfer.

Multilateral Development Bank (MDB): These are institutions created by a group of countries to provide development-related financing and professional advising. Unlike commercial banks, MDBs (such as the World Bank) do not seek to maximize profits for their shareholders, but prioritize development goals such as ending extreme poverty and reducing economic inequality. They often lend at low or no interest or provide grants to fund projects in infrastructure, energy, education, and other areas that promote development. MDBs are subject to international law.

NAFTA Certificate of Origin: This is a document used by NAFTA signatories (i.e., Canada, Mexico, and the United States) to certify that the goods being shipped were produced in North America, so they may receive reduced or eliminated duty in these countries. The same or a similar document will be required under the new United States-Mexico-Canada Agreement (USMCA), which is replacing NAFTA.

North American Free Trade Agreement (NAFTA): The former trade agreement between the United States, Canada, and Mexico featuring duty-free entry and other benefits for goods that qualify. In late 2018, NAFTA was replaced by the USMCA, which is basically an updated version of NAFTA.

OFAC Regulations: The Office of Foreign Assets Control (or "OFAC") oversees all U.S. boycotts, sanctions, and embargos. Sanctions are not always across-the-board, and they may be limited to just specific goods. For example, food and medicine can sometimes be shipped to sanctioned countries (www.treasury.gov/ofac).

Office of the U.S. Trade Representative (USTR): This is the U.S. government agency responsible for negotiating trade agreements.

Origin: This means the location where a shipment's transit begins with a pick-up scan. (The term may also be used by customs authorities to mean the country where the product was produced.)

Phytosanitary Certificate: A certificate issued by a government agency (for exports the USDA) to satisfy import regulations of foreign countries. The certificate indicates that a shipment has been inspected and found free from harmful pests and plant diseases.

Piggyback Export Marketing: An arrangement whereby one U.S. manufacturer distributes a second U.S. company's product or service overseas. The most common arrangement is where the exporting company has an overseas contract to supply a wide range of products or services (e.g., medical supplies). If this company does not produce all of the required goods, it must purchase some of them from other U.S. suppliers.

Primary Market Research: The collection of data directly from a foreign marketplace through interviews, surveys, and other direct contact with representatives and potential buyers. Primary market research is especially useful, since it can be tailored to your company's specific needs, but it can also be time consuming and expensive. For this reason, U.S. exporters contract for the work to be done by the USCS, through its overseas posts in more than 75 countries.

Pro-forma Invoice: The name of this document is misleading because a pro-forma is actually invoices, but price quotations that include the cost of the goods, plus all other costs borne by the exporter (e.g., shipping, insurance, payment terms, etc.). Because they provide so much information on the shipment, a pro-forma is often the central document from which the other shipping documents are generated.

Prohibited Commodities: These are products for which shipment is prohibited by law, regulation, or statute of any federal, state, or local government or by any country through which the shipment may be carried.

Restricted Commodities: These are commodities that rules and regulations require special approvals and documentation for shipping.

Schedule B: A 10-digit product classification code used by the U.S. Census Bureau to collect trade statistics. The first six-digits of this code are the standard international HS number, or Harmonized Code. The remainder further defines the precise commodity being shipped. There are about 8,000 Schedule-B classifications. A good way to look-up your product's code number is with the "Schedule-B Search Engine" (https://uscensus.prod.3ceonline.com/).

Secondary Market Research: The collection of data from various sources (mostly online), such as trade statistics for a country or a product. Secondary research is less expensive that primary research and is often used initially to determine which regions or countries have the most potential, and thus merit primary research.

SITC (Standard International Trade Classification): The SITC recommended by the United Nations for classifying trade statistics for economic analysis, is also used in many trade statistics reports. This is all highly theoretical until you are trying to decide which market is worth investing your money in.

Sight Draft: A form of payment used when the exporter wishes to retain title to the shipment until it reaches its destination and payment is made. Before the shipment can be released to the buyer, the original "order" ocean bill of lading (the document that evidences title) must be properly endorsed by the buyer and surrendered to the carrier.

Small Business Development Center (SBDC): A government-funded national network of business counselors for small enterprises. In many states, SBDCs offer service to help exporters.

Specially Designated Nationals: The Treasury Department maintains a list of foreign nationals and companies with whom you are prohibited from doing business (www.treasury.gov/SDN).

Subsidy: An economic benefit granted by a government to domestic producers of goods or services, often to strengthen their competitive position.

Supply: The quantity of a product that sellers will make available at a given price and time in a specific market. A supply schedule indicates the quantity of a product that might enter the market at a particular time. In a market economy, supply is principally determined by many individual firms trying to earning profits.

Surplus: The amount of a commodity that cannot be absorbed in a given market at the existing price.

Tariff: A tax imposed on a product when it is imported into a country. Tariffs may be used to raise the prices of imported products, thus making them less competitive with locally produced goods.

Technology Licensing: A contractual arrangement under which patents, trademarks, service marks, copyrights, trade secrets, or other intellectual property are sold or made available to an overseas licensee. The U.S. companies frequently license their technology to foreign companies that use it to manufacture and sell products in their country or region as defined in the licensing agreement. Technology licensing allows a company to enter a foreign market quickly and with fewer financial and legal risks than when operating a foreign production facility.

Terms of Sale: Terms that define the obligations, risks, and costs of the buyer and seller in an export transaction. These terms typically include the shipping Incoterms and the terms of payment.

TEU (Twenty-foot Equivalent Unit): This unit is based on the carrying capacity of a twenty-foot container and is used when calculating the carrying capacity of container vessels.

Time Draft: This is a document used when an exporter extends credit to the overseas buyer. It states that payment is due by a specific time after the buyer accepts the time draft and receives the goods. By signing and writing "accepted" on the draft, the buyer is formally obligated to pay within the stated time.

Trade Agreement: Also known as trade pact, this is a wide-ranging tax, tariff, and trade treaty that often includes investment guarantees. "Free Trade Agreements" are used to lower trade barriers, including import tariffs.

Trade Barriers: Government laws, regulations, policies, or practices that either protect domestic products from foreign competition or artificially stimulate exports of particular domestic products.

Trade Fair Certification Program (TFC): A U.S. Department of Commerce program that certifies international trade events so U.S. companies can know ahead of time if an event is high quality which offers business opportunities.

Trademark: A word, symbol, name, slogan, or combination of these that identifies and distinguishes the product or company. It may also serve as a sign of the product's quality.

Trading House: A company specializing in the export and import of goods produced by other companies.

TT (Telegraphic Transfer): This is a term used to refer to electronic bank transfers of funds, often internationally. It is initiated by the "debtor" who instructs the bank to debit its account and send money to the account of a person or firm. A transfer fee is often charged by the sending bank, and in some cases by the receiving bank.

UCP (Uniform Customs and Practice for Documentary Credits): These are rules of the International Chamber of Commerce (ICC) that govern a letter of credit issued to pay for imports and exports.

UNCITRAL (United Nations Commission on International Trade and Law): UNCITRAL was set up by the UN to help harmonize and international trade laws. The commission focuses on four principal international areas: sale of goods, payments, commercial arbitration, and legislation pertaining to shipping.

U.S. Agency for International Development (USAID): A U.S. government agency that procures goods and services from U.S. companies for use in assistance to developing countries (https://www.usaid.gov/).

U.S. Central Intelligence Agency (CIA): A U.S. government agency charged with gathering intelligence and statistics. The CIA publishes the World Factbook online, an excellent market research resource for U.S. exporters (https://www.cia.gov/library/publications/the-world-factbook/).

U.S. Commercial Service (USCS): The trade promotion arm of the U.S. Department of Commerce's International Trade Administration. The USCS operates U.S. Export Assistance Centers nationwide and has overseas offices to help American exporters in more than 75 countries (https://www.export.gov).

U.S. Department of Agriculture (USDA): The U.S. government department responsible for developing and executing federal government policy on farming, agriculture, forestry, and food. The Foreign Agricultural Service, within in USDA, is responsible for promoting U.S. food exports (https://www.fas.usda.gov/).

U.S. Department of Commerce (DOC): This U.S. government department is responsible for promoting domestic economic growth and handling other commerce-related responsibilities (https://www.commerce.gov/).

USMCA (United States-Mexico-Canada Agreement): This trade agreement, signed in late 2018, is a replacement for the NAFTA agreement. While similar in many ways to NAFTA, the new agreement is designed to increase the North American components used in cars assembled here. It also reduces the Canadian tariffs on U.S. dairy products. The USMCA also makes a number of significant upgrades to environmental and labor regulations, especially regarding Mexico.

U.S. Small Business Administration (SBA): The U.S. government agency that manages programs for U.S. exporters, including export finance loan programs. To learn more, view our free webinar on SBA export financing (https://www.sba.gov/).

U.S. Trade and Development Agency (USTDA): The U.S. government agency that provides grants for engineering and construction feasibility studies in developing countries using products and services sourced from the United States (https://ustda.gov/).

Abbreviations

AV	Adjusted Value
B2B	Business-to-Business
B2C	Business-to-Consumer
BIS	Bureau of Industry and Security
CAFTA-DR	Central America and Dominican Republic Free Trade Agreement
CDC	Centers for Disease Control and Prevention
CIA	Central Intelligence Agency
CIF	Cost, Insurance, and Freight (Incoterm)
CIP	Carriage and Insurance Paid To (Incoterm)
COO	Certificate of Origin or Chief Operating Officer (depending on context)
CPT	Carriage Paid To (Incoterm)
CS	U.S. Commercial Service (or USCS)
CTO	Chief Technology Officer
DOC	U.S. Department of Commerce

DOE	U.S. Department of Energy
DOS	U.S. Department of State
EMC	Export Management Company
ETC	Export Trading Company
ExIm Bank	Export-Import Bank of the United States (or EXIM)
EXW	Ex Works (Incoterm)
FAS	Foreign Agricultural Service, or Free Alongside Ship (Incoterm), (depending on context)
FCA	Free Carrier (Incoterm)
FOB	Free on Board (Incoterm)
FTA	Free Trade Agreement
FTZ	Free Trade Zone
GDP	Gross Domestic Product
IBP	International Buyer Program
ITA	International Trade Administration
LLC	Limited Liability Corporation
LLP	Limited Liability Partnership
MDB	Multilateral Development Bank
NAFTA	North American Free Trade Agreement
NC	Net Cost
ROI	Return on Investment
ROO	Rule(s) of Origin
RVC	Regional Value Content
SBA	U.S. Small Business Administration
SBDC	Small Business Development Center
TANC	Trade Agreements Negotiations and Compliance
TFC	Trade Fair Certification Program
TV	Transaction Value
USAID	U.S. Agency for International Development
USDA	U.S. Department of Agriculture
USPS	U.S. Postal Service
USTDA	U.S. Trade and Development Agency
USTR	Office of the U.S. Trade Representative
VNM	Value of Non-originating Materials
VOM	Value of Originating Materials
WTO	World Trade Organization

Appendix

INCOTERMS OUTLINE

Incoterms are one of the most important skill sets and areas of skill set training for all personnel engaged in foreign sales and business development.

It sets the foundation for sales transactions and relates directly to the risks and costs involved in global trade.

The International Chamber of Commerce (ICC) in Parvis is the lead organization responsible for Incoterms. Below direct from the ICC and other sources is an outline for international sales personnel to study and learn from.

The Incoterms® rules are a globally recognized set of standards, used worldwide in international and domestic contracts for the delivery of goods.

The rules have been developed and maintained by **experts and practitioners** brought together by ICC. They have become the standard in international business rules setting. The trade terms help traders avoid costly misunderstandings by clarifying the tasks, costs, and risks involved in the delivery of goods from sellers to buyers. The **Incoterms® rules** are recognized by UNCITRAL as the global standard for the interpretation of the most common terms in foreign trade.

Launched in September 2019, **Incoterms® 2020** will come into effect on January 1, 2020. Please note that all contracts made under **Incoterms® 2000** and any other previous editions remain valid and parties to a contract for the sale of goods can agree to choose any version of the Incoterms® rules. However, we recommend using the most current version of the rules, **Incoterms® 2020**. Nevertheless, it is important to clearly specify the chosen version.

Your Partner for International Logistics

SCARBROUGH

888-744-7749 | pricing@scarbrough-intl.com

INCOTERMS ® 2010 RULES
Chart of Responsibility

Charges/ Fees	Any Transport Mode		Sea/Inland Waterway Transport				Any Transport Mode				
	EXW	FCA	FAS	FOB	CFR	CIF	CPT	CIP	DAT	DAP	DDP
	Ex Works	*Free Carrier*	*Free Alongside Ship*	*Free on Board*	*Cost & Freight*	*Cost Insurance Freight*	*Carriage Paid To*	*Carriage Insurance Paid To*	*Delivered at Terminal*	*Delivered at Place*	*Delivered Duty Paid*
Packaging	Buyer or Seller	Seller	Seller	Seller	Seller	Seller	Seller	Seller	Seller	Seller	Seller
Loading Charges	Buyer	Seller*	Seller	Seller	Seller	Seller	Seller	Seller	Seller	Seller	Seller
Delivery to Port/Place	Buyer	Seller	Seller	Seller	Seller	Seller	Seller	Seller	Seller	Seller	Seller
Export Duty & Taxes	Buyer	Seller	Seller	Seller	Seller	Seller	Seller	Seller	Seller	Seller	Seller
Origin Terminal Charges	Buyer	Buyer	Seller	Seller	Seller	Seller	Seller	Seller	Seller	Seller	Seller
Loading on Carriage	Buyer	Buyer	Buyer	Seller	Seller	Seller	Seller	Seller	Seller	Seller	Seller
Carriage Charges	Buyer	Buyer	Buyer	Buyer	Seller	Seller	Seller	Seller	Seller	Seller	Seller
Insurance	**	**	**	**	**	Seller	**	Seller	**	**	**
Destination Terminal Charges	Buyer	Buyer	Buyer	Buyer	Buyer	Buyer	Seller	Seller	Seller	Seller	Seller
Delivery to Destination	Buyer	Buyer	Buyer	Buyer	Buyer	Buyer	Buyer	Buyer	Buyer	Seller	Seller
Import Duty & Taxes	Buyer	Buyer	Buyer	Buyer	Buyer	Buyer	Buyer	Buyer	Buyer	Buyer	Seller

*Seller is responsible for loading charges, if the terms state FCA at seller's facility.   **Negotiable between buyer and seller

***THIS IS FOR INFORMATIONAL PURPOSES ONLY. SCARBROUGH INTERNATIONAL, LTD. IS NOT RESPONSIBLE FOR THESE CONTENTS, REFER TO FULL VERSION OF INCOTERMS ® 2010 FOR FULL DESCRIPTION.

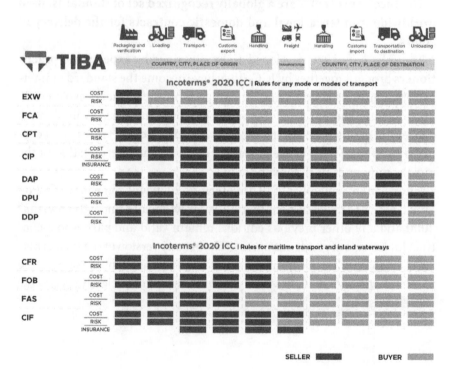

On January 1, 2020, Incoterms® 2020 ushered in a new era for the world's most essential terms for trade. The ICC explains some of the main changes.

Which Incoterms Rule Should I Use?

The **latest edition of the Incoterms® rules** features an in-depth introduction to help users select the appropriate Incoterms® rule for their sale transaction. The introduction explains the purpose and use of the Incoterms® rules, identifies differences between **Incoterms® 2010** and **Incoterms® 2020**, and outlines best practice for incorporating the Incoterms® rules into contracts and explores the relation of contracts ancillary to the sale contract, the concepts of risk and delivery, the role of the carrier, and the care to be taken when using variants of the Incoterms® 2020 rules.

Incoterms® 2020 also incorporates expanded explanatory notes for users at the start of each Incoterms® rule. These explanatory notes assist users with accurately interpreting the latest edition of the Incoterms rules to avoid costly misinterpretations or misapplications.

Why Has the FCA Incoterms Rule Been Revised?

Free Carrier (FCA) has been revised for **Incoterms® 2020** to cater to a situation where goods are sold, FCA for carriage by sea, and buyer or seller (or either party's bank) requests a bill of lading with an on-board notation. FCA in article A6/B6 now provides for the parties to agree that the buyer will instruct the carrier to issue an on-board bill of lading to the seller once the goods have been loaded on board, and for the seller, then to tender the document to the buyer (often through the banks).

Where Are the Costs Listed in Incoterms® 2020?

Within **Incoterms® 2020**, all costs associated with a given Incoterms rule now appear at article A9/B9 of that rule, allowing users to see the full list of expected costs at a glance. In addition to the aggregated presentation, the costs associated with each item – for example, carriage (article A4/B4) or export clearance (article A7/B7) – still appear in the respective articles to accommodate a user who wants to focus on a specific aspect of the sale transaction.

What Are the Different Levels of Insurance Coverage in CIF and CIP?

The Incoterms® 2020 rules provide for different levels of insurance coverage in the Cost Insurance and Freight (CIF) rule and Carriage and Insurance Paid To (CIP) rule.

Under the CIF Incoterms® rule, which is reserved for use in maritime trade and is often used in commodity trading, the Institute Cargo Clauses (C) remains the default level of coverage, giving parties the option to agree to a higher level of insurance cover. Taking into account feedback from global users, the CIP Incoterms® rule now requires a higher level of cover, compliant with the Institute Cargo Clauses (A) or similar clauses.

How Does Incoterms® 2020 Account for Arranging Carriage?

Incoterms® 2020 recognizes that not all commercial trade transactions from the seller to the buyer are conducted by a third-party carrier. In some cases, transactions are conducted without a third-party carrier at all, such as a seller using its own means of transportation, or a buyer using its own vehicle to collect goods.

Where is Information on Security-Related Requirements?

Building on the extensive security-related requirements established by **Incoterms® 2010**, the latest edition of the Incoterms® rules includes clearer and more detailed security-related obligations in articles A4 on carriage and A7 on export/import clearance of each Incoterms® rule. Costs relating to these requirements also appear in the consolidated costs article A9/B9.

Is the Incoterms Rule DPU New?

No, simply renamed and moved to more accurately reflect the content of the rule. The former Delivered at Terminal (DAT) has been changed to Delivered at Place Unloaded (DPU) to emphasize that the place of destination can be any place and not just a "terminal", and to underscore the sole difference from DPU – under DAP the seller does not unload the goods, under DPU, seller does unload the goods.

And since delivery under DAP happens before unloading, **Incoterms® 2020** presents the newly named DPU after DAP.

Beware of Untrustworthy Sources

There is a significant amount of **misleading information** concerning the Incoterms rules on the Internet and users should be aware of the existence of incomplete, inaccurate, and unofficial information. From referencing non-existing rules – such as Incoterms 2015, Incoterms 2016, or Incoterms 2017 – to selling deceptive training sessions, **these websites can result in unintended costs** for both buyers and sellers.

Unless sourced directly from ICC or ICC regional offices (known as ICC national committees), these **Incoterms® 2020** materials should not be trusted, as they may result in contractual mistakes and ensuing disputes.

Discover **Incoterms® 2020** and related products from ICC's **Knowledge 2 Go** eCommerce platform.

FREE TRADE AGREEMENTS

The United States has 14 FTAs currently in force with 20 countries.
Last Published: *3/22/2018*

With Which Countries Do the United States Have an FTA?

The United States has 14 FTAs in force with 20 countries: Australia, Bahrain, Chile, Colombia; DR-CAFTA: Costa Rica, Dominican Republic, El Salvador, Guatemala, Honduras, and Nicaragua, Israel, Jordan, Korea, Morocco; NAFTA: Canada, Mexico, Oman, Panama, Peru, and Singapore.

How Can U.S. Companies Identify Tariffs on Exports to FTA Partner Countries?

The **FTA Tariff Tool** can help you determine the tariff, or tax at the border, that U.S. FTA partners will collect when a U.S. exported product that meets the FTA rule of origin enters the country. You can look up the tariff rate for a given product today, as well as identify when in the future the tariff rate will go down further or be eliminated altogether.

Learn more about FTAs tips and how to get help by watching a video **Make the Export Sale: U.S, Free Trade Agreements**.

Prepared by the International Trade Administration. With its network of 108 offices across the United States and in more than 75 countries, the International Trade Administration of the U.S. Department of Commerce utilizes its global presence and international marketing expertise to help U.S. companies sell their products and services worldwide. Locate the trade specialist in the U.S. nearest you by visiting http://export.gov/usoffices.

CUSTOMIZED SALES TRAINING OVERVIEW

Overview

Management creates customized training programs in sales and sales management that recognizes the following:

- Quality sales personnel can make a company more successful, grow the business model, and impact profit and margin enhancement.
- Each salesperson and business model is unique and generic training only goes so far. Customized personalized training is a much more effective spend for a company as an investment in its sales personnel.
- Customized training takes very specific input from sales management, colleagues, and the sale person themselves in developing the content and delivery process to assure effective training results.

Deliverables

- Management meets with senior management to clearly define expectations and deliverables of the customized training programs.
- We develop specific training program to impact behavior and results in the sales process in those areas raising concern and we enhance those areas of accomplishment where we help raise the bar of performance.
- Sales is accomplishing five major areas of success:

  - Creating opportunities
  - Delivering proposals
  - Closing deals
  - Growing margins and profits

- Maintaining key clients.
- Impact behavior

We develop a customized program to:

- Develop skill sets: **relationship building, conflict management, problem resolution, best practices in customer service, negotiation techniques, communication and presentation skills, team participation, creating value add, and higher margins.**
- Continue the customized training for another six months on a weekly basis of follow-up with the student to make sure they are on track on making the training program successful.

Having a qualified and experienced trainer is key to a successful sales management development program.

Trainer:

Sales Management Trainer Thomas Cook

Tom is Managing Director of Management International, (bluetigerintl.com), a premier international business consulting company on business management, sales and sales management, marketing, supply chain, and international operations.

Tom was former CEO of American River International in NY and Apex Global Logistics Supply Chain Operation in LA.

He has over 30 years of experience in assisting companies all over the world in managing their business development in sales, marketing, and global operations.

He is a member and advisor to the AMA, American Management Association in NYC, sits on the board of numerous corporations, and is considered a leader in the business verticals he works in.

He has now authored over 19 books on business, one on sales management outlined below:

Tom is also the Director of the National Institute of World Trade (niwt.org) a 30-year-old educational and training organization, based here on Long Island.

Tom can be reached at tomcook@bluetigerintl.com or 516-359-6232

EXPORT SALES ARE RECOGNIZED BY POTUS ... THE PRESIDENT OF THE UNITED STATES

Exports are a chosen method for increasing business development and opening overseas markets. It is critical to the sustainability of any country to sell abroad.

The United States recognized companies that export successfully and contribute to overall foreign business development ... as outlined below excerpts from the Department of Commerce (DOC.gov).

"E" Award for Exports

- Air Innovations, Inc. – North Syracuse, New York
- Aleph Group, Inc. – Riverside, California
- CTSi – Lexington Park, Maryland
- Earth Networks – Germantown, Maryland
- Eco Global Sales Group – Sunrise, Florida
- Equilibar, LLC – Fletcher, North Carolina
- Garner Products, Inc. – Roseville, California
- Geophysical Survey Systems, Inc. – Nashua, New Hampshire
- Golden Malted – South Bend, Indiana
- MAC Aerospace Corporation – Chantilly, Virginia
- Mack Defense, LLC – Allentown, Pennsylvania
- Maine Coast – York, Maine
- Master Electronics – Phoenix, Arizona
- Maxtec – Salt Lake City, Utah
- MN8 LumAware/Foxfire – Cincinnati, Ohio
- Owl Cyber Defense Solutions, LLC – Danbury, Connecticut
- PDC Machines, Inc. – Warminster, Pennsylvania
- R & M International Sales Corporation – Fort Washington, Pennsylvania
- Safe Foods Corporation – North Little Rock, Arkansas
- SIFCO Applied Surface Concepts, LLC – Independence, Ohio
- SightLine Applications, Inc. – Hood River, Oregon
- Sigma Recycling, Inc. – Norcross, Georgia
- Smitty's Supply, Inc. – Roseland, Louisiana
- Warren Rupp, Inc. – Mansfield, Ohio
- Wenger Manufacturing, Inc. – Sabetha, Kansas
- WFN Strategies, LLC – Sterling, Virginia

Thirteen companies and organizations received the "E" Award for Export Service for assisting and facilitating export activities.

"E" Award for Export Service

- Arizona Commerce Authority – Phoenix, Arizona
- B-FOR International – Fredericksburg, Virginia
- Blue Tiger International – East Moriches, New York
- Broward County Office of Economic and Small Business Development – Fort Lauderdale, Florida
- Chicago Regional Growth Corporation – Chicago, Illinois
- Economic Development Partnership of North Carolina – Cary, North Carolina
- GVSU's Van Andel Global Trade Center – Grand Rapids, Michigan
- IAPMO – Ontario, California
- Intralink – Saratoga, California
- MSU Broad College of Business International Business Center – East Lansing, Michigan
- Prince George's County Economic Development Corporation – Largo, Maryland
- Robinson+Cole – Hartford, Connecticut
- The Provident Bank – Amesbury, Massachusetts

Six companies received the "E" Star Award for Exports, which recognizes previous "E" awardees that have reported four years of additional export growth.

"E" Star Award for Exports

- Ace Pump Corporation – Memphis, Tennessee
- Bespoke Group, LLC – Irving, Texas
- GENICON – Winter Park, Florida
- Quality Electrodynamics, LLC – Mayfield Village, Ohio
- Quality Switch, Inc. – Newton Falls, Ohio
- SPF Depot – Bossier City, Louisiana

Two firms were awarded the "E" Star Award for Export Service, which recognizes previous "E" recipients that have shown four years of continued support of exporters since first winning the "E".

Advanced Sales Class
Case Studies
Thomas Cook
2019

1. You are the sales manager for a team of eight sales personnel, four seasoned, and four new. The more seasoned are independent and make their numbers every quarter. But the four new seem to be struggling.

   What steps can you take?

2. You are the sales manager of a team of ten sales personnel. They are responsible for both new and renewal business.

   Sales have gone flat over the last year and the team seems to be struggling with holding onto their business rather than developing new opportunities. As they get paid on existing as well as new ... no one is very happy.

   What can you do?

3. As sales manager of a team of 12 sales personnel ... eight on-site and four remote. You notice that the on-site group is doing better. The remote group sales are lagging. How can you assess and what actions might you take?

4. You have responsibility for five sales personnel and also a team of ten customer service representatives who support the sales team.

   Over the last year, sales goals have not been met, and there seems to be a lot of angst between sales and customer service.

   The customer service team dislikes the sales group who they think are arrogant and condescending and the sales team believes customer service are not doing enough on their behalf.

   The atmosphere is becoming toxic ... what steps can you take to create a mutual resolve?

5. The sales team you manage is doing well but there seems to be a disconnect between them and your internal operations and management staff.

   The sales team is outside of the office most of the time and place huge demands internally.

   A resentment is building between the internal staff that the sales team is not working ... they hear about them doing a lot of entertaining, golf, ball games with clients, etc., and internal personnel view them as a waste of time.

Your senior management seems to side with everyone internally and is putting pressure on you to reign the sales team in.

How do you handle?

6. You have four direct sales reports all who are doing well and meeting their goals on existing products with existing clients.

However, when marketing introduces new products, there is a struggle to have the sales team work with these new products as they are comfortable in their existing product lines.

They all work over 50 hours a week and their plates are pretty full.

What steps can you take to get them to work on the new product lines?

7. You are trying to build a larger sales team but are having a hard time attracting new sales talent. In your existing sales team of 15, you have had turnover consistently of 20%–25% a year.

You are spending a lot of time dealing with personnel issues, client problems, and internal strife.

Complaints from the sales team regarding compensation, incentives, and having to deal with numerous internal issues that get in the way of their sales initiatives.

You are losing some of your team to two competitors who do not seem to have all these issues. Your boss is not happy and starting to raise concerns about your ability to lead the sales team.

How do you assess and what actions can you consider?

8. Your team of 35 sales representatives overall is doing pretty good but you have two remote sales team members whose sales are spiking unusually high.

After questioning the two, you become concerned about their sales process. You have an aggressive commission structure on new business and you are concerned that these two sales representatives, may be sharing commission incentives with clients or possibly other areas of concern … misrepresentation, overstating, etc.

How do you assess and if any concerns are uncovered, how do you handle?

A PRESENTATION OUTLINE ON DEVELOPING EXPORT SALES FROM THE UNITED STATES TO THE WORLD

Draft Presentation
For
Export Sales and Business Development Executives
Creating Robust Sales into Foreign Markets

Focus
Opening New Markets, Creating Robust Export Opportunities, Leveraging Export Options and/or Exporting Better!!!
Presenters Bio
Thomas A. Cook (tomcook@bluetigerintl.com), a 35-year seasoned veteran of global trade and international business development. He is the author of over 19 books on business, importing and exporting, global trade and working international opportunities.

Key Topics Discussed

- Defining the Export Opportunity
- Demand for American Made Products
- Market Opportunities Overseas
- Challenges in Selling in Foreign Markets
- Defeating the Challenges and Making for a Successful Export Strategy
- Leveraging the Global Supply Chain
- Risk Management
- Export Resources
- Resources for Exporting
- eCommerce

- Viable Exports
- Best Practices in Developing Foreign Sales Opportunities
- Summary, Questions, and Answers

Defining the Export Market:
- 95% of the consumer market
- 85% of the commercial market
- Includes North America ... Mexico and Canada (NAFTA)
- Currently U.S. exports over 1.6 trillion in total values
- To over 100 countries dominated in Europe, Latin America, Asia ... With growth in Africa and the Middle East

The "Demand" for U.S. Products
- Prestige
- Diversity
- Accessibility
- Quality
- Reliability

U.S. Demand Additionally
- Foreign Distribution Point
- Goods that are Imported
- Goods that are Assembled

Where exports create **"Opportunity"**, it also Creates **"Risk"**.

The key is to mitigate the risks ... thereby maximizing the opportunities.

Risks
- Finding Markets
- Going Direct vs. Distributors
- Export Logistics
- Getting Paid
- Export Trade Compliance
- Resource Development

Finding Export Markets
- Google searches
- Trade shows
- Market Research Consultants

- U.S. Department of Commerce
- Chambers of Commerce

Trade services:

Blue Tiger International
- Working all companies in a wide variety of market verticals ... As a "value-added" service
- Assisting companies in both exporting and global sourcing
- Specifically, in exporting:
  - Assessing export readiness
  - Finding potential markets
  - Finding potential customers
  - Negotiating deals and contracts
  - Getting you paid
  - Handling freight and logistics
  - Leveraging opportunities

Going Direct vs. Distributors: "PROS"
- Immediacy
- Local knowledge
- Costs
- Local headaches
- Getting paid

Going Direct vs. Distributors: "CONS"
- IPR (Intellectual Property Rights)
- Control of markets and customers
- Margins
- Relative importance
- Control of your own destiny

Export Logistics
- Moving the freight
- Obtaining professional assistance
- Dealing with foreign import regulations

Moving the Freight:
- Balance on timeliness, safety, and cost
- Truck, air, and ocean

- Insure the shipment
- Fixed vs. variable
- Establish quality service provider relationships
    Obtaining professional assistance:
- Service providers: Freight Forwarders, Customhouse Brokers, and 3PL's
- Vetting

Vetting Criteria
Pricing and terms
Value add
Reputation
Experience
Geographic areas
Size
Scope of capability
Door to door
Fulfillment

Dealing with Foreign Import Regulations
- Necessary evil and must do!!!
- Foreign customs
- Government agencies: Equivalent USDA/FDA, ATF, CDC, DEA, etc.
- Documentation, valuation, origin, and HTS (harmonized tariff schedule)

Export Trade Compliance Management
- Necessary evil and must do!!!
- Denied parties list
- Product and country exclusions
- Documentary requirements
- Utilize expert support

Getting Paid
- New customers ... Higher level of scrutiny
- Check references
- Ok to offer terms as relationship matures
- Sight Draft at the time of delivery
- Export credit insurance

Leveraging the Global Supply Chain
- Bonded warehouses
- Foreign trade zones
- Free trade agreements (FTAs)

Risk Management
- Cargo insurance
- Property and liability
- Travel
- Products liability

Export Resources
- Consultant: bluetigerintl.com
- Department of Commerce: DOC.gov
- Service providers
- National Institute for World Trade: (www.niwt.org)

eCommerce
- Export savvy
- Regulations
- Payment
- Website: Int'l User-Friendly ... Language and Culture
- Logistics: last mile delivery
- Import process
- Freight consolidations

Product Viable Exports
- Industrial products
- Automobiles and parts
- Medical equipment
- Aviation and defense
- Pharma and supplements
- Agriculture
- Energy related
- Optical related
- Plastics, gems, minerals
- Food products
- Educational and financial services

Export Countries

N. America: Canada and Mexico

Europe: France, U.K., Netherlands, and Germany

Asia: China, Taiwan, S. Korea, and Sri Lanka

Africa: S. Africa, Nigeria, Egypt, and Algeria

Latin America: Brazil, Argentina, and Chile

Summary and Best Practices

The United States manufactured, mined, and farmed ... Products have a huge opportunity where 95% of the consumer market lays awaiting

Take the time to understand the challenges and the risks ... Manage these through due diligence and reasonable care practices

Master accessing all the available resources ....

Of which numerous resources and Blue Tiger International ... Stands ready to assist!!!

U.S. FREE TRADE AGREEMENTS

WHY SHOULD YOU CARE ABOUT FREE TRADE AGREEMENTS?

If you are looking to export your product or service, the United States may have negotiated favorable treatment through an FTA to make it easier and cheaper for you. Accessing FTA benefits for your product may require more record-keeping, but can also give your product a competitive advantage versus products from other countries.

WHAT IS AN FTA NEGOTIATED BY THE UNITED STATES?

An FTA is an agreement between two or more countries where the countries agree on certain obligations that affect trade in goods and services, and protections for investors and intellectual property rights, among other topics. For the United States, the main goal of trade agreements is to reduce barriers to U.S. exports, protect U.S. interests competing abroad, and enhance the rule of law in the FTA partner country or countries. The reduction of trade barriers and the creation of a more stable and transparent trading and investment environment make it easier and cheaper for U.S. companies to export their products and services to trading partner markets.

HOW CAN FTAS BENEFIT U.S. EXPORTERS OR INVESTORS?

U.S. FTAs typically address a wide variety of government activities. One example is the reduction or elimination of tariffs charged on all qualified products coming from the other country. For example, a country that normally charges a tariff of 5% of the value of the incoming product will eliminate that tariff for products that originate (as defined in the FTA) in the United States.

Documenting how a product originates or meets the rules of origin, can make using the FTA negotiated tariffs a bit more complicated. However, these rules help to ensure that U.S. exports, rather than exports from other countries, receive the benefits of the agreement.

Some other types of opportunities frequently found in FTAs include:

- The ability of a U.S. company to bid on certain government procurements in the FTA partner country
- The ability of a U.S. investor to get prompt, adequate, and effective compensation if its investment in the FTA partner country is taken by the government (expropriated)
- The ability of U.S. service suppliers to supply their services in the FTA partner country
- Protection and enforcement of American-owned intellectual property rights in the FTA partner country
- The ability of U.S. exporters to participate in the development of product standards in the FTA partner country

WITH WHICH COUNTRIES DO THE UNITED STATES HAVE AN FTA?

The United States has 14 FTAs in force with 20 countries and is currently in the process of negotiating regional FTAs with several others.

U.S. FTA partner countries: Australia, Bahrain, Chile, Colombia; DR-CAFTA: Costa Rica, Dominican Republic, El Salvador, Guatemala, Honduras, Nicaragua, Israel, Jordan, Korea, Morocco; NAFTA: Canada, Mexico, Oman, Panama, Peru, and Singapore.

HOW CAN U.S. COMPANIES IDENTIFY TARIFFS ON EXPORTS TO FTA PARTNER COUNTRIES?

The FTA Tariff Tool can help you determine the tariff, or tax at the border, that U.S. FTA partners will collect when a U.S. exported product that meets the FTA rule of origin enters the country. You can look up the tariff rate for a given product today, as well as identify when in the future the tariff rate will go down further or be eliminated altogether.

FREE TRADE AGREEMENTS

- FTAs Home
- Australia
- Bahrain
- CAFTA-DR
- Chile
- Colombia
- Israel
- Jordan
- Korea
- Morocco
- NAFTA
- Oman
- Panama
- Peru
- Singapore

EXAMPLE OF TRADE DATA AVAILABLE FROM THE DOC: ITALY - ADVANCED MANUFACTURING

This is the best prospect industry sector for this country. It includes a market overview and trade data.
Last Published: *8/15/2019*

Overview

Italy is the second largest manufacturing country in Europe with an extraordinary know-how in strategic, diverse sectors such as machine tools, fashion items, food products, automotive, and pharmaceuticals. "Made in Italy" products continue to excel in areas where Italian manufacturers are very export-driven and make sizeable investments in advanced manufacturing technologies that improve production and reduce manufacturing inputs. These technologies include, among others, industrial automation, robots, and additive manufacturing.

Leading Sub-Sectors

The market for industrial automation in Italy is sizeable and growing: in 2018, it was valued at € 5.3 billion, with 7.1% growth over 2017. Specifically, the best performing technologies were the ones with a more direct link to digitization, namely man-machine interfaces (10.2% growth over 2017), Radio Frequency Identification (RFID) applications (+10.3%), industrial wireless solutions (+15.5%), and industrial networking solutions (+25.5%).

Italy is the sixth largest market in the world for robots, and it is the tenth largest global producer of such technologies. Italian companies now employ 172 robots per 100,000 workers, one of the highest rates of robot usage in Europe. In 2017, the Italian market for robots was estimated to be approximately $745 million, 8% growth over 2016. New installations of robots in Italy reached their historical record in 2018, for a total of 9,237 units, growing by 11.5% over 2017 (globally, installation of new robots in 2018 had only grown by 1%). Although their use in Italian manufacturing is still limited, collaborative robots (i.e., those that work side by side with humans on production lines) have been growing at rates close to 50%.

At the moment, comprehensive and reliable data on the size of the Italian market for additive manufacturing does not yet exist. Additionally, some

Italian users are large manufacturing concerns, ranging from racecars to oil and gas and defense, and they may be secretive about the number of 3D printers they employ and their purpose. The Italian association for the promotion of additive manufacturing, 100 member strong Additive Italian Technology Association (AITA), is cross-sectorial and does not have the specific focus that would enable it to gather precise data, although efforts are underway to resolve that issue. In any case, industry sources value the 3D printing market in Italy at anything in between $1.2 and 1.7 billion. Also, recent efforts by the U.S. Commercial Service in Italy to promote additive manufacturing technologies have gathered considerable interest from local manufacturers and are likely to be replicated.

Opportunities

The advanced manufacturing technologies with the best chances of success in Italy fall within the scope of the government of Italy's advanced manufacturing plan, known as "Piano Nazionale Impresa 4.0". The plan, aimed at boosting the adoption of advanced manufacturing technologies by Italian firms, was the latest among those developed by large European manufacturing countries but is considered by many to be the most advanced and comprehensive. The plan originally consisted of €13.5 billion in tax breaks (such as "hyper-amortization") for investments to be performed until end – year 2018, but it was later extended to cover orders placed through the end of 2019 as well; the tax breaks, cumulated with additional resources that span the 2017–2020 time frame, will reach a total value of €20.4 billion. The plan aims at "triggering" private investments worth €23.9 billion in the above-mentioned time frame. Its beneficiaries are Italian firms and foreign firms that have operations in Italy, regardless of sector and company type and size.

Below is a summary of the technologies eligible for incentives. Opportunities exist for U.S. firms that can provide these types of technologies to the Italian market:

1. Advanced Manufacturing Solutions: autonomous, cooperating industrial robots with numerous integrated sensors and standardized interfaces
2. Additive Manufacturing: 3D printing, particularly for spare parts and prototypes; decentralized 3D facilities to reduce transport distances and inventory

3. Augmented Reality: augmented reality for maintenance, logistics, and SOP; display of supporting information, e.g., through glasses
4. Simulation: simulation of value networks; optimization based on real-time data from intelligent systems
5. Horizontal/Vertical Integration: cross-company data integration based on data transfer standards; precondition for a fully automated value chain (from supplier to customer, from management to shop floor)
6. Industrial Internet: network of machines and products; multidirectional communication between networked objects
7. Cloud: management of huge data volumes in open systems; real-time communication for production systems
8. Cyber security: operation in networks and open systems; high level of networking between intelligent machines, products, and systems
9. Big Data and Analytics: full evaluation of available data (e.g., from ERP, SCM, MES, CRM, and machine data); real-time decision-making support and optimization

In May 2019, several proposals were advanced by the current government in order to widen the range of technologies that can benefit from the hyper-amortization scheme, for instance, the cloud-based ones for cyber security purposes; proposals were also submitted to retroactively extend hyper-amortization to periods for which it had not been previously available. Furthermore, as of late May 2019, the government seemed inclined to make the Piano Impresa 4.0 incentives "structural", and no longer tentatively extendable on a year-to-year basis, starting in 2020.

Web Resources

Italian Ministry of Economic Development document outlining Advanced Manufacturing Plan in English: http://www.sviluppoeconomico.gov.it/images/stories/documenti/2017_01_16-Industria_40_English.pdf
World Manufacturing Forum (WMF): September 25–27, 2019, Cernobbio, 2-day conference that seeks to raise awareness and identify cooperative solutions to global manufacturing challenges through discovery, dialogue, and sharing of best practices between government, manufacturing, and innovation leaders.
https://www.worldmanufacturingforum.org/
Hannover Fair: April 20–24 2020, Hannover. The world's leading industrial technology show, with many Italian exhibitors and attendees.

http://www.hannovermesse.de/home
AITA – Italian 3D Printing Association: http://www.aita3d.it/inglese/
U.S. Commercial Service Contact:
Federico Bevini, Commercial Specialist
U.S. Commercial Service, U.S. Consulate Milan
Tel: +39 026268 8520
E-mail: federico.bevini@trade.gov
http://www.export.gov/italy/

Excerpts from another book by Thomas A. Cook at Taylor and Francis ... Global Warrior Series:

Negotiation Skill sets in Global Customer Service

This Chapter outlines the necessary skill sets to negotiate with leverage, advantage and with success. Customer Service is not an easy responsibility but can be made manageable when an individual understands what is necessary to do to negotiate better.

> Negotiation is both an art and a science. Master both aspects and win more times!
>
> *Thomas A. Cook*

The Winning Premise of Negotiation

While we all want to win in every negotiation we enter, the likelihood is that is not probable.

Nor should it be a desired goal. We need to enter into our global customer service responsibilities in getting a job done.

Our primary responsibility in customer service is to manage our company's relationship successfully with our overseas clients and vendors.

Negotiation prowess is a tool to help us accomplish that goal. Winning may not necessary be the direct result.

Winning is achieving our goal, which may include various levels of compromise and sacrifice to get where we want to be:

1. *Obtain new customers*
2. *Grow with existing customers*
3. *Sustain relations with existing customers*
4. *Successfully working out he day to day issues and finding good problem resolution*
5. *Eliminating as much difficulty, frustration and angst as possible.*

In global trade, successful negotiation gets us to where we are achieving our goals 1–5, as outlined above.

This is a highly "emotionally intelligent" perspective that winning is not the critical goal ... achieving results in the areas outlined above are!

Negotiation is therefore a skill set that helps us achieve those desired results.

An Example, Based on True Events

You are the customer service manager (Marie) for a tool manufacturer in Ohio, who exports to over 19 countries. Your European salesman (Nigel) has opened a new account in Germany.

The terms of the first sale was DDP (Delivered Duty Paid). This meant that you the seller/exporter is required to ship the goods to final destination in Frankfurt and pay for all the expenses inclusive of the customs clearance process, duties and taxes (VAT).

It was a small kind of test order, with only four pieces of equipment valued at $21,300.00. The additional costs added another $1,100.00 to the transaction totaling $22,400.00.

The shipment left the Ohio plant on schedule, Tuesday afternoon was being shipped by airfreight and was scheduled to arrive and be delivered by Friday morning.

The exporter utilized an integrated carrier to handle the shipment. That carrier's office needed information from the buyer (Ultimate Consignee) enabling customs clearance. That office waited too late and only requested the information on Friday morning.

By the time it received the necessary information, it was too late, and they missed delivery on Friday morning. It was delivered on Monday morning.

At that point, the client was not very happy as they needed the equipment for tooling which was going to occur on Friday and over the weekend.

The client found another solution on Friday with a local tool company that was a "Band-Aid" fix. More costly and not exactly what they required or wanted.

The terms of payment were 30 days, and now the customer was making a case about not paying in their anger.

The salesperson is also unhappy as to how this was handled and is all over Marie, the Customer Service Manager to resolve the issue and the dissatisfaction with the shipping problem.

The resolve is in structuring a strategy that is fact based. When we discuss key elements later in this chapter ... mining for information is a strategy and tactic. Creating a plan is also part of the negotiation process.

It can work as follows:

- Part of problem resolution is negotiating a favorable outcome
- The outcome needed by the seller is to not lose the new client
- The outcome from the clients' perspective is not known at this time and must be found out. The mistake that Marie could make is by assuming she knows what the resolve is, rather than investigate what they need to bring back favor
- The German culture favors honoring commitments tightly, delivering as scheduled, and being on time!
- At some point, the salesperson won the confidence over from the buyer. He has the best relationship, at this point
- The responsibility for the problem lays clearly with the seller in Ohio and possibly Marie, herself.

Let me explain:

The shipment had a very specific delivery schedule. The freight arrived on Thursday morning in Frankfurt for customs clearance and last mile delivery.

Marie's office alerted the shipping agent in Frankfurt of the shipment and all the important documentation and delivery instructions. The customer service department followed up, when they arrived at 0900 EST, in Frankfurt the time was 2 PM.

By the time, the customer provided the necessary information for customs clearance ... it was after 5 PM local time in Frankfurt ... passing the time frame for customs clearance.

Marie's office should have had their integrated carriers' local agent in Frankfurt obtain the necessary information from the customer a few days before the needed delivery date. Proactively obtaining the required information. Then Marie's office establishing a follow-up procedure on Thursday to make sure that had been accomplished.

This would reduced the opportunity for service failure dramatically and may prevented any customer dissatisfaction to begin with.

Negotiation or Problem Resolution Strategy ...

... Have the salesperson visit with the customer on Monday morning or soon thereafter. Nigel will get Marie on the phone while he is present in the customer's office.

Remember the goal is to keep the client, for the long term, and mitigate the current problem.

When the call begins … Marie takes the lead. She apologizes for the problem, takes ownership of the problem, makes no excuses, and explains that her office failed to follow up proactively with the clearance and delivery agent in Frankfurt.

Marie advises that there will be no charge for the freight portion and will re-issue a discounted invoice. She also advises that within the next two orders, delivery will be made for free.

Marie also advised that her staff will proactively follow up on all their shipments to make sure delivery occurs as committed and she will personally supervise that responsibility.

The offer works and the customer places another order. A year later the relationship is good and is growing well.

The customer witnessed Marie's commitments being honored, and she stayed on top of all the shipping from that day forward. Marie and the client now developed a relationship based upon commitment and promises made. Trust was now established.

The goal of the negotiation was to keep the customer, and this was achieved. The negotiation:

- The negotiation accepted responsibility and faced the problem "head-on" without making excuses.
- The negotiation created mitigation in cost for the immediate problem and continued mitigation on the next two shipments.
- The negotiation offered commitments for preventive measures.
- The negotiation created a relationship between Marie and the customer which was based on "trust".
- The negotiation created a "win-win' for both parties.

There could have been another ending to that story for the company in Ohio. But Marie had taken a class with the National Institute for World Trade (niwt.org) and learned about how to resolve the problem and negotiate solutions … the best $375.00 she ever spent!!!

Negotiation is a tool, a process, and an action to obtain a favorable result. Negotiation can be utilized:

- To change behavior
- Influence a different outcome

- Overcome unwillingness
- Gain a more favorable decision

Negotiation is best accomplished by individuals who understand the psychology of human behavior and apply that to a reasonable thought process of communication and action to achieve desired results as outlined in the above four outcomes.

Cultural Issues in Negotiation

The premise of "negotiation" is the same everywhere in the world. But the strategy on execution will change based upon the cultures we are working with.

In many cultures:

- Relationship is more important than the product or service
- Time is not as important as it is here in the United States or in other western countries ... Germany, Switzerland, etc.
- Confrontation can be viewed as very offensive
- Price can be a huge factor outweighing any other aspect
- Contracts don't have the same meaning as in the "West"
- Looking into the eyes, can be seen offensive and confrontational
- Women are held in less regard
- Religion may play a big part in relationship and attitude
- Detail may have less importance
- Short-term considerations seriously outweigh and long-term benefits
- Certain mannerisms of people will be considered strange, rude, or hard to comprehend
- Politics may be "verboten" to discuss or be a major point of interest
- Compliance will have little meaning

Relationship is More Important Than the Product or Service

In the countries that border the Mediterranean and certain Latin American cultures ... relationship is the driving factor of building business opportunity.

While "relationship" is critical in all cultures ... in a place like Italy or in Venezuela ... you will need to work on creating a "bond" with your prospective customer or vendor before any opportunity will mature in your favor.

Time and effort need to be put forth to develop relationships with overseas buyers and vendors.

The financial side needs to be budgeted and the effort needs to be expended.

Time is Not as Important as it is Here in the United States or Other Western Countries … Germany, Switzerland, etc.

Americans run on tight schedules and generally responsible for being on time … but nowhere as diligent as the Germans and the Swiss … who are fanatics about being on time.

180 degrees opposite is the Latin Culture who from a time perspective treats it very liberally.

It is not a right or wrong matter … it is just different and we need to be sensitive to that fact!

Confrontation Can be Viewed as Very Offensive

Most Americans are pretty direct and very willing to speak our minds. In some cultures, this can be viewed as "confrontational".

Asians would be offended if we "stare" them down or be "in their face" in the midst of a discussion or meeting.

On the other hand, if you were in Australia or England ... a straightforward, no-nonsense approach would be welcome.

Again, we need to be sensitive to our approach and handle discussions and meetings accordingly.

Price Can be a Huge Factor Outweighing any Other Aspect

In most western cultures, proposal and business development contain a balance of service, value add, and price.

In China, as an example, price rules in business and outweighs most other factors. It sometimes becomes frustrating when dealing with China on the balance that needs to take place in a negotiation ... between cost and quality ... or ... price and value.

In making the best effort to manage this concern ...

- clear, concise, and detailed expectations are helpful
- financial consequences for service or quality failures
- being extremely diligent, demanding, and always "squeaking the wheels"

Contracts Don't Have the Same Meaning as in the "West"

In the west, a "contract" is a conclusion nary event at the end of a negotiation. In the East, the contract is that final event, but it is also a starting point of continued negotiations.

To be "frank" ... the Asian community does not feel as committed to a contract to the same extent as we do in the West. This is not ... a being honorable issue ... it is a difference in viewpoint on the basis of how we view a contract and their culture views a contract.

Again, this is not a right or wrong issue ... it is just a different approach.

Unfortunately, the consequences of this difference in how contracts are viewed do raise some serious issue in customer and vendor relationships and in how legal matters become handled or resolved.

The utilization of qualified counsel with local representation in the countries you do business in ... is valuable in mitigating this concern.

Looking into the Eyes, Can be Seen Offensive and Confrontational

As mentioned previously, conformation can be a liability. But behaviors that we have in the West that are not offensive can be construed as offensive in the East.

An example of this is "eye contact". In the West, we expect eye contact in a serious discussion. In the East, eye contact is minimized and viewed as an aggressive behavior.

And even more so with women.

This pint validates the need to learn the cultures of the people we are doing business with. The last thing we want to do is to start a relationship off, by being offensive, even though that is not our intent.

Sometimes we are called the "Ugly American". One of the reasons for that is our general lack of sensitivity to the cultural differences that exists in the world. Eye contact is one of them.

In the Middle East a good business rapport between men will have them holding hands, like a "couple" would.

In most of the world, this would be viewed as homosexuality or a feminine behavior. In Saudi … this is a sign of business confidence and a relationship mannerism acceptable in that world.

Women are Held in Less Regard

Women have risen to serious levels of leadership in western businesses. This is not true in a number of countries throughout the world.

Factors influencing this behavior and pattern are tied into politics, religion, and traditions in those societies.

I have a number of women executives as clients who operate globally and in some western cultures have no problem navigating their responsibilities. But in countries dominated by Islamic.

Culture ... they struggle. In some cases are not even accepted.

In other cultures, women are still considered to be the matriarch of their family and have little or no place in the world of business.

The clothes women wear, whether they can drive or not, vote, hold public office, own assets are all challenges in many countries. This then creates some issues when we do business in cultures where women have less relevance.

We have to modify our behavior to work successfully in these arenas that keep women down and out.

Religion May Play a Big Part of Relationship and Attitude

There are over 100 religions or sects in the world.

As reported by Project World Impact .... On average, eight in ten people in the world currently align themselves with a religious group.

A recent religious demographic study shows that 2.2 billion, or 32%, of the world follows Christianity, 1.6 billion, or 23%, are Muslims, 15% are Hindus, 7% are Buddhists, and 0.2% of the world is Jewish.

Additionally, 400 million people are affiliated with indigenous, folk, or other traditional religions, and 58 million people are religiously affiliated with smaller-scale/lesser-known religions such as Zoroastrianism, Wicca, and Sikhism. Christianity is currently the most evenly distributed religion with roughly equal amounts of Christians residing on the various continents. Muslims, Hindus, and Christians all tend to live in countries in which they are the majority.

People who claim to be religiously unaffiliated are beginning to grow in number and are the majority groups in China, the Czech Republic, Estonia, Hong Kong, Japan, and North Korea.

At the beginning of 2014, organizations noted that religious conflicts had reached a new high from observations taken over the past six years.

In 2012, nearly one-third of all countries in the world recorded religiously motivated conflicts. For example, Middle Eastern countries are still rebounding from impact the Arab Spring uprisings.

China has recently increased the amount of religious conflict in the Asia-Pacific region. Additionally, nearly 29% of the world's nations had high levels of government-sanctioned religious restrictions for their citizens.

The most common form of religious discrimination over the past year has been the abuse of citizens who are members of religious minorities.

Around 47% of countries reported that this was the type of persecution that they face.

Religiously motivated terrorist activities have also increased in frequency over the past 2 years. Sectarian violence, especially in Syria, has increased to nearly one-fifth of the world.

Sectarian strife has created strain on neighboring countries since violence has caused entire groups of people to seek asylum in other countries.

Religious relationships between clergy and governments impact business relationships and how business people react in business situations.

Understanding the role religion plays in business and culture can be another important factor on how we proceed in managing our sales and customer service responsibilities in global trade.

Detail May Have Less Importance

Attention to detail and its incorporation into business relationships are important in most cultures around the world.

But there are individuals in certain cultures that "detail" is not as critical factor in the decision-making process as is "relationship". In the Middle East and North Africa, you sometimes witness this circumstance.

They weigh the relationship to their business partner so heavily that the details are not so important. The big picture will take care of the little picture or in other words ... if the important relationship and confidence level is in place ... the details will take care of themselves.

This becomes a much more relaxed way of doing business and carries a lot more trust in the equation of negotiating for favorable results.

Short-Term Considerations Seriously Outweigh and Long-Term Benefits

A consequence of a majority of companies all over the world, having to go "lean and mean" as a result of the 2008 Recession ... have them looking at short-term results at the expense of longer-term benefits.

Most of this mind-set was considered a "survival strategy" which has continued on into 2017 and beyond.

In certain places in the world, economic malady continues, those cultures still foster a spirit for short-term benefit.

We need to make sure that we understand who these buyers are and respond in our customer service strategies accordingly.

Certain Mannerisms of People Will be Considered Strange, Rude, or Hard to Comprehend

In the Middle East, "burp" after a meal and you just congratulated the chef. Burp in the middle of a Manhattan restaurant ... and you might be thrown out onto the street.

In India ... the right hand is always offered the left hand is not ... as that is the one we do "potty" with.

In rural China, it is ok for children to defecate in the streets, as part of their learning process. Clothing is slotted to accommodate that occurrence.

In the United Kingdom, roundabouts replace most stoplights.

In Chile and Ecuador, it is fashionable to show up to 30–60 minutes late for an appointment.

In Russia, which has a serious rate of alcoholism … you can never put a glass back on to the table after a toast, with any liquor left in the glass.

Children in Greece place their lost teeth up on the roof and not under their pillow.

In Japan, the practice of Bushido teaches strength, integrity, and loyalty and is incorporated into their business practice.

In Brazil, "showers" by people are often taken several times a day and is often discussed as a daily topic among Brazilians at meetings.

In Taiwan, handing a business card over to another person as if it was a sacred document.

In Egypt, regularly driving in traffic in the opposite direction as the means to get where you need to go.

Above are a few of the thousands of customs around the world that we have to be aware of and be sensitive to when we operate in those countries and deal with their people.

The more we understand and be reasonable about … the better our negotiations and outcomes.

Politics May Be "Verboten" to Discuss or be a Major Point of Interest

Early in my career, I learned quickly to leave politics behind in my conversations with clients, vendors, prospects, and business relationships.

It served for no real value, and it was a lose-lose proposition.

In European and Middle Eastern cultures, there is a deep passion about politics and the role America has played in the years 2009–2017, under the Obama Administration.

Discussing politics will lead to arguments and a less-than-desirable outcome.

Leave it to the dignitaries to politicize.

Compliance Will Have Little Meaning

The entire world views the United States as being too compliant in almost every area of governance, such as but not limited to:

Occupational Safety Health Administration (OSHA)
Labor Laws
Trade Compliance
Sarbanes Oxley
Internal Revenue Service
Securities and Exchange Commission
Federal Aviation Administration
Transportation Safety Administration

Compliance creates cost, infrastructure, and personnel standards greater than most countries have around the globe. Many foreign business managers look with disdain and uncertainty at the amount of regulation and compliance issues when doing trade with America.

Pundits would argue that regulation and compliance make for a safer and more secure world.

Adversaries say the United States goes too far.

Either side of the issue … compliance is an area of concern when trading with the United States and must be navigated diligently to be successful in global trade.

Key words to live by in compliance are:

- Due diligent
- Reasonable care
- Supervisor and control
- Proactive engagement

Key Elements in Global Negotiation

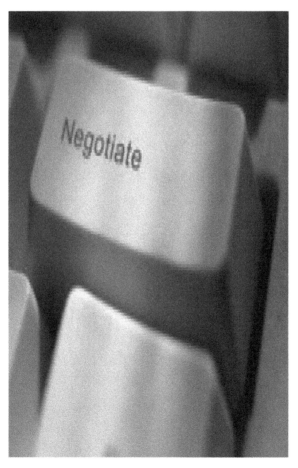

Why study negotiation?

Why Study Negotiation?

- More responsible and favored results
- Lead people to make better, more favored decisions
- Protect you and your company.
- In supply chain/purchasing/domestic/international business … a critical skill to define success!!!

    And personally translates to big benefits, as well!!!

    Transaction by transaction and long-term that provides sustainable results!

Negotiation

The key issues in negotiation that show favorable results are:

- Change
- Behavior modification
- Influencing decision-making
- Leading in various directions

When you negotiate, you are creating a "win-win" scenario for all parties involved.

We are not processing a "zero-sum" conclusion where only one party wins and the other loses.

International business requires a certain degree of détente' in order to be successful.

Trust!!!!! here only one party wins …

What are Our Primary Responsibilities in Negotiation Management?

- Create a win-win scenario for all parties
- Obtain favorable outcomes

What are our primary responsibilities?

If we "negotiate" better … we increase our chance of successful business management in every area of responsibility ***

And personally, as well!!!

Trump … Art of the Deal

Everything is Negotiable!
Is it?

Most senior and experienced executives in global trade will prefer to say that everything can be discussed and all matters are up to change ... or put in other words ... Everything is negotiable!
Negotiation ...
is it innate or can it be learn?

There is a continued debate on whether or not negotiation skill sets are innate or can they be learned?

The author has concluded the following:

There are people who have an internal strength for negotiating better than others. There are some people who cannot negotiate anything well.

In either situation … some people "got it" and some people "don't".

In either situation, though, there are negotiation skill sets that can be learned, developed, and honed.

The key is obtaining education, training, and hands-on experience from those that can negotiate well and teach others to do so.

Maslow and Negotiation

The author believes the better one understands human behavior … the better one can negotiate.

Maslow wanted to understand what motivates people. He believed that people possess a set of motivation systems unrelated to rewards or unconscious desires.

Maslow (1943) stated that people are motivated to achieve certain needs. When one need is fulfilled a person seeks to fulfill the next one, and so on.

The earliest and most widespread version of Maslow's (1943, 1954) hierarchy of needs includes five motivational needs, often depicted as hierarchical levels within a pyramid.

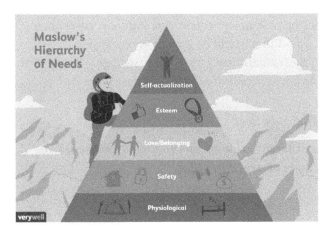

This five-stage model can be divided into basic (or deficiency) needs (e.g., physiological, safety, love, and esteem) and growth needs (self-actualization).

The deficiency or basic needs are said to motivate people when they are unmet. Also, the need to fulfill such needs will become stronger the longer the duration they are denied. For example, the longer a person goes without food the more hungry they will become.

One must satisfy lower-level basic needs before progressing on to meet higher-level growth needs. Once these needs have been reasonably satisfied, one may be able to reach the highest level called self-actualization.

Every person is capable and has the desire to move up the hierarchy towards a level of self-actualization. Unfortunately, progress is often disrupted by failure to meet lower-level needs. Life experiences, including divorce and loss of job may cause an individual to fluctuate between levels of the hierarchy.

Maslow noted only one in a hundred people become fully self-actualized because our society rewards motivation primarily based on esteem, love, and other social needs.

In business, motivation for individuals is usually linked to three key areas:

Career
Security
Money

Business motivation comes in the three forms above for most people everywhere in the world. Some might add "patriotism" as a motivator, which might be true in some cases for military, government, and career politicians ... but that would be serious exceptions.

Knowing these motivators in business will help us in how we approach a negotiation when people are driven by these factors.

International Business

Requires a differentiation of methodology incorporating ... political, economic, and cultural allowances

International negotiation incorporates all the skills we have outlined above combined with the nuances of culture and the variables unique to those people and countries they represent.

The better we understand these cultural issues, the better outcomes we will have in moving forward in our negotiations.

Global negotiation …

Deals with:

- General negotiation skill sets
- Negotiating domestically versus internationally

Global Negotiation....

Deals with:

- Biggest differences between domestic versus international …
- Consequences when a mistake is made
- Cultural issues
- Mind-set of a "contract or an agreement"
- Commitment to mine and exercise patience

Basic Strategy

- Win-win negotiation theory
- Outcome for both sides or numerous parties and benefits
- Internationally ... just maybe more complex

Basic Strategy

The Psychology of Negotiation in Business:

- Change behavior
- Impact decision-making
- Persuade
- Change mind-set
- Move in a different direction
- Convince
- Create

On a "softer" note ...
   "Influence"

Basic Strategy

The Psychology of Negotiation in Business:

- Win-win-win
- Compromise
- Timing ... process
- Lifespan
- In steps ... timing?
- Pieces
- Short-term versus long-term
- Patience is a virtue
- Potential consequences ... of winning or losing?

Basic Strategy

The Psychology of Negotiation in Business:

Which "animal" are you … and which one are they?

Some theorists believe that the majority of people can be grouped into four categories of personality style.

The owl, the eagle, the dove, and the rooster.

The owl is the thinker, conservative, and knowledge seeker.

The eagle is driven by a greater goal and does not get lost in minutia. A+ personality types, quick, and decisive.

The dove is a "social butterfly", relationship driven, and approached things cautiously and is very trusting.

The rooster is aggressive, outspoken, opinionated, social, and clearly the loud one at the party.

Knowing these traits would then allow us to create the best approach and negotiation strategy.

Basic Strategy

The Psychology of Negotiation in Business:

Basic Strategy

CHART

The Psychology of Negotiation in Business:

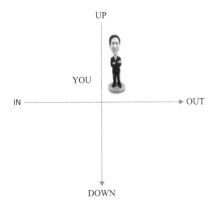

Remember that negotiation has to occur internally, as well. The pictorial above depicts the scenario where one has to negotiate in four directions. Bosses above. Reports below. Colleagues laterally along with vendors, suppliers, and customers.

Some negotiation thoughts …

- Quantify price anticipation
- Determine other issues or benefits/value added
- Send "tests"
- Don't get "lost" in the detail or minutia
- Determine decision-makers … meet if possible
- As an example … longer-term commitments, bundling, purchasing options … may add to price lowering opportunity
- Importance of knowledge, wherewithal, and specific awareness of the issues
- Bring to closure … Example as it relates to an Request for proposal (RFP)!

Some additional thoughts ...
What are some of the things we regularly negotiate for?

- Price
- Business process improvements
- Terms
- Contracts/Statement of Work and Master Service Agreement (SOW's/MSA's)
- Risks

Strategy versus Tactics

Goals ... Strategies ... Tactics ... Action Plans ... Accountability and Responsibility Systems

ACTION PLANS: Focus & Prioritize

Project

Tasks

Who

When

Status

Step one: Set goals
Goal setting
S ... specific
M ... measurable
A ... attainable
R ... relevant
T ... timely and trackable
Goals that utilize SMART characteristics have the best chance to succeed and is a good "marker" to determine just what goals you want to achieve.

In a negotiation, goals are determined for both or the multiple sides involved.

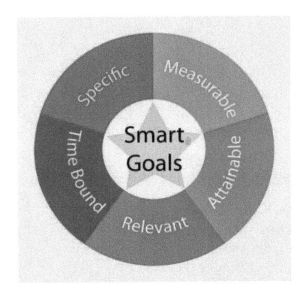

Twelve steps in successful negotiation

1. Understanding what you are looking to accomplish ... Goals!
2. Gaining senior management support
3. Creating a team approach
4. Mining
5. Setting the stage
6. Executing initial strategy
7. Outline what will be necessary to earn an agreement
8. Tactics/execution/problem resolution
9. Closing the deal

10. Implementation
11. In ongoing negotiations that will repeat ... evaluate and set the stage for next year
12. Follow-up (win or lose)

Twelve steps in successful negotiation
Understanding what you are looking to accomplish:

1. What you have determined?
2. What others have determined?
3. If goals ... SMART?
4. Parameters and timing
5. This effort will be successful if we accomplish ....?
6. Emotional intelligence reigns supreme!

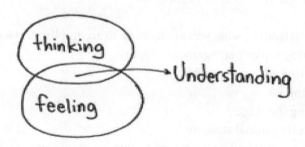

Twelve steps in successful negotiation
Gaining senior management support ...

- Why?
- How to obtain?
- How to utilize?
- Risks and rewards ... take notice!
- Keep them appraised
- Leadership to help get the deal done!

Mining ...
Knowledge can be the most critical element of any negotiation ...

- Resources
- Spending and investing time ... everyday!
- Building a "rolodex"
- See vendor options
- Internet
- Networking ... trade shows, industry events

Setting the stage

Bringing a plan together ... first in your head, second with your management, then with a written outline

- Relationship building
- Initial information gathering
- Determine decision-makers

Executing Initial Strategy

- Short-term goals versus long-term goals
- Meetings ... business and social
- Establishing relationship and "trust"
- Qualifying
- Commit ... then honor!
- Ask questions ... probing ... "SWOT Analysis"
- Time frames are potentially established
- Next steps ... intellectual confrontation on what to expect ... action plan is created
- Prioritize issues, needs, and wants ... "must haves versus maybes?"

Outline what will be necessary to earn an agreement

- Ask, ask again and again ... be creative in your approach
- Obtain an understanding and maybe even an agreement

- Establish actions and next steps
- Set up next meeting or action time frame
- Beginning of the "close".

The framework or foundation is established, which everything will rest upon ... in the negotiation initiative!!

Tactics/Execution/Problem Resolution

- Straight forward ... no nonsense
- Make sure you are heard
- Persistence, pushy, aggressive, forward
- Set stage for close ... the close should happen naturally!

Closing the Deal
- Should happen "naturally" and without asking
- Closing questions … indirect approach

- Direct approach
- Prior agreements in writing
- Action plan… creating comfort level and continued sensibility that a correct decision was made
- RFP proposals … go back to the proposal!

Implementation
- Deal not successful until implemented
- Should be part of all understandings and agreements
- Big area for failure in new relationships

Ongoing negotiations ...
That repeat or renew
Strategy and execution

Follow-up (win or lose)

Maybe the most important step(s)
In new customer care or in what was accomplished!

Workshop review:
Straight Forward, No nonsense, honest, to the point
... grip it and rip it!

Approach to relationship and negotiation????

Workshop Review:

Relationship Building:

Accomplish more with good relationships.
   eCommerce????
   Good means quality and honesty/transparency.
   Gets you through the difficult times.
   Allow more honesty.

Workshop Review:

Emotional issues:
Anger
Dissatisfaction
Trust or lack of
Trying to make everyone "happy"
Which hat to wear?
Control and balance …is the critical element.

SWOT Analysis
S trengths
W eaknesses
O pportunites
T hreats
Some thoughts …
SWOT
S … price, valued added
W … incumbent may have relationship
O … capture business
T … one time chance, do you know what you need to do, how you are perceived, current strength of existing relationships (change issue)
Leading to … strategies … then tactics
Tactics/Execution/Problem Resolution

- You want the close to come naturally
- You want to identify and counter all issues
- You want to place yourself in the best position to be able to close the deal
- Sidebar: Problem Resolution (Crisis Management)
- Stop bleeding

- Information gather (intensely)
- Meet and conference call with all concerned parties
- Obtain options
- Create a strategy
- Execute
- Tweak
- Review and follow-up

Closing the deal

- Get a feel of where they are at?
- Ask open-ended questions?
- Ask soft questions? (suggestions)
- Timing is critical
- Bring closure

Follow-up (win or lose)
Win or lose......follow-up is critical.

Lose

Sets the stage for a future opportunity.

Win

- Demonstrates concern
- Assures success
- Proactive problem resolution

What motivates prospects:

- Price
- Service
- Timeliness
- Value added
- Personal issues (Maslow)

International

- Complications
- Mind-set
- Challenge
  - When things go wrong!
  - Cultural issues …. China, Latin America, Middle East
  - One shoe fits all … nada!
  - Strategies are very diverse and customized

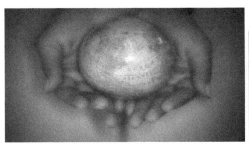

International contracts export sales and import purchase orders

- Terms of sale
- Terms of payment
- Freight
- Insurance
- Title
- Revenue recognition*
- Marking, packing, and labeling
- Permits and registrations
- IPR
- Disputes

Incoterms®
    Incoterms® are:
    Point in time and trade ...
        Responsibility
        Liability

Transfer

Seller <-> Buyer
    Importer <-> Exporter
    Costs and Risks – that's it!

Incoterms® ... Negotiating a better price or reducing risks
   Examples:

   Landed costs and risks
   Export >>> trade compliance
   Ex works
   DDP
   Import >>> landed costs
   Ex works versus FOB

Negotiation Character Traits?
   Outline ten character traits that will help a person more successfully close deals:
   Negotiation Character Traits

   1. Honesty
   2. Sincerity
   3. Caring

4. Product and industry knowledge
5. Problem solver
6. Responsive
7. Quality communicator
8. Leadership
9. Charisma
10. Serious, but not too much so
11. Funny, but not too much so (sense of humor)
12. Make them feel good
13. Cater to their ego, needs, and wishes
14. Learn how they listen and learn
15. Think on your feet
16. Credible
17. Authority figure
18. Do what you say you will
19. Be persistent

Negotiation Questions
Identify ten questions you can ask to obtain a sense of where a prospect is at....without being offensive or too obtrusive.
Negotiation Questions

1. In a perfect world, what would make you 100% satisfied with your supplier/vendor?
2. What things do you like best about your current supplier/vendor?
3. What things would you change, if you could?
4. What would motivate you to change suppliers?
5. You have seen our proposal...what is attractive about it? Where does it fall short?
6. Who else is involved in the decision-making process? Is there an opportunity to dialogue with them directly?
7. In your RFP/RFQ....what are the deliverables you are specifically looking for? ....that would cause a vendor to receive a favorable result?
8. Will there be an opportunity to revise our proposal, once the dialogue and the purchasing process are moved along?
9. Is price your only issue?
10. When are you looking to make a final decision?

Some thoughts ...

- SWOT Analysis of all serious competitors
- Get past non-negotiation issues ... how?
- Build offering and sales process to make it as difficult as possible to say no ... negotiate with "leverage"
- Short-term considerations for longer-term benefits ... market share versus margins
- Landed cost analysis ...

Some additional thoughts ...

Landed Costs Analysis

List of all the costs involved in a domestic or import/export trade.
How can we impact these costs?
Develop strategy to implement negotiations to make impact happen!

RFP Management
- What are you trying to achieve?
- Deliverables?

- Process ...
- Science versus art?
- Identify options?
- Qualify options?
- Price equation ...
- Value versus price
- Steps ...

Supplier Agreements (SLA)

How do we manage, hold accountable, and gain the greatest value ... while paying competitively??? Please provide your responses in the blank bullet lists below.

-
-
-
-
-
-

Lack of technical expertise

When I work in a field that is technical ... how do I not step on technician's toes and how best to manage my negotiation responsibilities???

-
-
-
- Intonation
- Repeating points
- Soft tone versus Firm
- Different language
- Order of topics in a discussion.

Summary

- Negotiation skills can be learned ...
  "learning/training is a process"
  -
- Develop a "win-win" mentality, identify with your other side
- Patience is a virtue ... overall and transactionally!
  -

- Create a strategy, develop tactics
- Learn to manage up, down, in and out
- Goals, expectations need to be **SMART**!
- Execute with consistency, persistence, and structure

Advanced Sales Management ... Sales Personnel Key Performance Indicators (KPIs) May 2018 Thomas A. Cook

Sales Personnel Evaluation Criteria:

Performance Metrics:

Visits:	Numbers	Goal	% of Goal
Renewal:			
New:			
Penetration:			

Team Player:		
Internal Support:		
Demand Planning Assistance:		

On-Time Performance:	
Addressing Areas of Improvement:	
Internal Committee Participation:	

Marketing:
Customer Service:

Sample Sales Contract
Template ...Sales Agreement

INTRODUCTION

This Sales Agreement is a method of identifying some of the core expectations of XYZ Corp. and outlining Performance and Commission Plans for the sales team. The goal of this Sales Agreement is to create sales excellence, achieve company goals, and compensate sales performance through a defined commission structure. Sales personnel will also be responsible for meeting other sales-related criteria. These will include specific KPIs and entry into the company's Customer Relation Management system (CRM).

All sales personnel must sign this Sales Agreement to be eligible to earn sales commissions.

XYZ CORP. SALES PERSONNEL

All sales personnel will be expected to generate gross profit (gross revenue less transportation-related expenses) sufficient to achieve their anticipated goals.

Compensation is based upon an agreed draw. Compensation includes car allowance and employee benefit expenses. Accounting against the draw is done quarterly. If money is due employee, then it is paid quarterly. If there is a deficit, it is carried quarterly, and a determination is made to reduce the draw or take any agreed appropriate action.

Thirty percent of the gross profit is the basis of his formula and will be accounted against the expected Gross Profit (GP) on all freight business. For consulting ... 20% of 80% of the amount billed and collected from clients' billing.

New XYZ Corp. Sales Personnel will be expected to show progress towards achieving their GP threshold under the following progression schedule:

Progression	Schedule
1st quarter	25% of threshold
2nd quarter	50% of threshold
3rd quarter	75% of threshold
4th and future quarters	100% of threshold

TRANSITION/MAINTENANCE ACCOUNTS

Legacy and house accounts of XYZ Corp. where no other salesperson is earning a commission that are assigned to a salesperson for ongoing maintenance and development will be subject to a reduced rate of 50% of the agreed commission structure.

GLOBAL/CORP/KEY ACCOUNTS (MAJOR ACCOUNT)

Accounts secured as a part of a major account selection where the salesperson was not the owner of the Overall customer relationship/selection will be subject to a reduced crediting level. XYZ Corp. recognizes that many major account selections often require to follow up and sales at each local location. 10% of the GP will be allocated to National Account Team (NAT).

WAREHOUSE/DISTRIBUTION

Commission for warehouse and distribution services will be calculated at 5% of the gross revenue. To qualify for commission, the account must generate a minimum of $2,000 per month in gross revenue. The 5% of gross revenue will be treated as GP for calculation towards the threshold.

SALES KPIs

All XYZ Corp. Sales Personnel will be required to meet KPIs. Performance against these KPIs will be reviewed along with GP performance each quarter and will be included in the sales performance evaluation each quarter. KPIs along with GP performance are requirements of sales positions.

COMMISSION PAYOUTS SUBJECT TO THE FOLLOWING:

- Commission will be paid out via payroll only.
- Commission will be calculated and administrated by a designated individual/individuals.
- Commission results will be sent to sales personnel for review, sign off, and return.
- A signed Sales Agreement must be on file to be eligible.
- Accounts must be entered and maintained in the Corp CRM system to qualify for gross profit eligibility in threshold calculation.
- Commissions will terminate on the last day worked. Final commission will be calculated against shipments which have been paid in full prior to the last day worked.
- Commissions will not include GP occurring during any leave of absence.
- Accounts must have a signed credit application on file to qualify for gross profit eligibility in threshold calculation.
- Sales Commission Addendum will be reviewed annually by the Sr. Management Team.
- Sales Commission Addendum may only be altered by the Corp VP of Sales, Managing Director of Americas, or President of XYZ Corp.
- Commission will only be paid on activity where the customer pays within 60 days of their obligation unless extenuating circumstances exist and management agrees to waiver on this procedure.

Business Interests and Obligations

The following are the parties' agreements as to the legitimate protectable business interests of the company:

- *Trade Secrets/Confidential Information*: Employee agrees that employee shall not disclose any of the trade secrets or confidential information directly or indirectly, nor use them in any way, either during the term of this agreement or at any time thereafter, except as required in the ordinary course of employee's employment for the benefit of the company. Trade secrets may include, without limitation, compilations of market information, customer lists, and business plans of the company. Confidential information may include, without limitation, internal financial statements and analysis, personnel files and evaluations, internal pricing and cost information, customer lists and contacts information, salary and compensation information, and information concerning specific customer needs.

- *Competing Business*: Customers of the company and all related information regarding customers of the company are proprietary and employee agrees that for a period of 12 months after employment with company ends, employee with not call on, solicit, or engage in any type of competing business with any customers of the company unless specifically agreed by the company.

- *Restriction on Interfering with Employee Relationships*: Employee agrees that during employment with company, and for a period of 12 complete calendar months following the termination of employee's employment with the company, employee will not, either directly or indirectly, hire, call on, solicit, or take away, or attempt to call on, solicit or take away any of the employees or officers of the company or encourage any employees or officers of the company to terminate their relationship with the company.

- *Survival of Covenants*: It is expressly understood that no employee, officer, or director of the company has the authority to waive, release, modify, alter, or limit any of employee's obligations except in a writing executed by the Corporate Vice President of Sales, Managing Director XYZ Corp. Americas, or President of XYZ Corp.

- *Arbitration of Disputes*: All salespersons agree that any dispute or claim in law or equity arising between them regarding the obligation to pay commission under this Agreement shall be decided by neutral arbitration as provided by California Law and you are giving up any rights you might possess to have the dispute litigated in a court or by a Jury trial. In all other respects, the arbitration shall be conducted in accordance with the California Code of Civil Procedure.

- *Governing Law:* It is the intention of the parties that the laws of the state where employee primarily performs the duties he or she has been assigned should govern the validity of this Agreement, the construction of its terms, and the interpretation of the rights and duties of the parties hereto. The agreed venue and jurisdiction for any claims or disputes under this Agreement are stated to be advised. (dispute resolution via arbitration)

Exceptions

An exception to the above policy will only be granted under extraordinary circumstances. In order to receive an exception, the salesperson and his/her direct supervisor must provide the Corporate Vice President of Sales with a written request for an exception.

EMPLOYEE ACKNOWLEDGEMENT OF
RECEIPT AND UNDERSTANDING

This Agreement is designed with the intent to outline a sales performance and commission agreement for Sales Personnel at XYZ Corp.

This Agreement should not be considered an employment contract which in any way limits your freedom, or the company's freedom, to terminate the employment relationship at will or pursuant to any current or future Employment Agreement, if one exists between the salesperson and XYZ Corp. XYZ Corp. reserves the right to revise, supplement, or rescind any Policies and/or Agreements or portion of their Policies and/or Agreements as it deems appropriate, and at its sole and absolute discretion. This Agreement may not be modified, altered, or amended except in writing, and such amendment is not effective until approved and published by XYZ Corp. Should any of the clauses in this Agreement be declared invalid, null, void, or unenforceable, the rest of the Agreement shall remain in full force and effect. This agreement shall be the sole agreement between company and employee and can only be amended by the Corporate Vice President of Sales or other approved officer

The above is understood and agreed to:

_____

_____
Sales Person

_____
Date

_____
Signature VP Sales - Corp VP Sales

_____
Date

Note: This Sales Agreement supersedes and replaces all other Sales Agreements previously established whether written or verbal.

XYZ COMPANY

Draft Draw Compensation Program (Ex… Freight Company)

Outline for an alternative and possibly more responsible commission structure for sales personnel:

Overview

The current XYZ Corp. commission program for sales personnel is difficult and arduous to manage.

An alternative that is simpler and easier to administer and provides a greater incentive to sales personnel who are succeeding in the Draw Program.

Structure

A salesperson receives a "draw" based upon historical commissions, books of business, sales plans, or sales experiences.

This draw is an "advance' of anticipated commissions.

Tied into the overall draw is a car allowance, cost of employee benefits, and T&E.

Station managers therefore need to keep a tight rein on T&E costs.

Example 1

Bob's draw is $4,000/monthly or $12,000/quarterly.
  His car allowance for the quarter is $1,200 and his benefits cost if $1,500.
  His T&E was $1,100.
  His total costs for the quarter is $15,800.
  His GP for the quarter is $75,000.
  30% of that GP is $22,500.
  Bob would get a check for the difference … $6,700.

Next quarter …
  Bob's GP is $70,000 at 30%   … 21,000.
  Same costs.
  He would receive a check for $5,200.
  Next quarter …

His GP is 46,000 at 30%   ... 13,800.

He would be in a deficit mode of $2,000.

This would be monitored and if it continued to drop ... either lower draw ... is matter became serious ... evaluate if any draw is required and go on straight commissions or maybe termination is warranted.

Additional Considerations:

Monies must be collected within 60 days.

The commission structure will be calculated quarterly at 30% rate against GP but ....only 25% will be paid out quarterly. Five percent will be held in arrears and will only be paid when the salesperson reaches his or her target at year end.

As an additional incentive, once the salesperson exceeds their target, by $100,000 of GP they will be paid an additional 5% of the GP of the additional amount.

Minimum GP by lines of business must be achieved as set by the station managers and communicated to the individual sales personnel/

- Minimum GP guidelines (subject to individual station manager guidelines)

Ocean Import ... 10%	Ocean Export ... 25%
Air Import ... 15%	Air Export ... 20%
Domestic: TBA[1]	Warehouse: TBA*

- There will be no aging of accounts ... as long as the salesperson achieves their minimum target renewal and growth goals.

    Failure to meet target growth will lead to a loss of full commissions on existing accounts.
- Silo managers have the responsibility to assign commission percentages that might deviate from 30% depending upon extenuating circumstances around each client situation. As an example: Corporate accounts assigned sales would fall into a 50% reduction of GP in allocated commission.

---

[1] Silo managers will review each account, the GP and the merits of each situation ... and work with the sales person to come to an agreed commission structure in domestic and warehousing services.

WHITE PAPER ON ECOMMERCE SALES INTO CHINA 1/15

Apex Global Logistics

eCommerce Solutions in China

The last two years have seen a huge window open in China for eCommerce. The United States followed by Europe has led in eCommerce the past ten years.

Until 2013, China has been slow to offer cost-effective eCommerce. This was due primarily to legal, documentary, and customs clearance challenges.

Many of the largest eCommerce companies have had difficulty in entering China and moving eCommerce sales with any degree of a comprehensive until the past year and half.

Officials in China have now paved the way for an easy structure for eCommerce companies to enter this market successfully.

Though only a year or so old eCommerce is showing significant signs of success. There is tweaking going on each day but eCommerce continues to move forward. The Twelfth Five Year Plan created by the Ministry of Industry and Information Technology which set China's growth strategy for 2011–2015 has provided impetus for the growth of eCommerce.

Today in 2020, E Commerce is a major business vertical in both business and consumer sales growing at a dramatic pace, as their middle-class segment continues to expand and have the disposable income to spend.

The plan acknowledges the great potential of China in leading business-to-business and business-to-consumer eCommerce opportunities as China continues to grow into a consumption-based economy.

The number of internet users in China, along with online payment systems and the physical delivery systems (logistics), was minimal until an explosion of internet usage took place in 2010 causing China officials to enact legislation and regulatory changes favoring eCommerce.

The market potential in China exceeds US $500 million. This amount is larger than all westernized markets and continues to grow exponentially every quarter.

Advancements in technology, the needs of China consumers requiring accuracy, speed and timely accessibility, along with a developing consumer mind-set is driving eCommerce to higher elevations.

Almost every U.S. eCommerce company has or is posturing to gain their share of the expected growth and opportunity in China.

Apex Global Logistics, a premier logistics provider based in Shanghai, Los Angeles, New York, and a host of other key international cites has taken a leadership role in providing solutions to eCommerce companies entering the China market.

Apex has created a separate and distinct business unit designed to provide customized service solutions for eCommerce companies. Apex is currently serving over one hundred companies in eCommerce solutions in China, such as but not limited to Amazon, Alibaba, and Ebay.

This new operating company is called ECMS. ECMS, based in Shanghai, is now the established leader in China with outreach throughout China.

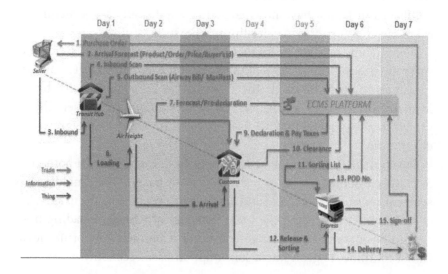

ECMS has been operating successfully as a logistics provider solution for eCommerce companies.

ECMS has developed six steps necessary for companies engaged in China eCommerce to follow:

- *Ensure landed cost models earn required margins.*
- *Align with quality service providers.*
- *Maximize utilization of technology options.*
- *Establish secure technology and payment systems.*
- *Create a cost-effective return policy and capability.*
- *Trade compliance is a necessary evil.*

Ensure Landed Cost Models Earn Required Margins

Control of costs is a critical evaluation strategy to make sure you can influence margins to earn the required profits.

Landed costs include an array of add-on(s) to the purchase price, inclusive of freight, customs clearance, insurance, duties, and taxes.

The schedule below outlines some of the duty charges in China.

Product Catalog	Tax Rate
Foods & Drinks	10%
Leather, Bag & Luggage	10%
Home healthcare equipment	10%
Kitchen & Small appliance	10%
Furniture	10%
Photographic equipment	10%
Computer & accessories	10%
Toy & Office supplies	10%
Stamp	10%
Instrument	10%
Fabrics & manufactured product	20%
Home appliance	20%
Bicycle & accessories	20%
Watch, Clock & accessories	30%
Sports products	30%
Liquor & Tobacco	50%
Cosmetics	50%
Others	10%

These costs along with others must be factored into the "landed cost". Designing comprehensive landed cost models is both an art and a science, which protects anticipated profits and makes it easier for the consumer to understand their total costs of eCommerce purchases.

Align with Quality Service Providers

Shipping goods internationally will require accessing quality and comprehensive service providers.

The opportunity for successful eCommerce depends on the ability and capability of service providers like Apex/ECMS to offer logistics solutions.

eCommerce companies need to seek out China eCommerce service providers and create "partnerships" that will enhance their ability to move the product from source to consumer ... safely, timely, and cost-effectively.

Apex/ECMS has created partnerships with a host of companies that enables them to service all the supply chain needs of their eCommerce clients.

Maximize Utilization of Technology Options

The technology interface from consumer to seller to logistics provider to customs clearance and to final delivery inclusive of payment creates a closed circle of service that meets everyone's needs in the eCommerce supply chain.

Technology prowess will drive eCommerce, and those companies that master "technology" will better control costs and improve customer access to future purchases.

Technology for the utilization of marketing, purchase, logistics, shipment status, billing, etc. ... will be the stalwart of the eCommerce business model.

Establish Secure Technology and Payment Systems

Secure technology and the security of the online payment system are a critical element of eCommerce that must be in place in order for it to work for the consumer. The entire eCommerce market flourishes only when the consumer is confident the system is secure as if the consumer has a lack of confidence in the security of the transaction, they will not process online sales and purchases.

Recent security breaches in the United States against retailers, manufacturers, and distributors are worrisome but have aided in the continual enhancements of better security technology and procedures to prevent fraud and criminal access.

Create a Cost-Effective Return Policy and Capability

Just as in any other business, items that are sold through eCommerce may not meet the customer's expectations and may be returned to the company. Internationally, this poses another whole set of challenges to the eCommerce company as no customs regulations and business processes in two countries have to be being managed.

Consider a company may have a billion U.S. dollars of eCommerce sales into China and have USD $200,000 of returns. While this USD $200,000 represents less than ½ of 1% of the sales activity, these returns have the potential to become the biggest nightmare to the logistics team if the returns are not structured proactively in advance.

Apex/ECMS has developed a comprehensive closed-end system to deal with the challenges of reverse logistics and smooth out the entire return process.

Trade Compliance is a Necessary Evil

Trade compliance is a necessary management function for exporting and importing. Paying attention to:

- Harmonized Tariff System Classification (HTS)
- Valuation
- Documentation
- Record-keeping
- Customs entry process
- Logistics options
- Compliance communication responsibilities

Each of these areas is important and needs to be addressed proactively at the time of export to China and also when anticipating that some percentage of goods will be returned to point of shipping.

Dealing with customs regulations on exports, imports, and return shipments will need to be mastered in eCommerce trade.

SUMMARY

eCommerce is a booming event in China. It is saturated with opportunity for every company that develops web bases and internet sales.

However, the opportunities are fraught with risks. The key is to assess those risks and develop strategies that mitigates exposures.

Failure to heed the risks can lead to disaster. Managing the risks can protect growth and profit margins and allow the success of any eCommerce initiative.

This white paper provides an overview of many of the solutions found through "hands-on" experience of the Apex ECMS team of professionals who are successfully managing the eCommerce solution into China.

Following the steps reviewed above will provide the best opportunity to succeed in China with eCommerce will be realized.

Author:
Thomas A. Cook
tomcook@bluetigerintl.com

Contact:
Apex Global Logistics
Mike Piza, Sr. VP
mikepiza@apexglobe.com
516-640-2249

Index

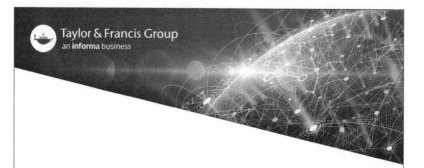